Beyond the Bake Sale

Beyond the Bake Sale

The Essential Guide to Family-School Partnerships

Anne T. Henderson, Karen L. Mapp, Vivian R. Johnson, and Don Davies

THE NEW PRESS

NEW YORK
LONDON

Support for this book was generously provided by the Charles Stewart Mott Foundation. The interpretations, conclusions, and recommendations in this book represent the views of the authors and not necessarily those of the Mott Foundation, its trustees, or its officers.

Requests for permission to reproduce selections from this book should be mailed to: Permissions Department, The New Press, 38 Greene Street, New York, NY 10013.

Published in the United States by The New Press, New York, 2007
Distributed by Perseus Distribution

LIBRARY OF CONGRESS CATALOGING-IN-PUBLICATION DATA
Beyond the bake sale : the essential guide to family-school partnerships /
Anne T. Henderson.
 p. cm.
Includes bibliographical references.
ISBN: 978-1-56584-888-7 (pbk.)
1. Education—Parent participation—United States. 2. Home and
school—United States. I. Henderson, Anne T.
LB1048.5B49 2007
371.19'2—dc22 2006019254

The New Press was established in 1990 as a not-for-profit alternative to the large, commercial publishing houses currently dominating the book publishing industry. The New Press operates in the public interest rather than for private gain, and is committed to publishing, in innovative ways, works of educational, cultural, and community value that are often deemed insufficiently profitable.

www.thenewpress.com

Book design and composition by Lovedog Studio
This book was set in Goudy Old Style

Printed in the United States of America

19 18 17 16 15 14 13 12

*This book is dedicated to all the wonderful teachers,
parents, principals, community members, organizers,
advocates, and other leaders in public education
who are out there working every day to make
the vision of this book a living reality.*

Contents

Section III Guidelines for Action from Research

Contents

. . .

viii

Section IV Resources and Tools

Preface and Acknowledgments

One of our goals in writing this book is to recognize the wonderful work of our friends and colleagues across the country. Not only have we tried to capture their spirit in the many examples, tips, research briefs, and quotes sprinkled throughout the book, we have also asked for their suggestions as we went through several drafts. These parent leaders, researchers, school administrators, state and federal officials, teachers, and organization and foundation leaders readily responded with examples of excellent practice, advice for our readers, and ideas about how to present this information. We cannot thank them enough.

The history of this book began in 1982, when Anne and Basil Henderson were collaborating on a national study of parent involvement in the federal Title I program. Congress had replaced ten pages of parent involvement mandates in the law with a two-line requirement that school districts hold an annual meeting for parents to explain the program. A central question of the study was whether Title I administrators were continuing to involve parents in decisions about the program now that they no longer had to do so.

As Anne and Basil interviewed teachers, Title I coordinators, principals, parents, and district administrators, it became clear that many saw family involvement as helping kids with homework. Parent advisory councils had been eliminated in favor of "make-and-take" workshops. One day, Basil said, "Anne, you've got to write a book about parent involvement for educators."

Anne took the idea to the National Committee for Citizens in Education (NCCE). Carl Marburger, an NCCE founder and senior associate, said, "Let's do it." Bill Rioux, NCCE senior associate and director of publications, added, "I've had a title in mind, and this is the book to match—*Beyond the Bake Sale*." Theodora Ooms, a colleague at the Family Impact Seminar, wished to contribute the findings of her study on parent involvement in Connecticut and Colorado.

In 1986, *Beyond the Bake Sale: An Educator's Guide to Working with Parents* by Henderson, Marburger, and Ooms was published by NCCE. When NCCE closed in 1994, the Center for Law and Education acquired and generously continued to distribute the book. It sold many thousands of copies through nine printings. That book was parent involvement 101. This book builds on the great gains in both research and practice since then.

In 2000, Norm Fruchter, at the Institute for Education and Social Policy at New York University, advised Diane Wachtell, the executive director of The New Press, to call Anne about her work. Anne turned to her colleagues Don Davies, Vivian Johnson, and Karen Mapp at the Institute for Responsive Education. The Mott Foundation, which had generously supported their work over the years, agreed to provide funding.

In 2002, the Southwest Educational Development Laboratory asked Anne and Karen to write a research synthesis about the impact of parent involvement on student achievement. That review was published as *A New Wave of Evidence: The Impact of School, Family and Community Connections on Student Achievement*. The body of research it covers is the backbone of this book.

A second literature review included current publications on this topic and examples of innovative practice. This was done by Don Davies, with the able assistance of Dominique Astier.

The authors conducted focus groups and interviews with parents, teachers, principals, and administrators. We want to thank everyone who organized and participated in these sessions. In Los Angeles, Ruth Yoon, director of Families in Schools, graciously arranged for a meeting at what was then District F, with Richard Alonzo, Mary Lou Amato, Tom Delgado, and Linda Ariyasu. Their innovative ideas and practices enrich several chapters in this book. We are saddened by the death of Dr. Ted Alexander Jr., associate superintendent of Los Angeles Unified School District. He was the head of the district's parent advisory committee and a great supporter of family involvement.

In Alexandria, Virginia, Karen Parker Thompson set up a meeting with principal Karl Smith and staff at Ramsay Elementary School and collaborated with Ruth Dinzey at Tenants and Workers United to organize a focus group of Latino families.

At a national conference on community organizing at the Kennedy School of Government at Harvard, Kavitha Mediratta convened several experienced organizers and principals who work with them: Amanda Rivera, Luz Ruiz, Melania Page-Gaither, Father John Korcsmar, Sister Mignonne Konecny, Marvelyn Maldonaro, Lisa Robertson, and Alma Purvis.

In Massachusetts, principals Claire Crane at the Ford School in Lynn and Bill Henderson at the O'Hearn School in Boston arranged for focus groups with parents and teachers. In Florida, Sally Wade of the Florida Partnership for Family Involvement in Education identified outstanding principals to interview, and Karen Willoughby at the Family Involvement office in Fairfax County, Virginia, did the same.

Many principals and educators candidly shared their wisdom and experience: Cathy David, teacher, principal, and district administrator, in Alexandria, Virginia; Doug Becker and Laura Bartkowski in Kansas City, Kansas; Tom Bentson at Olde Creek Elementary School in Fairfax, Virginia; Mary Ledoux of Brooksville Elementary School and Joe Clifford of West Hernando Middle School, in Brooksville, Florida; Roberto Pamas of Holmes Middle School in Annandale, Virginia; Christine Lamb of Groveton Elementary School in Groveton, Virginia; Steve Constantino, founder of the consulting group Family Friendly Schools and former principal of Stonewall Jackson High School in Manassas, Virginia; Yvonne Torres, an associate superintendent in New York City; Emma Paulino, parent and organizer, Oakland Community Organizations; and Laura Flaxman at the Coalition for Essential Schools in Oakland, California. Their contributions have greatly enriched this book.

For their assistance on Title I compacts, we thank Bob Witherspoon at RMC Research for sharing examples and Stephanie Fama, an active parent in Kansas City, Missouri, for creating a compact development process. For wise counsel on issues of class and cultural difference, we thank John Diamond, assistant professor of education at the Harvard Graduate School of Education, and Glenn Singleton of the Pacific Educational Group in San Francisco. For collaboration on developing a tool to assess attitudes, we thank Pardeice McGoy and Peter Kleinbard at the Youth Development Institute at the Fund for the City of New York.

For other advice at critical points, we are grateful to Joyce Epstein at Johns Hopkins University, Kathy Hoover-Dempsey at Vanderbilt University, and Sue Ferguson of the National Coalition for Parent Involvement in Education. Melissa Whipple, coordinator of the Parent Academic Liaisons program in San Diego, went far beyond the call of duty to give us tools, specific examples, stories and quotes from her colleagues, and tips for our readers. All your good counsel and encouragement are deeply appreciated.

Our readers offered invaluable ideas and constructive criticism. We are tremendously grateful to Claire Crane, principal of the Ford School in Lynn, Massachusetts; Sally Wade of the Florida Partnership for Family Involvement in Education; Bea Fernandez, director of the San Diego Parent University; John Diamond of the Harvard Graduate School of Education; Warlene Gary, executive director of the National PTA; Lee Shumow at Northern Illinois University; Karen Parker Thompson, coordinator of family involvement and community resources in Alexandria Public Schools; Norm Fruchter of the Community Involvement Program at the Annenberg Institute for School Reform; Joyce Epstein at Johns Hopkins University and the National Network of Partnership Schools; Mark Warren at the Harvard Graduate School of Education; Jeana Preston at the California Parent Center in San Diego; and Jemina Bernard at the New York City Board of Education.

At the Institute for Responsive Education, Rashaud Pettway, Linda Peterson, Carol Strickland, and Brendan McCaffery graciously yielded space, ordered food, gave advice, and offered logistical support. At The New Press, Ellen Reeves has been a patient, understanding, perceptive, and rigorous editor, just the right mix of qualities to guide the unwieldy collaboration of four authors. Jessica Colter has also been unstintingly helpful.

The Charles Stewart Mott Foundation has steadfastly supported parent and community engagement in education and community development since 1935. For all their guidance and encouragement over the years, we want to express our appreciation to the foundation's board of trustees and to program officers Pat Edwards, Chris Sturgis, and Christine Doby.

Finally, we want to thank our families, who have given us their unqualified love and support throughout the entire process. We couldn't have done it without all of you.

Chapter 1

Introduction

Why Bother to Read This Book?

In this book, we argue that partnerships among schools, families, and community groups are not a luxury—they are a necessity. In passing the No Child Left Behind law, Congress and the president made a promise to our children that all will have an equal opportunity to get a high-quality education and master high academic standards. That means *all* our children—no matter what language they speak, how much their families earn, what disabilities they may have, what God they worship (if any), or what holidays they celebrate.

Quality public education may be national and state policy, but it is not yet a civil right. There remain tremendous disparities in funding, facilities, and instructional resources across our sixteen thousand school districts, and this inequity underlies the poor outcomes that the law attempts to address. Consequently, our public schools need all the help they can get—from parents, family members, community residents, local organizations, and anyone else whom we can engage in children's learning.

Demands for reform continue to mount. Federal and state action has produced a strong move toward higher standards of achievement, increased testing, and accountability to the public for results. There is considerable backlash, however, especially against using high-stakes standardized tests to hold schools liable for poor performance and to prevent students with low scores from graduating.

While some see progress, many corporate and foundation leaders are impatient with the pace of change. Educators and policy makers are arguing over whether funding is adequate to meet all the new federal mandates. Public support appears to be growing for vouchers and competition from the private sector as the main tools for reform. We think that parents and community members, working as partners with educators, can accomplish change within the public sector—but this will take a new model of working together, one that goes way beyond the bake sale.

There are five reasons why you should read this book.

1. Partnership and student academic achievement are closely linked. Many years of research show that involving families and the community contributes to children's academic and social success.

> The evidence is consistent, positive, and convincing: families have a major influence on their children's achievement. When schools, families, and community groups work together to support learning, children tend to do better in school, stay in school longer, and like school more.[1]

This statement summarizes the conclusion of *A New Wave of Evidence: The Impact of School, Family and Community Connections on Student Achievement*, the most recent and comprehensive review of the research. Here are some key findings:

✦ Students whose families are involved in their learning earn better grades, enroll in higher-level programs, have higher graduation rates, and are more likely to enroll in postsecondary education.
✦ When families take an active interest in what they're learning, students display more positive attitudes toward school and behave better both in and out of school.

- Children do best if parents can play a variety of roles in their learning: helping at home, volunteering at school, planning their children's future, and taking part in key decisions about the school program.
- Middle and high school students whose families remain involved in these ways make better transitions, maintain the quality of their work, develop realistic plans for the future, and are less likely to drop out.
- Children from diverse cultural backgrounds tend to do better when families and school staff join forces to bridge the gap between home and school cultures.

From early childhood through high school, families make key contributions to student learning. School improvement programs are much more effective when schools enlist families in the process. Regardless of income level or education background, all families can—and do—support their children's success.

When parents become involved at school, they tend to become more active in the community. Well-planned family learning and support activities tend to increase self-confidence, so parents and family members go on to pursue a high school diploma, additional job training, and higher education. Knowledge is power. Well-informed parents can be more effective and productive partners.

The more the relationship between families and the school is a real partnership, the more student achievement increases. When schools engage families in ways that are linked to improving learning, students make greater gains. When families are engaged in positive ways, rather than labeled as problems, schools can be transformed from places where only certain students prosper to ones where all children do well.

Community groups make important contributions, too. One key difference between high- and low-achieving children is how (and with whom) they spend their time outside school. Community groups offer important resources for students and families, and schools can provide a critical link to these resources.

Be warned: positive results are not automatic. They are more likely to be achieved when school, family, and community partnership programs are well planned and carefully executed. How to do this is what this book is all about.

2. Partnerships help build and sustain public support for the schools. In this era of market-driven education reforms, including vouchers and charter schools, public schools are seeking increased support. The traditional approach is public relations. We think that three other partnership strategies offer more direct benefits, both to schools and to the community:

1. Conducting active programs to engage the public, including parents and families
2. Working with community organizations to help students and families and to improve educational quality
3. Promoting greater citizen participation in our democracy

Schools that embrace the partnership idea in practice enjoy higher levels of respect and trust in the community, as well as among school staff and families. Partnership schools tend to have better teacher morale and higher ratings of teachers by families. They also have more support from families, better reputations in the community, and more success at implementing school reform initiatives.

TIP:

Public engagement is a way to build support for public schools that gets beyond PR.

Public Agenda, a nonprofit polling and research organization, emphasizes:

✦ Extensive outreach to make sure that activities include regular people—people who do not hold leadership positions and whose voices are not commonly heard

✦ Discussions geared to average citizens instead of just experts

✦ A civil exchange of ideas among participants without grandstanding or polemics

✦ Tolerance for people with different points of view[2]

Collaborative approaches can contribute to strengthening the human, social, and economic foundation of neighborhoods. One goal of school-community initiatives is to develop a neighborhood's ability to identify its own issues and marshal sufficient resources to solve problems. This kind of community capacity can help not only to improve the safety and economic vitality of neighborhoods but also, as it evolves, to improve the quality of teaching and learning in the schools.[3]

Community agencies and institutions benefit, too. When they collaborate with schools, they can reach more easily the people they want to serve and gain access to school services and expertise. In the process, they can increase public support for their work—and even save money by eliminating overlapping services.

Families are more stable and healthy if they can meet basic needs for housing, food, transportation, and employment. When schools team up with community organizations, families can gain access to a range of social services. Then they are in a better position to take advantage of other opportunities, such as counseling, additional education, and job training. Many studies have documented the resulting benefits for families and children, including:

+ Increased knowledge of child development
+ Greater confidence in their role as their child's first teacher
+ More frequent attendance at school meetings and a stronger sense of responsibility for children's schooling
+ Improved literacy and other skills
+ Better communication with schools and teachers

3. Families and the community can help schools overcome the challenges they face. The challenges for America's public schools are great and growing, and many schools are making heroic efforts to address them. Serious gaps in achievement persist between more affluent children and those from low-income families. New waves of immigration from Central America, Asia, Africa, and the Middle East are bringing to many schools more children and families whose English is limited and who are not familiar with our school system or society.

During the 1990s, between 14 million and 16 million people entered the country, far more than in any decade in the nation's history. This pace was sustained during 2000–2004, with the foreign-born population increasing by over 1 million per year. By 2000, immigrants represented one in nine of all U.S. residents, and their children represented one in five of all children under eighteen. While these children are at first concentrated in the great gateway cities, they are rapidly dispersing across the country.[4]

As poverty rates rise and manufacturing jobs decline, families and communities face multiple economic and social problems. These have a direct impact on the schools. For example, the number of highly mobile families has increased. Of the more than 290 million people in the United States, 43 million move each year. In many communities, the shortage of affordable housing has put numerous families on the street. Homelessness affects children's health, their mental stability, and their work in school.

RESEARCH BRIEF:
Children in poverty

According to the National Center for Children in Poverty at Columbia University, more than 73 million children (birth to age eighteen) live in the United States. About 40 percent of them live in low-income families.

✦ Low-income means being unable to provide basic necessities. Most families of four must reach twice the federal poverty level ($40,000) before they can provide their children with adequate housing, food, and health care.

✦ Twenty-nine million children in this country are growing up in low-income families.

✦ More than 81 percent of them have at least one working parent whose income is not sufficient to provide basic necessities.

✦ Eighteen percent of children—13.5 million—live in families that are at or under the federal poverty level.

✦ The number of children in poverty has been rising steadily since 2000.[5]

The findings of a new, rigorous study on the actual dropout rate between ninth and twelfth grades are summed up in its title: *Losing Our Future: How Minority Youth Are Being Left Behind by the Graduation Rate Crisis*. In predominantly black and Latino urban districts, high school graduation rates are well under 50 percent.[6] Where do the students who drop out go? According to the National Center for Education Statistics, about half of prison inmates are dropouts, and a high proportion of these have been in special education programs.[7]

RESEARCH BRIEF:
Chicago Parent Centers dramatically reduce dropout rate

A long-term study of the Chicago Parent Centers (serving families with children from ages three to nine) found that parent participation in the program had a major impact on their children's social and academic outcomes. The longer parents took part in the program, and the more they were involved at school, the less likely their children were to repeat a grade, be abused, be arrested, or require special education. Each year that parents took part in the program increased the odds that their child would complete high school by 16 percent. **Over 80 percent of students whose parents were involved for the whole six years graduated from high school, compared to 38 percent of students whose parents were not involved at all.**[8]

Changing family patterns also present schools with challenges. For example, the 2000 Census shows that over 4 million children are living with grandparents, and that one-fourth of these grandparents have sole responsibility for the children. Nearly half of low-income children, those in the bottom 20 percent, live with only one parent, and nearly half move every year.[9]

These changes in society and the economy have spawned what the media call the "culture wars." Many communities are beset with sharp debates about religious expression in schools (including prayer, religious clubs, and how to teach evolution); appropriate treatment of gay, lesbian, and transgendered students; and how to prevent bullying and sexual harassment. School staff are coping with changes in traditional sexual roles and values, and with cultural differences in food, dress, and music. Language differences trigger debates on whether instruction for English-language learners should be given in the home language or focus strictly on English. Safety in and around schools is another pervasive challenge, intensified by headline-grabbing incidents of violence.

There is wide disagreement about solutions to these controversies. School leaders are in the uncomfortable position of having to mediate the disputes and build a consensus about what to do. They know that schools can address few, if any, of these challenges effectively by themselves. Principals, teachers, and other staff already work long hours and volunteer time during vacations to work with families and coordinate programs. Common sense and years of experience suggest that a collaborative approach is needed to define the problems, discuss productive approaches, and design and implement possible solutions. Ideas and examples for how to do this are presented throughout this book.

4. Teachers can benefit from parent and community partnerships. Teachers say they want more support from parents and are troubled by what they see as low parent involvement and poor student behavior. Yet they are unsure about how to collaborate productively with families. Many tend to be more comfortable with helping families to be involved with their children at home than with engaging families in their classrooms and school buildings.

School leaders can help teachers and their unions understand how partnership approaches can be of direct benefit to them. Plans for partnerships are often developed with little or no teacher input, and teachers are told, "Just do it." A top-down, management-driven approach confirms many teachers' perception that their views are often ignored. This can doom the effort from the start. If, instead, teachers are involved in planning at the outset, they can become powerful allies for expanding the connections among schools, parents, and community members.

In addition, educators can learn a great deal from parents. Parents and other family members bring knowledge and perspectives about their children, their culture and values, and the strengths and problems of their communities.

RESEARCH BRIEF:
Partnership programs benefit teachers

Involved families are more likely to understand the goals of the teacher and the school and to be more supportive of proposed changes. They also rate teachers more highly. Teachers who involve parents positively and consistently tend to rate families more positively. They also hold fewer social class and racial stereotypes than teachers who do not. In addition, teachers who involve parents and other volunteers report that they have more time to devote to teaching and to giving children individual attention.[10]

5. The No Child Left Behind Act provides partnership opportunities that can help schools meet the requirements of the law. No Child Left Behind (NCLB) holds public schools accountable to provide all students with a quality education, putting educators under intense pressure. School officials who ignore the requirements of this federal program are at considerable financial risk.

For example, families in a Title I school (Title I of NCLB provides funding to schools serving concentrations of low-income children) may transfer their children to a higher-performing school if the current school does not make "adequate yearly progress" for two years in a row. Students who do not transfer must be offered supplemental services, such as after-school tutoring or classes in reading and math, paid for by the school district.

It is wise to pay careful attention to the law's obligations and opportunities for parent involvement, for they can offer resources to make that adequate yearly progress. According to the report *NCLB: What's in It for Parents*, parents must be involved at several points:

1. **School-parent compact.** Every Title I school must have a school-parent compact, developed with and approved by parents. The compact must describe how the school and parents will build a partnership to improve student achievement.

Progress in a teachers' union–school collaboration in California

Parents and teachers at the 28th Street Elementary School in Los Angeles decided to organize against a chrome-plating factory across the street. Emissions from the factory were polluting the air and ground around the school, making students and teachers fear for their health. The teachers' union, United Teachers of Los Angeles, began to work with the local branch of ACORN, a community-based group that had been organizing parents. Their joint work at this school has led them toward the next step—planning for a collaborative effort to address academic performance at a cluster of south Los Angeles schools.[11]

2. **School and district policy.** Each Title I school and district must write a parent involvement policy that has been developed with and agreed upon by parents. The district policy must describe how parents will be involved in developing plans to improve schools and engage families.

3. **Report cards.** Each year, the school district must distribute a report card specifying how every school and the district as a whole are performing. Both the school and district report cards must be in a language and format that parents can understand.

4. **Parent choice.** If a Title I school has not made adequate yearly progress in improving student performance, parents have two options. They may request a transfer, or they can ask for supplemental services and become involved in developing a school improvement plan.

5. **State review.** The state education agency must monitor the school districts' Title I programs to make sure they carry out the law. If the district is not involving parents as the law requires, parents can appeal to the state.

6. **Communication.** For the first time, federal law defines parent involvement as regular, two-way, and meaningful communication about student learning and other school activities.[12]

Some provisions of NCLB apply to all public schools, not just Title I schools. Every school district or school can choose to develop a strong partnership program, even if such action is not required. Almost every chapter of this book contains tips, examples, or advice about how to use these provisions to your advantage.

Read On

The benefits we have sketched above are real. We feel that they can be achieved through effective partnership programs in any public school, from preschool through high school, and in every kind of community. We hope you will want to read on and discover how our book can be of practical help to you, your school, and your community.

Our goal has been to make this book easy to read and easy to use. The chapters are short and full of tools, tips, stories, research briefs, and advice from colleagues. Each one ends with a succinct checklist designed to help you assess the current state of your school, family, and community partnerships, identify areas in need of improvement, and develop strategies to strengthen and enhance your partnership programs. We encourage you to use these checklists as discussion tools at staff meetings, professional development events, and meetings with family and community members.

We draw most of the ideas in this book from our years of work with schools, teachers, parent groups, community members, organizers, and advocates of public education. This book truly is your book. We dedicate it to you.

Chapter 2

What Is a Family-School Partnership Supposed to Look Like?

Behind this book is a vision, an idea we want to share about schools that are successful in creating partnerships to help all their students reach high levels of social and academic achievement. Our vision is not utopian at all. We know that it is, in fact, practical and achievable in all kinds of communities, urban, suburban, or rural—and rich, poor, or in-between.

We know it because we have seen it. The ideas in this book are rooted in two types of experience. The first is what we have learned from reading hundreds of research studies. The second is what we have seen over many years in actual schools.

Strong leadership by principals, teachers, and parent and community leaders can turn these ideas into reality. They have learned that well-executed partnership goes hand in hand with school improvement, whether prompted by their own desire to create a better school or in the process of effectively implementing state educational reform efforts and federal programs, including No Child Left Behind.

We suggest that you and your colleagues, joined by the families in your school, think hard about your own vision. As you use this book, you'll have an opportunity to decide what you want your school to be like, and how to employ partnership strategies as an important tool for school change.

Four Versions of Partnership

Where is your school when it comes to partnering with families? Does your school cling to attitudes and practices that confine parents to limited, traditional roles? Has your school tried to define what it means by parent involvement and partnership with families? How is your school connecting with community resources?

 Ask yourself this question: what might a school look like that has created a genuine culture of school-family-community partnership, *and* that has made real progress toward high social and academic achievement for all students?

We would like to offer a rubric, or description, that sets a high but achievable standard for partnership.[1] The four levels of achievement are called:

+ **Partnership School**
+ **Open-Door School**
+ **Come-if-We-Call School**
+ **Fortress School**

Using this scoring guide, you can get a rough idea of where your school falls. The subheadings link to the chapters that follow, and the descriptive statements under these are intended as leading indicators, not as definitive criteria. At the end of each chapter is a detailed checklist to help you examine your school's practice more closely.

Look at the bulleted descriptors under each heading and mark the ones that best describe your school.

Partnership School

All families and communities have something great to offer—we do whatever it takes to work closely together to make sure every single student succeeds.

❑ BUILDING RELATIONSHIPS
- Family center is always open, full of interesting learning materials to borrow
- Home visits are made to every new family
- Activities honor families' contributions
- Building is open to community use and social services are available to families

❑ LINKING TO LEARNING
- All family activities connect to what students are learning
- Parents and teachers look at student work and test results together
- Community groups offer tutoring and homework programs at the school
- Students' work goes home every week, with a scoring guide

❑ ADDRESSING DIFFERENCES
- Translators are readily available
- Teachers use books and materials about families' cultures
- PTA includes all families
- Local groups help staff reach parents

❑ SUPPORTING ADVOCACY
- There is a clear, open process for resolving problems
- Teachers contact families each month to discuss student progress
- Student-led parent-teacher conferences are held three times a year for thirty minutes

❑ SHARING POWER
- Parents and teachers research issues such as prejudice and tracking
- Parent group is focused on improving student achievement
- Families are involved in all major decisions
- Parents can use the school's phone, copier, fax, and computers
- Staff work with local organizers to improve the school and neighborhood

Open-Door School

Parents can be involved at our school in many ways—we're working hard to get an even bigger turnout for our activities. When we ask the community to help, people often respond.

❑ BUILDING RELATIONSHIPS
- Teachers contact families once a year
- Parent coordinator is available if families have questions or need help
- Office staff are friendly
- Staff contact community agencies and organizations when help is needed

❑ LINKING TO LEARNING
- Teachers explain test scores if asked
- Folders of student work go home occasionally
- School holds curriculum nights three or four times a year
- Staff let families know about out-of-school classes in the community

❑ ADDRESSING DIFFERENCES
- Office staff will find a translator if parents ask in advance
- Multicultural nights are held once a year
- "Minority" parents have their own group

❑ SUPPORTING ADVOCACY
- Principal will meet with parents to discuss a problem
- Regular progress reports go to parents, but test data can be hard to understand
- Parent-teacher conferences are held twice a year

❑ SHARING POWER
- Parents can raise issues at PTA meetings or see the principal
- Parent group sets its own agenda and raises money for the school
- Resource center for low-income families is housed in a portable classroom next to the school
- PTA officers can use the school office
- A community representative sits on the school council

Come-if-We-Call School

Parents are welcome when we ask them, but there's only so much they can offer. The most important thing they can do is help their kids at home. We know where to get help in the community if we need it.

❏ **BUILDING RELATIONSHIPS**
- Better-educated parents are more involved
- "Many immigrant parents don't have time to come or contribute"
- Staff are very selective about who comes into the school

❏ **LINKING TO LEARNING**
- Parents are told what students will be learning at the fall open house
- Parents can call the office to get teacher-recorded messages about homework
- Workshops are offered on parenting

❏ **ADDRESSING DIFFERENCES**
- "We can't deal with twenty different languages"
- "Parents can bring a translator with them"
- "This school just isn't the same as it used to be"

❏ **SUPPORTING ADVOCACY**
- School calls families when children have problems
- Families visit school on report card pickup day and can see a teacher if they call first

❏ **SHARING POWER**
- Principal sets agenda for parent meetings
- PTA gets the school's message out
- "Parents are not experts in education"
- Community groups can address the school board if they have concerns

Fortress School

Parents belong at home, not at school. If students don't do well, it's because their families don't give them enough support. We're already doing all we can. Our school is an oasis in a troubled community. We want to keep it that way.

❏ BUILDING RELATIONSHIPS
- Families do not "bother" school staff
- "Minority families don't value education"
- Parents need security clearance to come in
- It is important to keep community influences out of the school

❏ LINKING TO LEARNING
- Curriculum and standards are considered too complex for parents to understand
- "If parents want more information, they can ask for it"
- "We're teachers, not social workers"

❏ ADDRESSING DIFFERENCES
- "Those parents need to learn English"
- "We teach about our country—that's what those parents need to know"
- "This neighborhood is going downhill"

❏ SUPPORTING ADVOCACY
- Parents don't come to conferences
- Problems are dealt with by the professional staff
- Teachers don't feel safe with parents

❏ SHARING POWER
- Principal picks a small group of "cooperative parents" to help out
- Families are afraid to complain: "They might take it out on my kid"
- "Community groups should mind their own business; they don't know about education"

Where Does Your School Fall?

Check the boxes that have the most statements under them marked or circled. Check only one box in a row.

✦ If three or more of your checked boxes fall in the Fortress School section and none under Open-Door or Partnership, your school is trying to keep parents away rather than work with them. In standards-based terms, it is **below basic.**

✦ If three or more of your checked boxes fall under Come-if-We-Call and none under Partnership, your school may want parents to be involved only on its terms. In standards-based terms, it is at the **basic** level.

✦ If at least four of your checked boxes fall under Open-Door or Partnership and none are under Fortress School, your school welcomes families and supports them to be involved in a number of ways. In standards-based terms, it is **proficient.**

✦ If at least three of your checked boxes are under Partnership and the rest are under Open-Door, your school is willing and able to work with all families. We bet the student achievement level goes up every year. In standards-based terms, it is **advanced.**

Now, suppose you have put partnership into action at your school, using this book and your own ideas. Imagine what a group of thoughtful observers would see and report when they visit your school. Let's assume that these visitors are conducting a Welcoming School Walk-Through, a process that schools and school districts are adopting to help schools see themselves through the eyes of others. (For more about the Walk-Through, see Chapter 9, "Scaling Up.")

Four members of the visiting team are school staff. The other eight are parents and community members. Your team might look like this: administrator, teacher, cafeteria worker, guidance counselor, bus driver, business leader, PTA board member, two parents with diverse backgrounds, community leader, high school student, and professor from the local college of education. In addition, four district staff are facilitating.

The team members break into four groups to look at these aspects of your school:

1. Focus on academic achievement
2. School climate
3. Communications and information
4. School-wide practices and policies to engage families

What would the visitors observe? What would teachers, parents, and students from your school tell them? Would they say that you have the "right stuff"? Let's look at the comments from one such walk-through.

What Do Visitors Say About the Focus on Academic Achievement?

"The school's test results are posted on the front bulletin board and portfolios of student work displayed all through the building. We could see that most students are performing at 'proficient' in language, math, and science. These good results seem to hold across all lines of race, ethnicity, gender, and family income. Many teachers credit the heavy involvement of parents in this success." (*College professor*)

"Parents are kept up on how their kids are doing—or not doing. Teachers send notes home on Fridays—and I make sure the kids don't stash them on the bus. Plus, I see the learning packs that teachers send home. Parents really like those video games—it helps them learn English." (*School bus driver*)

"The collaboration with the local college really impressed me. Student teachers intern here and help out the staff. In return, teachers can take courses at the college, for low fees. The faculty come and help staff plan new programs. Parents can take college classes right here. The council is working on a kids-to-campus program so they can start planning for college." (*District facilitator*)

"I really like it that they've made the things for parents smaller. It feels more personal—like the open house is a different grade each night.

I always felt lost at the big things. And they always include something for parents to help their kids. Now, we serve a lot more food at the open houses!" (*Cafeteria worker*)

"The Boys and Girls Club after-school program has homework help for kids. A lot of them are going. My son says it's kind of fun." (*African American parent*)

What Do Visitors Say About School Climate?

"I walked in and the school looked neat and clean. There were signs and a map of the school in the front lobby, and clear instructions about signing in at the office. The secretary and security guard greeted us professionally. They understand customer service here." (*Business leader*)

"The principal really 'walks the walk.' She was out front greeting parents when we came in, and she does it at the end of the day too. She seems to know all the student's names! Teachers say she is very clear about how she expects them to involve parents, but she listens to their ideas, too. Partnership is the way they do business in this school." (*Guidance counselor*)

"In the front office, someone who doesn't speak English came in, and a secretary found a translator right away. They answer the phone nicely—they don't say, 'We're busy, call back later.' And there's no counter for them to hide behind." (*District facilitator*)

"The people who work in this school are very nice. They treat us like people. The handouts don't say 'workshops for immigrant parents' and 'language minority nights.' We don't see ourselves as immigrants and minorities; we're Latinos. And they take the time to learn how to pronounce our names." (*Bilingual parent*)

"When I needed to use the restroom, I asked a student where I could find an adult bathroom, and he took me right there, no problem." (*Anonymous*)

What Do Visitors Say About the Quality of School Communications and Information?

"Teachers really care about the students. I saw an awesome student model of a roller-coaster. They include students in conferences, so we can talk about how we're doing. This is definitely cool." (*High school student*)

"The Parent Center a good place to go. I can grab a cup of coffee and sometimes catch my girl's teacher. The parent coordinator has a kid with disabilities, too, and she gets the special ed parents together once a month to talk. It's hard sometimes, but she's willing to go to bat for our kids." (*Special education parent*)

"I've visited the school at night—it's really busy. It's like a community center—adults and students come for classes, basketball, computer lab, job training. There's a great drumming group, too." (*District facilitator*)

"As a teacher, I noticed that the newsletter isn't full of jargon, and the terms and acronyms are explained clearly. The pictures show all kinds of students, not just the prizewinners. Brochures for parents about school programs and community services are translated in the main languages. The Web site is family-friendly, too." (*ESL teacher*)

"The partnership with a local health clinic is great. Quite a few students have gotten eyeglasses and hearing aids." (*Social worker*)

What Do Visitors Say About Practices and Policies to Engage Families and Community Members?

"We had some student behavior problems a while ago. African American and Latino parents told me they felt that their kids were being blamed. They wanted to help make rules that would be clear and consistently enforced for all students. The students got in the act, too—they wanted the rules to be for everyone, not just them. Being on time and treating others with respect apply to everybody—and that includes me. This really helped me set a positive tone." (*Principal*)

"The school works with a community group that's taking the lead on economic development in this ward. It's an election year, and they're organizing a candidate forum to get commitments for a new science lab—this is the only school in the district without a lab." (*Community leader*)

"When we started our partnership program, teachers worried that 'pushy parents' would try to 'take over.' The PTA worked with teachers to develop guidelines for parents' rights and responsibilities—what's good advocacy for kids and what's over the line. We wanted to get beyond the 'bake sale' model." (*PTA board member*)

"The school council members include several civic and business leaders, which gives it real political influence in the city. When the council started, they surveyed families and other residents and used the results to set council priorities." (*District facilitator*)

A Final Note

In this brief chapter, we have presented our vision of effective family-school partnership as a way to summarize the main ideas and themes in this book. We encourage you to develop a vision for your own school. We hope this book will stimulate your thinking. The ideas and examples are drawn from the research and from many real schools that seem to have the "right stuff." There is, of course, no magical combination of partnership practices that produces results every time. There are many successful schools where partnership is the rule, and they come in a wonderful variety of shapes, sizes, and structures.

As you will see, the book follows a progression. The first section, "Why Partnerships Are Important," ends with this chapter on vision. It explains why family-school-community collaborations are worth the investment of your time and energy.

The second section, "Getting Started: Building the Relationship," has two chapters. Chapter 3, "Ready, Set, Go!," will help you take a look at your attitudes and practices. How ready are you to step forward? How can you build a team committed to partnership? Chapter 4, "Developing Relationships," lays the foundation for working together—building trust. The "joining process" that it describes can help transform your school into a real community.

The third section, "Guidelines for Action from Research," has five chapters. Chapter 5, "Linking to Learning," is about improving student achievement. It offers clear, practical advice about how to focus your activities and programs for families on what students are learning and doing. Chapter 6, "Addressing Differences," explores how differences of culture, race, and class can create powerful barriers to engaging parents, and what to do about it. Chapter 7, "Supporting Advocacy," defines this tricky subject and lays out how schools can work with families in planning for their children's future and guiding them through our complicated educational system. Chapter 8, "Sharing Power," builds the case for families' having a voice in school governance and community affairs. Not only does developing "political capital" signal respect for families of all backgrounds, but it also makes them full-fledged members of the community. Chapter 9, "Scaling Up," steps back and looks at the context in which schools operate—the school district. It covers what a district can do to develop system-wide policies and practices that support families to enhance their children's experience in school.

The fourth section, "Resources and Tools," has two chapters. Chapter 10, "Help!," includes a selected list of useful materials, organizations, contacts, Web sites, and suggested readings organized by various topics. Chapter 11, "Tools," contains a kit of handy items, such as a school climate survey, a job description for a family involvement coordinator, and a conference checklist. The introduction suggests ways to use these tools, as well as the checklists at the end of each chapter, to evaluate your work and assess whether it is making a difference.

We hope you will use this guide in many ways. School leaders, including school council members, parent group officers, and the parent involvement action team, can use it to design and carry out a comprehensive family engagement program. Principals can find ideas for stimulating discussions at faculty meetings and retreats, at gatherings with families and in the community, and within the school council. Teacher and parent action research teams can use the checklists to assess school practice and make recommendations. Leaders of community organizations can get together with the principal and parent groups to talk about how to increase school-community exchanges.

Parent leaders and organizations such as the PTA or PTO can use the tips and checklists to make their groups more inclusive and responsive to parents who have stayed on the margins. Teachers, counselors, and other staff can get ideas for specific practices to apply to their own interactions with families. The front office can use it to develop a code of customer service.

At the district level, planners can use it to design a family involvement component of a school reform program, a literacy or math program, or an after-school program. Staff responsible for professional development can use the examples and suggested activities to plan workshops and coaching at school sites. Evaluators can convert checklists and surveys to assessment tools, to develop a higher level of practice throughout the district. District leaders can gain ideas for how to link parent and community engagement strategies to school improvement initiatives.

We hope that you use this book in the spirit with which it is offered—to build a vital, trusting, productive community of people who enjoy learning from each other and can work through their differences in the interests of the children. A school is a treasured place in a community, a place where people of all backgrounds can come together and thrive. Every school can be such a place. How to get there is what this book is all about.

Chapter 3

Ready, Set, Go!

How Do You Know if You're Really Open to Partnership?

In most districts and schools throughout the country, educators will readily agree that families must be involved in their children's education and that home-school partnerships are vitally important. With such overwhelming agreement, why can't we find real partnerships in every school? The reality is that educators and parents have many beliefs, attitudes, and fears about each other that hinder their coming together to promote children's education.

So the answer to "Are family-school partnerships important?" tends to be "Yes, *but* . . ."

Before we can create strong and effective partnerships with families, we have to believe not only that it's important but also that it can be done—and that we can do it. That means it's necessary for school staff to hold a set of positive beliefs about family engagement.

From our conversations with district leaders, principals, teachers, and other school staff, we have identified four core beliefs that serve as the foundation for the work of engaging families. In partnership schools, these beliefs infuse every aspect of the school. Ilene Carver, a teacher at

Orchard Gardens School in Boston (a K-8 school), expresses them all when she says:

> How do we get families involved? The most important thing is our mind-set. First, we have to absolutely believe in our souls that families want to support their children and that this support or partnership can make a significant difference in a child's educational experience. Second, we need to prioritize reaching out to families. Often this requires personal phone calls and sometimes even home visits. Many family members have experienced horrendous treatment in the schools, as students and/or as parents.

When teachers reach out with the goal of building partnerships based on mutual respect and common purpose, families will respond.

Core Belief 1: All Parents Have Dreams for Their Children and Want the Best for Them

It is vital for educators to understand that the families who send their children to them each day want their children to succeed in school and in life. Yes, families may say or do things that lead us to wonder if they respect the importance of education. But these actions and behaviors often are triggered by other stressful factors in parents' lives.

In her book *The Essential Conversation*, sociologist Sara Lawrence Lightfoot writes, "I believe that all parents hold big expectations for the role that schools will play in the life chances of their children. They all harbor a large wish list of dreams and aspirations for their youngsters. All families care deeply about their children's education and hope that their progeny will be happier, more productive, and more successful than they have been in their lives."[1]

Unfortunately, the verdict that "parents don't care about their children's education" often falls on parents of color, immigrant parents, or families from poor communities. The many reasons for this misunderstanding of families' desires and beliefs are discussed further in Chapter 6, "Addressing Differences."

Roni Silverstein, an assistant principal in Montgomery County,

Maryland, a diverse suburb, says, "The belief that minority parents don't care couldn't be farther from the truth. When you talk to them you realize that our American schools are the answer to their dreams. What they had to go through to get their children here is remarkable. Many of them work two or three jobs to stay here. They have the American dream in their hearts. If anything, they care more."

What about parents who really don't want to be involved? There are some parents who are so overwhelmed with personal problems that they don't have any energy left for their children's education. In that case, we recommend finding another person in the child's life who can act as a parent. This can be another family member (over 4 million children are being raised by grandparents) or a close family friend or neighbor. If you can't find such a person, turn to a community organization that is active in the family's neighborhood or that provides mentors, such as Big Brothers/Big Sisters.

> "When we go up to that school, they treat us like dirt."
>
> "They think we don't care about our kids because we live here [in a low-income housing project]."
>
> "There's no bus to get there—we have to get a ride from somewhere. So we don't go. Why would we?"
>
> *(African American parents, Kansas City, Missouri)*

RESEARCH BRIEF:
Families of all backgrounds feel college is essential

Not only do many parents of color value K-12 education, they feel college is essential for their child. In a survey of African American, Hispanic, and white parents, Public Agenda found that the parents of color actually placed a greater priority on higher education than the white parents.[2]

This first core belief is the most important of the four. Assuming that all families want the best for their children is the first step in cultivating and maintaining strong partnerships. One way to change attitudes is to lay out experiences and information that contradict those attitudes.

Parents and Teachers Talking Together

The Prichard Committee for Academic Excellence in Kentucky has developed a program called Parents and Teachers Talking Together, or PT3. A PT3 brings together parents and teachers to discuss their hopes for children and what should happen to improve student achievement.

The sessions involve up to thirty people (fifteen teachers and fifteen parents) and are held in local settings such as community centers, schools, churches, and private homes. Each one lasts four to five hours, including a meal, and is run by a trained facilitator.

Step One: After coming together to learn about the purpose of the PT3, parents and teachers break into separate groups. Each group brainstorms the answers to two questions: (1) "What do we want for our students?" These are wishes and dreams. (2) "What do we need to do to get what we want?" These are actions.

Step Two: Everyone convenes into one large group. After looking at the lists generated by the small groups, the participants identify similar responses and categorize them by topic. Then each group sets priorities by voting for the items they feel are the most important.

Step Three: The whole group discusses what parents and teachers can do to make these things happen. Working in small groups, they develop action plans to address their top priorities.

At the end, both parents and teachers report greater understanding and appreciation of each other's perspective. In follow-up research on participating schools, the Prichard Committee has found an increase in parent involvement, improved two-way communication, parent-teacher projects to improve student achievement, and continued discussions.

"The PT3 is exciting. What happens is that the two sets of adults who work directly with children realize that they share the same concerns and want many of the same things for the children. It's heartwarming, and it changes the perspectives they have of one another," notes Bev Raimondo, the director of the Prichard Committee's Center for Parent Leadership and a veteran PT3 facilitator. (For more information about the Prichard Committee and its programs, including PT3, see Chapter 10.)

Suggested Steps for Action

To support families' dreams, educators must demonstrate their belief that parents can help their children achieve them. First, we need to find out what those dreams are and figure out how to support families in realizing them.

Dreams can be the focus of a discussion between parents and teachers at an open house or other event at school. Pick someone to facilitate who has earned the trust of both sides. Here are some suggestions about how to organize the conversation:

1. In small groups, ask parents (and teachers who are parents) to talk about their dreams and expectations for their children's future.
2. Ask parents to write down or dictate some dreams for their children. Make two copies, one to keep and one to hand in.
3. Post the dreams on a chalkboard or newsprint. (Tip: These could go on a bulletin board later.)
4. In their small groups, ask parents to pick a few dreams from those posted and discuss what's required for a person to achieve them.
5. As a whole group, ask for ideas about the steps needed to achieve our dreams. For example, what's required in terms of education, programs, and courses? In-school and out-of-school activities? Personal qualities? Supports from family? Finances? Other?
6. Ask teachers to respond by commenting on how the school's curriculum is connected to families' dreams, and how parents can support their children to gain the skills they need. (For example, why is math an important skill to master for students wanting to be a doctor?)
7. Ask parents to discuss these dreams with their children. Do their children share the same dreams and goals? How are their dreams connected to what they're learning in school? What else do they need to be learning to reach their goals?

If the response to this activity is strong, consider developing a program called "Supporting Our Dreams." Encourage school staff and parents to engage students in discussing how their goals relate to future careers, and how those possible careers relate to the skills they are learning in school.

These discussions can be followed up with workshops that:

✦ Show families effective ways to support their children's learning at home.
✦ Give parents ideas about how to talk with their children about their goals and dreams.
✦ Explain the steps that children at their current grade in school must take to complete the classes and programs required to reach their goals. What programs are available at the next level that will give them the knowledge and skills they need for postsecondary education or training?

More ideas like these are discussed in the rest of the book, especially Chapter 5, "Linking to Learning," and Chapter 7, "Supporting Advocacy."

Core Belief 2: All Parents Have the Capacity to Support Their Children's Learning

Regardless of how little formal education they may have or what language they speak, all parents can contribute to their children's learning. Parents' knowledge, talents, and experiences in life give them plenty of capacity for assisting their children with school skills—but school staff may need to help parents understand and use that capacity. All parents have "funds of knowledge" about their children and the community that should be respected and tapped by school staff.[3]

The expression "Parents are their children's first teachers" is so widely used it has become a cliché. But it is true. We should view and treat parents as the experts that they are.

Still, many parents do not appear to be involved, at least at school. What goes through parents' minds as they consider whether to become involved—or hold back? For starters, they need to feel that they have something to offer, and that they would be welcome if they came.

In their important studies, Kathleen Hoover-Dempsey and Howard

Families' knowledge is often underestimated

Luis Moll, an expert in bilingual literacy at the University of Arizona, has studied barrio schools in the Southwest. He notes two troubling observations: teachers give students lessons that are filled with drills on facts and rules but have little connection to their home life, and they consistently underestimate their students' and families' "intellectual fund of knowledge." When Moll visited students' homes, he found that most Latinos he met had a "formidable understanding" of many topics, including agriculture, mining, medicine, religion, biology, and math.[4]

Sandler found that three key concepts influence the choices parents make about being involved in their children's education:

1. **How parents develop their job description as a parent.** (Researchers call this "role construction.") What parents think they're *supposed* to do to help their children and what their family and friends say about what's important and *acceptable* deeply affect what parents decide to do. Will they decide to be active and involved, passive and deferential, or angry and critical? Their cultural background and surroundings strongly influence this decision.

2. **How confident parents feel about their ability to help their children.** (Researchers call this "efficacy.") Parents are more likely to become involved if they feel that:
   - They have the skills and knowledge needed to help their children
   - Their children can learn what they have to share and teach
   - They can find other sources of skill or knowledge if needed
   - What they do will make a positive difference in their children's learning

Ready,
Set, Go!

. . .

3. Whether parents feel invited—both by their children and by the school. This "sense of invitation" is strongly influenced by signals that parents receive from their children and school staff. These signals let parents know what their children and teachers want and expect. Their children's age and how well they're doing in school also have an impact.[5] In her current research, Hoover-Dempsey notes that of the three factors, invitation is very often the most important.

In other words, we know that parents are more motivated to support their children's learning when they receive clear invitations and support from teachers and other school staff to be engaged, are confident about their ability to help their children, and are clear about what they should do to support their child's learning.

Obviously, school staff can have a big impact on these considerations, especially on making parents feel invited and welcome. In Chapter 4, "Developing Relationships," we discuss how schools can put out the welcome mat, honor families' strengths and interests, and explain clearly how they can help their children.

Suggested Steps for Action to Promote Parents' Capacity to Support Their Children's Learning

Let's explore the framework about what motivates parents to decide that they'll become involved. How does your school help families develop their job description as involved parents? How is it building their confidence so they can help their children and contribute to the school community? How is it making sure that families—all families—feel welcome and accepted?

This checklist can help you assess your school's belief in and support for families' capacity. Mark the statements that describe what school staff and parent volunteers are doing.

1. Developing the "job description" of an involved parent

   ○ Working with families each year to develop and approve a school-family compact that makes clear what parents can do, at home and at school, to promote learning. Making clear what school staff will do to support parents.

○ Recruiting parents who can act as "role models" to new families. For example, a buddy system to pair experienced parents with new arrivals, and storytelling to share experiences of raising children.

○ Asking families from different cultures to share their values and traditions, and to describe how they talk to their children about the value of a good education. (For more ideas, see the Family Welcome Questionnaire in Chapter 11.)

○ Listing the school's expectations for parent involvement in the school handbook and explaining at open houses and other activities why it's important.

○ Other: _____

2. **Building families' confidence in their ability to help their children**

○ Offering workshops and materials that give families skills and information.

○ Sending home learning packets, educational games, and videos that are linked to what children are learning in class.

○ Inviting families to observe in the classroom so they can see how subjects are taught and how children learn.

○ Making sure that at parent-teacher conferences, teachers say, "You are your child's first teacher; tell me about your child." (For a sample Parent Review form, see Chapter 11.)

○ Other: _____

3. **Making sure all families feel welcome and invited by school staff and their children**

○ Making home visits to get to know families and build a personal connection. (Most children love this, but first ask parents if they want a visit. The Needs Assessment Survey in Chapter 11 can be filled out during the visit.)

- ○ Following up flyers and notices of activities with personal phone calls to families and notes from their children inviting them to come.
- ○ Holding smaller meetings in the neighborhood and at school to build a sense of community, and inviting the whole family.
- ○ Surveying families about how they would like to be involved. Offering a range of opportunities, such as yard sales, science fairs, talent shows, reading clubs, plays, and musicals.
- ○ Other: _____

STORY:

I didn't think they meant *me*.

An African American parent was attending her first parent event at a school in St. Louis, after the parent coordinator had personally invited her. A teacher asked, "Did you ever get the flyers we sent home about workshops for parents?" The parent replied, "Yes, I got the flyers and stuff about what's going on at the school. But I didn't think they meant *me*. I didn't think they wanted *me* to come."

Core Belief 3: Parents and School Staff Should Be Equal Partners

The relationships between school staff and parents are commonly built on a lopsided power base. Parents often see school staff as the "professionals," who have the power to assign children to their teachers, dole out discipline, make the rules, and control access to desirable programs. As a result, parents may feel that they are supposed to help their children at home and come to the school only when asked. This seems to be more likely when parents come from different racial, ethnic, or class backgrounds than those of school staff.

Lopsided power relationships between educators and parents are played out in various ways. For example, teachers may feel they are expected to give parents specific directions about how to work with their children. The principal may feel the need to be seen as "in charge" and not as "giving in" to parents. Parents may react by staying away or not responding to the school's requests for volunteers.

We suggest that power should be shared. Every person who is interested in supporting children's development should have equal status, value, and responsibility. That means starting from the premise that everyone has something to offer, and that everyone should get something positive out of the relationship. In contrast to lopsided power relationships, Richard Elmore, a professor at the Harvard Graduate School of Education, suggests a principle of *reciprocity*.

> Every increase in pressure on schools for accountability for student performance should be accompanied by an equal investment in increasing the knowledge and skills of teachers, administrators, students, and their families, for learning about how to meet these new expectations.[6]

This means that people shouldn't be expected to do something well—or, worse, be punished for not doing it well—if they haven't been properly prepared. A school should not be labeled as "failing" if teachers haven't been offered high-quality professional development. If students haven't been taught effectively, or parents shown how to support learning at home, they can't be considered "failures" either. In a reciprocal system, they have a right to demand access to high-quality learning opportunities in return for being held accountable. In other words, their accountability will increase as their capacity is strengthened.

This chart contrasts what school staff might say about different topics, depending on whether the relationships in their school are lopsided or mutual.

Topic	Lopsided relationships	Mutual relationships
ACADEMIC SUPPORT	"Have your children follow my directions about their homework and other assignments."	"Here are some ways to monitor your children's homework and build their skills. Tell us what else you do to help your children."

Topic	Lopsided relationships	Mutual relationships
PARENT SUPPORT	"Train your children to respect and obey school staff at all times."	"Let's work together to develop a code of conduct and promote appropriate behavior."
STATUS	"We are the professionals; don't question our decisions."	"Share your knowledge, skills, and culture with our students. Please let us know when you can come to class."
PARTICIPATION	"Parents are welcome at school during designated times and events."	"You are welcome anytime! Please let us know what you want to know more about and when you can come to workshops and other activities that interest you."

Suggested Steps for Action

One way to determine if your school treats families as equal partners in improving children's learning is to assess how often parents are consulted in important decisions. The No Child Left Behind law has a number of requirements for parent involvement. Think honestly about whether, and how often, your school follows these practices listed in the federal guidelines. Our school:

1. Engages families in planning how they want to be involved in school. ____ YES ____ NO

2. Consults a representative group of parents, not only those who attend PTA/PTO. ____ YES ____ NO

3. Invites families to observe in classrooms, review books and materials, and visit other schools for ideas. ____ YES ____ NO

4. Invites families to attend staff develop-
    ment and faculty meetings.

    _____ YES _____ NO

5. Offers workshops about topics they
    suggest.

    _____ YES _____ NO

6. Involves families in action research—
    for example, surveying families about
    school climate, what workshops and
    activities families are interested in, and
    the best ways and times to communi-
    cate about their children's learning.

    _____ YES _____ NO

How well did you do? Are any of these
activities missing in your school? At the next
faculty meeting, discuss what's missing and
develop an action plan. School staff can support parents' capacity to help children with
school skills through in-school as well as out-
of-school activities. (To explore staff and family attitudes further, use the Attitude Check
exercise in Chapter 11.)

It's the Law

Each school served [by the
Title I program of No Child Left
Behind] shall jointly develop
with parents for all children
served . . . a school-parent
compact that outlines how
parents, the entire school staff,
and students will share the
responsibility for improved
student academic achievement
and the means by which the
school and parents will build
and develop a partnership
to help children achieve the
State's high standards.

—NCLB, Title I, Section 1118 (c)(3)

Core Belief 4:
The Responsibility for Building Partnerships Between School and Home Rests Primarily with School Staff, Especially School Leaders

To create a climate and culture that supports partnership with parents,
strong leadership is essential from both the principal and teachers. The principal plays the key role, but teachers also have to step up as advocates for
family involvement. Leadership from both sets the tone for all school staff.

That lopsided power dynamic we were just discussing also plays out
here. Many families see schools as powerful and forbidding institutions.

Ready,
Set, Go!

. . .

Reaching out to parents is easier for educators than "reaching in" to teachers and other staff is for parents. The principal and teachers must take the first step, especially when parents already feel intimidated by school staff. Certainly, there is a responsibility on both sides, and parents must continue to connect with teachers and other school staff on behalf of their children.

Everyone who works in the school, especially the principal, must "walk the walk," not just "talk the talk," of mutual partnership. This means exhibiting a real passion for partnership.

Of course, school staff must feel confident that they can generate the leadership necessary to carry out these partnership initiatives. The Hoover-Dempsey and Sandler research about what motivates parents applies to educators as well. Teachers will be more eager to engage families when they receive clear invitations and support from their colleagues, are confident about their ability to work with parents, and are clear that it's their responsibility to help families support their child's learning.

For example, Rick Dufour, an educator and expert on professional development, describes an activity with school staff in which he asked teachers to come up with ideas to improve student achievement in their school. The first list that teachers generated included things such as more money, fewer tests, and better-motivated students—all controlled by forces outside the school. He calls this "looking out the window."

Dufour told the staff that he could endorse most items on their list. But he suggested another list that he wanted them to consider for improving student achievement. This list of proposals he called "looking in the mirror." Compare the two lists.

Looking out the window	Looking in the mirror
• More financial support from the state	• Clear, focused academic goals for every student
• Smaller class size and more planning	• Close, timely monitoring of each student's learning to identify problem areas

Looking out the window	Looking in the mirror
• More staff to assist students—teacher aides, counselors, social workers	• Extra support for struggling students
• More-supportive parents	• Strong partnerships with parents based on frequent two-way communication
• No more state testing	
• Fewer mandates from central office	• A collaborative culture—teachers work in teams to help each other improve student achievement
• Higher salaries and support for teachers to attend professional workshops or graduate courses	• Understanding that it's the school's job to ensure that students learn, and are not just taught
• Students with a stronger work ethic and reduced sense of entitlement	• Expecting that all students can learn at high levels
• More current textbooks and instructional materials	• A safe, orderly school with clear, consistently enforced guidelines for student behavior and a powerful culture of mutual respect

The "looking out the window" wish list requires someone else to take action. In contrast, the "looking in a mirror" proposals call for leadership within a school and taking the responsibility for getting the job done.[7]

Suggested Activity

Try this same activity with school staff. Start by asking the group to brainstorm what would improve parent and family involvement at your school. Put the ideas that shift the responsibility to someone outside the school in one column, and ideas that take responsibility in another. Don't label the columns; let the readers figure it out. Then talk about the contrast between what's in the two columns.

Here are some ideas that might come up.

What would improve family involvement—looking out the window	What would improve family involvement—looking in the mirror
• Families who speak English and understand the culture here in the United States • More respect for the value of education • Parents who are more motivated • More money to hire staff who can work with families • More parent involvement programs run by the district • More discipline and better behavior in the home	• A more welcoming school building and front office • Positive phone calls home at least once a month • Translation available in the office and for conferences and other contacts • A family center stocked with learning materials that families can take home • Workshops on reading and math • More planning time to meet with families

School leaders must provide the resources, energy, and leadership to implement and sustain partnership programs. The principal, assistant principal, and master teachers can create a culture of partnership by modeling their beliefs, in both words and deeds, to the entire school community.

At a faculty or school council meeting, take some time to think about who in your school does the following:

✦ Meets and greets parents before, during, and after school, out in the schoolyard as well as in the building
✦ Provides staff with evidence about the importance of collaborat-

ing with families and with professional development to develop partnerships and programs

- ✦ Structures time and occasions during the school year for teachers to collaborate with families in small groups or one-to-one
- ✦ Holds colleagues accountable for communicating regularly with families about their children's progress
- ✦ Presents regular opportunities for staff to share strategies that have worked for building partnerships with families

Conclusion: Barriers to Achieving the Beliefs

What are the barriers to achieving these beliefs? When the faculty and other staff are from a different cultural and social background than students and their families, fears and feelings that people carry may prevent them from embracing these beliefs:

- ✦ Fear of being called "racist" or insensitive

- ✦ Worry about losing power and control

- ✦ Fear of unfriendly oversight or micromanagement of classrooms

- ✦ Concerns about physical safety

- ✦ Fear of being misunderstood

- ✦ Feeling inadequate to deal with conflict and controversy

- ✦ Low confidence in parents' knowledge and judgment

- ✦ Clinging to "safe" and traditional types of family involvement

Cathy David, who has been a teacher, principal, and administrator in Alexandria, Virginia, a diverse urban school district, has considerable experience with these issues. She advises principals to give teachers and other staff a safe space to talk about their fears and concerns, then to deal decisively with each one.

David tells this story: "The Parent Advisory Committee at my school proposed opening the computer lab from six to eight one night a week.

When I took the idea to the faculty, they reacted negatively: 'We can't do this, it won't work. They'll break the computers and mess up the software.'

"I decided to meet with my team leaders to address the objections one by one.

Teachers said:	I said:
"The parents and kids will break the computers."	"The PTA has agreed to replace any computers that are broken."
"They'll mess up the software."	"They can't really damage the software. Besides, we have lots of copies and it's free."
"The children will roam the halls and go into our classrooms un-supervised."	"We really should lock our doors when we leave for the night anyhow."
"Equipment might get stolen or misused."	"The PTA and PAC members will monitor the room to make sure everything is done properly."

"Once the objections were dealt with, the faculty agreed to a three-month trial. It worked just fine," David said.

Getting Started

As you read through this book, you may wonder, "Who is going to do all this?" We suggest that you appoint an action team. It's too big a job for one person, and it can't be delegated to the parent coordinator. A partnership initiative needs to be owned by all the partners, according to Dr. Joyce Epstein, the founder of the National Network for Partnership Schools and director of the National Center on School, Family, and Community Partnerships at Johns Hopkins University. One of Epstein's major contributions to this field is the concept of the action team for partnerships. Epstein told us: "Our studies indicate that it is important to have a 'partnership team' of teachers, parents, and administrators who work together to make sure that school, family, and community partnership are well designed, well integrated, and goal oriented." (For more information about resources to support action teams, including Epstein's definitive guide, see Chapter 10.)

The action team is a working group of a school council or school improvement team. It has the responsibility to plan and continually improve family and community involvement. "This makes a difference, our studies show, in what gets done, how much outreach there is, which parents become involved (who otherwise would be excluded), and how involvement affects students," notes Epstein. The team should include teachers, administrators, parents and other family members, and, at the secondary level, students. Epstein's guide, *School, Family and Community Partnerships: Your Handbook for Action*, is an excellent resource for action teams.[8]

Here are some things that action teams do:

1. Listen to families, teachers, other staff, and community members to identify ideas, needs, and priorities. The Fortress School–Partnership School framework in Chapter 2, the School Climate Survey in Chapter 11, and the checklists at the end of each chapter can also be used to flag areas that need attention.

2. Organize into committees, based on the priorities you set. Epstein recommends creating a standing committee for each of her six types of involvement: parenting, communicating, volunteering, learning at home, decision making, and collaborating with the community.

3. Develop a one-year action plan that covers each area you will work on, create a budget, and identify sources of funding.

4. Meet regularly (at least monthly) as a whole team and establish goals and guidelines for teamwork. How will you communicate? What decision-making process will you use? When will you allow time to discuss issues and solve problems?

5. Gather ideas and plan programs and activities.

6. Publicize activities and team meetings. Include all families and the school community.

7. Evaluate your work and report regularly on progress in meeting the plan.

Throughout the book, we refer to action teams or parent involvement committees, because we consider them essential for doing this work. Of course, individual teachers, administrators, parent leaders, other school staff, school council members, community leaders, and others can pick and choose ideas from this book. Developing the systemic action to transform a school requires a dedicated team working over the long term.

In the following chapters, we will provide your team with strategies to overcome fears and create effective practices that support children's learning. The next chapter deals with the issue of trust, which underlies all productive relationships, and outlines a process to bring families and school staff together.

Chapter 4

Developing Relationships

How Can You Build Trust Instead of Blaming Each Other?

Parents tell us that feeling welcome and being treated with respect by school staff is the number one key to their connection with a school. When school staff construct caring and trustful relationships with parents, treating parents as partners in their children's education, parents are far more likely to become involved—and stay involved.

From talking with principals, teachers, and other school staff, we've learned that many would like advice and tools about *how* to build trust and cultivate warm relationships with families. In this chapter, we explore steps that school leaders and your action team can take to create a school culture that fosters positive relationships with families and community members.

Trust Makes the Difference

When people feel liked, valued, and respected, they collaborate more readily. In their study of trust in Chicago public schools, Tony Bryk and Barbara Schneider found that schools where staff trust parents and their colleagues tend to have higher levels of student achievement. For example, teachers at schools with test results in the top quarter tend to have "strong" and "very strong" levels of trust, while teachers at schools in the bottom quarter tend to have "none" or "minimal" levels of trust.[1]

Bryk and Schneider's definition of trust is based on four qualities that people see in one another: respect, integrity, competence, and personal regard. They used these to develop a framework to look at the trust level in schools.[2] The chart on the following page uses their framework to show how school staff might describe relationships in a school where people trust each other.

The Joining Process

In her research on how and why parents are involved in their children's education, Karen Mapp asked parents to identify what school staff actually did to create trusting and respectful relationships. What parents told her led to Mapp's development of the "joining process." (The material about the joining process in this chapter is drawn from Mapp's 2003 article in the *School Community Journal*, "Having Their Say: Parents Describe Why and How They Are Engaged in Their Children's Education." This research was conducted at the O'Hearn School in Boston.)[3] Designing and implementing a joining process is a crucial job for your action team.

RESEARCH BRIEF:
Schools' practices of involvement are key

Epstein and Dauber note, "The strongest and most consistent predictors of parent involvement at school and at home are the specific school programs and teachers' practices that encourage and guide parent involvement. Regardless of parent education, family size, student ability, or school level ... parents are more likely to become partners in their children's education if they perceive that the schools have strong practices to involve parents at school."[4]

Element of trust	How school staff may describe a high-trust school
RESPECT: mutual esteem that recognizes the important role each person plays in a child's education	• People listen genuinely to one another. • Parents can talk with teachers and feel they have a say in what happens to their children. • Teachers can voice their concerns and feel that administrators will heed what they say. • Principals feel that teachers care about school and will seriously consider their proposals.
COMPETENCE: a feeling that colleagues work together to create an effective working environment and get the job done	• Our colleagues work hard, control their classrooms, and provide challenging teaching. • Administrators provide an orderly, safe building. • Parents provide for their children's basic needs and support education at home.
INTEGRITY: a feeling that colleagues keep their word and do what they say they're going to do	• People's words and actions are consistent. • Our school places the highest priority on children's best interests, and this is the highest purpose of the school.
PERSONAL REGARD: a feeling that colleagues care about one another and are willing to go out of their way to help	• Teachers stay after hours to meet with parents. • Teachers go the extra mile to help each other and advise a new teacher. • Teachers are willing to give students extra help. • School staff get involved in local community matters.

In the three-part joining process, the school community:

1. Welcomes parents into the school
2. Honors their participation
3. Connects with parents through a focus on the children and their learning

Developing
Relationships

• • •

49

Welcoming, honoring, and connecting with families creates a school community in which everyone says they feel like "members of a family." Parents respond to this culture by becoming loyal members of the school community, and by taking part in their children's education in ways they had never envisioned.

Welcome All Families to Your School Community

Parents report that a welcoming process creates a sense of belonging. Not only do parents feel that they belong to the school, but they also feel that the school belongs to them. This sense of belonging motivates parents to be more active in their children's schooling. How do school staff and leaders create a welcoming environment? Here are some good practices:

The Welcome Mat Is Out

Even before families enter the school, they look for reassurance that they will be welcomed when they step through the door. Here are some signals:

- Friendly signs (in all major languages spoken by your families) point out the entrance and say that families and visitors are welcome.
- Parking spots for parents and visitors are clearly marked and are near (or at least not very far from) the entrance.
- School staff and parents greet visitors in a friendly way and ask if they can help.
- Teachers, administrators, and other school staff go outside the building to greet and talk with parents.

The Whole Family Enrolls in the School

It's not just the student who joins a school community, it's the whole family. An enrollment process for new families might include tours of the school in the spring or before school starts in the fall, as well as welcome phone calls and special events to introduce new families to other parents and to school staff.

At the beginning of the school year, hold a "Welcome Night" for parents to meet the staff and follow their student's schedule. Assign "buddies" for new students and their families. Why not do the same for new staff—including custodians, secretaries, and cafeteria workers? Greeting them with a welcoming celebration will set the tone for the whole school community.

The School Feels Warm and Friendly

When first coming into your building, what do families and visitors see? What happens when they enter the front office or sign in at the security desk? What's on the walls to tell them about students and the great work they are doing? Parents tell us they love coming to school when they see things like this:

✦ The entryway is obvious (not behind the Dumpster in the back parking lot). It's clean, attractive, and well-lit. It's wheelchair-accessible. A sign welcomes visitors.

✦ Colorful signs (in different languages, as needed) direct you where to go.

✦ Brightly colored walls are decorated with student artwork or colorful murals the students have painted.

✦ Displays of student projects and other celebrations of student accomplishments outnumber warning posters about alcohol, drug abuse, teen pregnancy, and dropping out.

> "When your child first starts at this school, other parents call you up and welcome you. That's really nice. Then they have a new-parent breakfast, which they have every year. I managed to drag myself there with my screaming child. He was really good there, and I met many of the parents that I see all the time now, and everybody was very friendly. That started the interest for me, to see how involved everyone was. I felt like it was a 'welcoming-into-the-school' kind of thing, and that made me feel like, 'Look at all these people, doing all this for the parents.' So I try to do whatever I can whenever they have parties, make food, or something. I do something to help out."
>
> *(Parent, Boston)*

"The Counter"

Steve Constantino, a former principal, tells this story about his first day as a high school principal in Virginia:

Walking into the front office, the new principal noticed the worn carpet, mismatched plastic chairs, and the clocks that told the wrong time. Then there was *the counter*. There it stood, fifteen feet long and four feet high, covered with peeling laminate, a man-made barrier between the school and those who dared to enter. Behind the counter were the tops of two heads. After a few minutes, he coughed. No luck.

Finally, he said, "Good morning." The secretary closest to him looked up and said, "Yes?" (He later learned that it was her job to greet people.)

"I'm the new principal."

"Oh, your office is over there." She pointed and went back to work.

The message? *Welcome to our broken-down school where we hope we will make you feel as though you are imposing on us. Please take a seat in the mismatched uncomfortable plastic chairs while we decide if we are going to help you or not.*

That afternoon, the counter was taken down, forever. [5]

People Are Accessible

Being ignored or treated rudely is dispiriting. To have a family-friendly culture requires some standards of welcoming behavior, not to mention an open-door policy. This is how parents describe schools they see as inviting:

+ All the staff greet students, families, visitors, and each other in a genuinely friendly way.
+ The front office staff look up as soon as you come in and greet you warmly. If you don't speak English well, they quickly find someone who can interpret.
+ The principal is open and available. Not only are there regular

office hours to meet with families, but the principal also walks the halls and schoolyard, attends school events without a bodyguard, and visits community hangouts.

✦ At the beginning and end of the school day, teachers are outside greeting students and their families as they come and go.

✦ The PTA or parent group offers lots of opportunities to network and meet different people.

✦ The school publishes a directory or has a bulletin board that includes pictures of all the staff (including classified and support staff).

Smaller Is Better

Sometimes, school-wide events such as open houses can feel like cattle drives. Families are herded into the building, go through their paces, and leave without ever talking to someone long enough to make a real connection. Consider breaking down big events into smaller ones that are more inviting and less intimidating.

✦ Class meetings, grade-level socials, book groups, clubs, and other activities offer opportunities for small group conversations.

For ESL families, offer interpreters or special activities in their home language.

✦ Back-to-school nights can be spread out over a week, with one grade per night.

✦ One-to-one interactions, such as informal conversations on the school grounds and home visits by parents or staff, can build deep personal connections.

✦ A family center provides a place where small groups of parents can gather spontaneously or meet with school staff. (Make sure it's in a handicapped-accessible area of the school.) The center can be the home base of the family-school coordinator.

✦ The school library is open at night for families to use and take classes.

Tip from a Principal:
Restructure back-to-school nights so they're less rushed and more intimate

Hold back-to-school nights or open houses one grade level per night, on six different nights—or at least have one night for primary grades, the next for elementary. This way, parents with several children can meet all their children's teachers. Design them so that parents go to the classrooms, spend time with teachers, and learn about the expectations for learning. In middle school, organize teachers into teams, then have them meet with the families in their team.

(Karl Smith, Ramsey Elementary School,
Alexandria, Virginia)

If schools don't make this kind of effort to engage families, all too often the families will stay away. School staff may not consider the possibility that the school environment and culture are unfriendly to families. Building partnerships requires developing purposeful and systematic initiatives that welcome families into the school community. One way to start is to do a Welcoming School Walk-Through. For more information about this process, see Chapter 10.

A Formula for High Turnouts.

A fourth grade teacher at a low-income elementary school in Johnston County, North Carolina, routinely draws about 90 percent of her families to school activities. She sends handwritten notes home, inviting families to teach a lesson, join their children for a barbecue chicken lunch, or plant a class garden. She is on a first-name basis with all her students' parents and makes sure each one has her cell phone number.

Cathy David, who served as a principal at a diverse urban school in Virginia, says, "Make sure that the parents know that you care about their child. More than anything else, this builds trust." David suggests several ways to win the trust of families:

- Invite families to come into the school to drop off and pick up their children at the classroom door. This brings them into the building, so you can greet and get to know them.
- Keep confidential information to yourself—don't share it with your colleagues in the faculty lounge.
- Make *no* assumptions about families—get to know them and their kids.
- Give tours for new families.
- Be at a parent-teacher conference if there is a problem.

Honor Families by Recognizing Their Strengths and Contributions

In this second part of the joining process, the school community honors families by respecting and recognizing their strengths—and validating and affirming their efforts to be involved in their children's learning. As we discuss in the next chapter, you have to meet parents where they are, not where you think they ought to be.

Parents say they feel honored when school staff treat them as true partners in their children's educational development and invite them to work on decision-making committees and projects. Pairing newcomers with veteran parent volunteers builds their self-confidence further. This encouragement and support often motivate parents to become involved in new ways.

Tip from a Principal:
Don't be afraid to ask parents for help or advice

If you're discussing a tough issue, ask them: "What do *you* think we should do?"

(Claire Crane, principal,
Ford Elementary School, Lynn, Massachusetts)

Adopt a Partnership Philosophy

This means *sharing power,* and setting up mechanisms such as councils, committees, and focus groups. Giving families a voice in decisions and real jobs to do are convincing signals that the school recognizes and values parents. Parent input should be welcome in all aspects of the school, from personnel selection and evaluation to the curriculum and academic programs, and from discipline policy to extracurricular activities. For more information about this, see Chapter 8, "Sharing Power."

+ Give parents a real voice in governance, not just a rubber-stamp role. Be sure they have equal representation on all matters put to a vote.
+ Send out a School Climate Survey (see Chapter 11) every year, and give the results to parents. Post them on your school Web site. Ask the parent association to manage this process.
+ At school council meetings and school discussion groups, take on tough issues, not just the safe stuff. Tackle questions such as tracking (who gets into the gifted program or AP math?), racism and prejudice, and teacher treatment of students. Start by circulating a newspaper article or e-mail on the topic. Ask a neutral person to moderate.

- Give families a voice in selecting and evaluating the principal and staff. Ask what qualities are important to them. Put parents on the interview team and selection committee.
- Make sure a diverse group of families is involved in committees and leadership positions, not just the in-crowd or the "principal's pets."

What about the "rabble-rousers" and "troublemakers"—the parents who always seem to have a negative point of view or complain that they're never consulted? It is wiser to include them than to isolate or ignore them. Find out their interests and skills, and build on what they're good at. Team them up with people who have a positive attitude. Find out what's really bothering them and respond to that. Often, just feeling respected and included will take care of the problem.

"My school asks for parents' participation and advice all the time. It seems like the school lets the parents make the decisions, and that makes the parents become more involved. We feel like we're really a part of it. At the meetings, it's just like a family. Issues [are] being discussed, parents talk about what we feel is best for our child or for the school as a whole. Then we vote on it. If you have any suggestions, they're always open to that."

(Parent, Boston)

Embrace Your Families

Every single family can make some contribution to the school. Recognize all forms of family engagement (not just fund-raising) and offer different outlets for involvement, at home and in the community. Celebrations and awards ceremonies are a good way to honor their contributions. Send thank-you notes or little certificates of appreciation. Here are some ideas that school-family coordinators have given us:

- Invite and include all families and all family members.
- Hold activities at times that are convenient for families, such as six to eight in the evening, or at varying times to fit families' different work schedules.
- Make events fun and involve the whole family. Invite a local jazz combo to play at the open house. Ask parents to be greet-

ers, welcoming families as they enter and introducing them to others.

✦ Provide food and child care.

✦ Recognize the whole family—dads, grandparents, older siblings, aunts and uncles.

✦ Make it easy for families who speak little English to take part. Offer translation and interpreters; make sure they're welcomed and feel included.

Tip from a Principal:
Don't hesitate to apologize

"If you have the trust of your community, you can weather a storm and have time to get your side of the story out," says former principal Cathy David. "Show you care, follow through and do what you say you will, and own up to your mistakes.

"A parent wrote a check for a student activity, and it didn't get deposited for two weeks. The check bounced. The parent was furious, because there was money in her account when she wrote it, but not two weeks later. Instead of accusing the parent of not keeping track of her account, I apologized for the delay. That was the end of the problem."

Parents have told us that they felt respected and validated when their ideas and concerns are heard and taken seriously. Even if teachers and parents disagree over an issue, it is not a problem when both sides are willing to listen and take each other's feedback seriously. When the teacher view prevails, parents feel that the relationship is still one of equals, because the parents' contributions to the discussion were given equal weight and importance.

Listen and Respond to Families

Ask families about themselves and their children. Find out what their interests are and what they would like to learn more about. Ask them about

HONORING FAMILIES

Do more	Do less
• "Hello! Welcome to our school. How may I help you?"	• "Who are you? What do you want?"
• Welcome signs with name of the school and principal.	• NO TRESPASSING signs.
• Parent meetings that break into small discussion groups, each picking a leader.	• Parent meetings dominated by a few "officers."
• One-to-one and small group meetings.	• Large meetings in the school gym.
• Thanking parents for contributions large or small.	• Complaining that parents don't do more.
• Meeting and greeting parents before and after school, and going to community events.	• Hiding in the office and assigning parent involvement to the assistant principal or teacher's aide.
• Rotating meetings before school, evenings, and weekends.	• Meeting only during school hours.
• Involving families in selecting a new reading program.	• Announcing a new reading program.
• Surveying families to get their ideas and opinions about activities and programs.	• Planning events, then publicizing them to parents.

the most convenient times of day, and days of the week, for meetings and activities. Find out the best ways and places to get information to them— for example, by cell phone, land line, Web site, or e-mail. Post notices at the grocery store, church, nail shop, or community center. Act on their suggestions, and, if you can't do it right away (or ever), explain why.

Developing
Relationships
· · ·

Questions such as these are included in the School Climate Survey, Needs Assessment Survey, Parent Review, and Parent Volunteer Survey tools in Chapter 11. Learning from families about their concerns, skills, strengths, and ideas is essential to planning effective programs.

"We Need to Learn How to Listen!"

Melissa Whipple, coordinator of the parent academic liaison program in San Diego, tells this story:

I was at a staff development training where teachers were discussing an issue in small groups. One teacher was very good at listening. After a colleague offered an opinion, she repeated what she understood that person had said. Then she checked to make sure the group understood the speaker's point of view.

This really let us work efficiently and avoid misunderstandings, because she could listen and rephrase the ideas of others so well. After the meeting, I complimented her on this skill and asked her if she had received it through teacher training.

"Oh no," she said. "I used to be a bank teller. I received what they call 'active listening' training because most people are so sensitive about their money. We were thoroughly prepared on how to discuss money-related issues with customers."

This really struck me: if people are that sensitive about issues related to money, they must be super-sensitive about issues related to their children. Even when people share a common language and culture, we still have miscommunications. Think what happens when differences in upbringing, language, social class, religion, and personal experience change the relationship dynamic!

Teachers deserve training to increase their confidence and capacity to have sensitive conversations with parents. Parents deserve to be treated with insight, skill, and finesse when discussing their child's education and development. If bank tellers get this training, teacher prep and staff development programs should offer it, too.

BRIGHT IDEA

Ask for suggestions

Engelhard Elementary School in Louisville has a suggestion box, with forms and pencils next to it, prominently placed in the front entryway. Parents are invited to write down their ideas and are promised a response within twenty-four hours. Even if the suggestion will take more than a day to consider, the parents receive a call of thanks and a promise to get back to them soon.

Map Your School's Parent-Teacher Contacts

A. Teachers, counselors, or advisors are expected to communicate with families:

- ○ 1. When there is a problem
- ○ 2. At parent-teacher conferences
- ○ 3. At least once a month if the student is struggling
- ○ 4. At least once a month with every family
    Other _____

B. School-family communications tend to focus on:

- ○ 1. Student problems and misbehavior
- ○ 2. General news about the class
- ○ 3. Progress in specific problem areas
- ○ 4. Overall student progress
    Other _____

C. When do parents and teachers have face-to-face contact (besides parent-teacher conferences)?

- ○ 1. Some teachers attend PTA meetings and other events for families.

○ 2. All teachers attend at least one family-oriented activity each semester

○ 3. Teachers greet families before and after school

○ 4. Teachers routinely meet one-on-one or in small groups with families

Other _____

D. How often do teachers send home materials that will help parents work with their children, such as learning kits or interactive homework assignments?

○ 1. Rarely

○ 2. Maybe once a month

○ 3. It varies by teacher

○ 4. Every week

Other _____

E. How is student work shared with parents?

○ 1. Our school displays the work of top students only

○ 2. Parents can come to school and see work on the bulletin boards

○ 3. Teachers send home student work about once a month

○ 4. Student work goes home every week; parents and teachers comment on progress

Other _____

Add up your score. Give yourself a point of extra credit for each "other" response that moves your school toward open communications with families. The higher the number, the more your communications with families are open and trusting. If your score is 10 or below, develop a plan to open up communications with families.

Set Ground Rules for Involvement

Obviously, a school can't be wide open all the time. Involve families in designing the terms of engagement. For example, the school can honor families by having an open-door policy, and this policy should set the terms for the visits. Some rules that parents and teachers at the O'Hearn School in Boston have suggested for classroom visit days are listed in the table below.[6]

Do	Don't
1. Walk right into any classroom that does not already have three visitors.	1. Go into any room that already has three other visitors.
2. Go into the room along the side or back.	2. Disrupt the students' learning.
3. Observe what is happening in the room.	3. Take pictures without prior permission.
4. Talk with staff members only if approached by them.	4. Ask staff questions while they're engaged in teaching.
5. Leave when you want. Spend no more than twenty minutes in one room unless otherwise arranged.	
6. Leave messages or questions for staff in their mailboxes.	
7. Ask the principal any question you want.	

Developing

Relationships

· · ·

63

BRIGHT IDEA

VIP security ID cards

Security is always a concern, to parents as well as school staff. Because not all parents have a driver's license or other form of official picture ID, a middle school in St. Louis came up with the idea of a special security badge. They called it a "Very Important Parent (VIP) card." To get one, parents came to the office, got their photo taken with an instant camera, and filled out their name on cardstock labeled "VIP" in large, bright letters. Then the card was laminated. Parents wore them proudly.

Make Parent-Teacher Conferences Family-Friendly

These encounters between parents and teachers can provoke anxiety on both sides.

✦ Pull together a group of families and teachers to talk about how to make conferences less intimidating.

✦ Build a resource file of tips on good parent-teacher conferences.

✦ Consider organizing student-led conferences (see the next chapter, "Linking to Learning," for more details), and emphasize information sharing, rather than passing judgment.

✦ Prepare for the conference by using the Conference Checklist in Chapter 11.

✦ Above all, don't rely on conferences as your school's main contact with families. It's not possible to build constructive working relationships in one or two meetings a year.

Accentuate the Positive

Sorting and selecting students is one function of a school. Unfortunately, this often results in tagging students (and their families) with negative labels. For example, children in special education classes are often referred to as "the ADD kids" or "the LD kids." Don't think that students, and any parents within earshot, don't hear these labels!

Associate people with a talent or strength, and try to give everyone a positive identifier. Instead of "special ed student," say "the boy who built that amazing model" or "the girl who draws the beautiful pictures." Instead of "single mom" or "trailer park family," say "wonderful cook" or "math whiz" or "the mom who's such a help in the office" or "great storyteller." If a family has fixed up a house, planted a garden, helped out a neighbor, coached a team, or repaired a broken window, get that story out.

Connect with Families Through a Focus on the Children and Their Learning

Putting children at the center allows school staff to connect with families on ways to improve teaching and learning. When every family involvement activity, from school plays to open houses, has a focus on educational achievement, parents get the message: this school has high expectations for students. This show of caring not only for children's education but for their overall welfare allows parents and school staff to share a deep common interest. (For more detailed information on linking to learning, see the next chapter.)

Enhance Families' Confidence

All families want to help their children, but they may not know how. Offer workshops and classes for families about what their children are learning, how to help them at home, how to have productive meetings with teachers, and ways to establish discipline. These topics are popular with families. Several national organizations have developed such programs. See the resources on parent training in Chapter 10 for more information.

> "They made me feel like they were there to teach my son. They were always giving me little insights that they saw about him. I knew they were paying attention, that made me feel good. . . . They were telling me things about him that I would have told them, which was so cool. Before the words were coming out of my mouth, they were telling me about his strengths and weaknesses and what should and shouldn't be done. I said to myself, 'They know my son.'"
>
> *(Parent, Boston)*

In an online discussion group sponsored by MiddleWeb, teachers recommended looking at student work with parents. (For more information on this interactive Web-based resource, see Chapter 10.) In small groups, parents look at student work, describe what they see and don't see, and discuss what they wonder about. (To protect privacy, no student or teacher names are left on the work.) As Debbie Bambino, one of the teachers, put it: "Parents can add new layers of understanding that will inform our plans to improve our instruction and assignments."

A planning team of parents and teachers at Conway Middle School in Louisville, Kentucky, came up with this Looking at Student Work (LASW) strategy:

1. Every student in the school (grades six to eight) worked through an item from the previous year's state science test.
2. On a staff development day, parents were invited to join teachers in the cafeteria for a LASW session, examining the student work on the item. All items were anonymous.
3. All the teachers participated, not just science teachers, so there were parent and teacher "nonexperts" at each table.
4. They used a rubric (a scoring guide to assess student work) and an LASW protocol that went like this: Small groups looked at a piece of work, using the rubric to evaluate it. Each person rated the work on a sticky note and posted their ratings anonymously. The group discussed the reasons for the ratings, then agreed on one rating.
5. After rating several pieces, the groups revisited their ratings, discussing the level and quality of work and what they learned from the exercise. About thirty parents participated.

John Norton, an education writer and editor at MiddleWeb, observed the process. "This was one of the faculty's first experiences with looking at student work, too, and there were lots of 'ahas' among the parents and the teachers. Parents said they came away with a much clearer idea of what it means to view student work from a standards/mastery point of view."

Home Visits

A lot of home-school communication is limited to one-way notices and newsletters. Home visits can gain parents' trust, build rapport between families and school, and provide information about how the school works. If parents are reluctant to come to school, a home visit can be a critical link, and often leads to more participation at home and at school.

Who makes home visits? Sometimes teachers, aides, counselors, and principals visit families. Another approach is to recruit and train family advocates or parent-support workers to make home visits. Adults from

Steps for Making a Home Visit

In elementary school, a home visit can proceed in this way:

1. Arrange a visit at a time convenient for the family, usually evenings or weekends.
2. Begin by asking parents to talk about their children's skills, talents, and interests.
3. Relate these abilities to skills students are learning at school. Discuss how chores and other family activities can be ways to build those skills.
4. Introduce short, simple learning activities. For example: using cooking recipes to teach reading, sequencing, and measuring; playing counting and spelling games; doing outdoor science projects.
5. Show how to work with the children, and then observe as parents practice with their children. Leave learning materials behind for families to use.

In middle school, children can serve as hosts for home visits. They meet with teachers before the visit and discuss what kinds of assistance they would like. The home visit can include information about tutoring; special programs in math, science, or other subjects at local museums or colleges; and family activities to improve skills. In any home visit, the focus should always be on helping children to succeed in school.

the community who'd like to work part time are good candidates. They can build relationships with families, explain how the school works, take learning materials such as spelling lists and math learning kits, and show how to use them with children. Title I funds can be used for this purpose.

Home Visits to Improve Reading Skills

Even though it's in a low-income area, the O'Hearn school has posted some of the highest reading scores in the city, up from near the bottom. How was this transformation achieved?

First, teachers *and* parents had extensive discussions about how to improve. They tested strategies until they figured out what worked. To their surprise, they found that awarding prizes to students for reading the most books did *not* increase reading for most students. Instead, they found that home visits were far more effective. Parents trained as home visitors went to the homes of every new student and took books for each child in the family. Now, 95 percent of students and their families regularly take part in a home reading program. During their discussions, teachers and parents realized that the parent visitors had become an important resource to promote learning:

+ Families received visitors warmly because they called as friends who share their experience of raising children on a small income.

+ As these relationships continued, parents felt encouraged to visit classrooms and participate in school activities.

+ Parents speaking a second language read to their children in their native language and borrowed easy-to-read books in English from the school library.

+ As a result, home reading increased, trusting adult relationships developed, and children's academic performance steadily increased.

Show Parents That Staff Care About Their Children

In their description of the "Holiday School," a Chicago elementary-middle (K-8) school with a high trust level, Bryk and Schneider describe how the teachers have high expectations for the students, even though they live in an impoverished area. That teachers and parents share the same goals did not happen by chance.

"Holiday teachers knew that they had to make a concerned effort to help parents understand what they needed to do for their children to progress in school. [They say] 'I talk to my parents. I let them know what I really expect from them and their kids . . . and what I'll be doing.' In addition, Holiday staff encouraged parent visits to their classrooms and sought to use those opportunities to model how parents could better support their children's learning."[7]

According to Holiday School parents, teachers showed that they care in these ways:

> "When I was a teacher, I made home visits. I went with my aide, who spoke Spanish. When the child went home, then I went home with them, because I knew somebody was going to be there who knew that child. That was a really effective way to connect with my families."
>
> *(Pam Miller, retired teacher, Alexandria, Virginia)*

1. "There's a teacher who talks to those kids like he's their father."
2. "The teachers can relate to me. We talk. They listen to what I have to say. It's not like they look down on me."
3. "They're not concerned about just a part of the child, they're concerned about the holistic well-being of the children."
4. The principal "treats everybody in this school as equal. I don't care if you're black, white, Puerto Rican, he don't treat you different. . . . He don't have no racial nothing about him."
5. The principal is "funny, great sense of humor, but he's about the business of educating the children . . . I really admire [him]."[8]

Advice from a Principal:
Use school support staff

"We try to use the reading team, psychologists, guidance counselors, the nurse, and social workers. They do workshops for parents about strategies to work with their children and offer MegaSkills workshops that include refreshments and packets of school supplies or learning games to take home."

(Karl Smith, Ramsey Elementary School, Alexandria, Virginia)

Establish a Family Center

The family center can be the place where families and staff can form personal relationships. The Saltonstall School in Salem, Massachusetts, has a family center in a full-size classroom that looks more like someone's home than a schoolroom. A stove, oven, refrigerator, and microwave allow families to fix meals for meetings and get-togethers. Comfortable seating, toys, games, and reading materials make it feel "like home." Family centers are often staffed by the school's Parent Coordinator, but they can also be run by volunteers.

A family center can give a school a whole new approach to engage and inform families. First of all, it's a nonthreatening place to have meetings, workshops, informal discussions, and social exchanges. Here are some activities that family centers have sponsored:

+ A Father's Luncheon, at which over 350 fathers, grandfathers, uncles, brothers, and cousins ate lunch with children, visited classes, and signed up for school activities
+ A "parent presence" that teachers can call upon to visit class and help with students' unruly behavior
+ Food and clothing banks, lending libraries, and health fairs
+ "The Light's On" after-school program promoting students' interest in math, science, art, dance, drama, computers, and foreign languages

What Is a Family Center?

"Special places in schools where family members can meet, plan, and implement programs, family centers are also places where school staff and community volunteers are invited to collaborate in support of children's academic and social development. Particularly important to participants in the family center was the *designation* of a special place in schools for families. . . . 'A place of their own' for parents in schools . . . represents a significant symbolic and structural change in a school's relationship with families."[9]

(Vivian Johnson)

+ Yard sales to make household goods and clothing available to families
+ Talent shows at which parents, students, teachers, and other staff can show off their skills
+ Child care so that families can meet with teachers or help out in class
+ "Coffee with the Principal" on the first Monday of each month
+ Adult and family literacy programs, ESL and citizenship classes, job skills training, and GED programs
+ Parent education workshops on child development and other topics suggested by parents
+ Tutoring, mentoring, and "homework clinics"

Most family centers are located in the schools they serve—in converted storage areas, unused classrooms, ends of hallways, even a former girls' shower room. When lack of space is a problem, schools have been creative. San Diego transformed a school bus into a Mobile Parent Resource Center, with tables, chairs, a copier, a laminator, and resource materials. Fairfax County, Virginia, has opened a family center in an apartment complex near the school, in a two-bedroom apartment donated by the landlord.

Steps for Starting a Family Center

1. Find out what your community wants in a family center.

    *   Welcome the entire school community to take part.
    *   Conduct a needs assessment and map the resources in the school community.
    *   Distribute the results to everyone in the school community.

2. Based on the results, develop a plan.

    *   Invite everyone to meet to plan a Family Center.
    *   Determine goals, tasks, and a time line.
    *   Report progress regularly and share ideas frequently.

3. Celebrate the opening and keep planning.

    *   Be sure everyone is included when the Family Center opens.
    *   Consistently invite participation to create and maintain supportive strategies for the Family Center.[10]

Family centers are just as important in middle and high schools as they are in elementary schools. Where else in a high school could parents go if not to a family center? At all levels, they're a gathering place where families, school staff, students, and community members are welcomed and supported. In middle and high school, students become more involved. They drop in, talk about what's on their minds, ask for advice, and check things out. They see family centers as a place like home, but in school.

For example, a student who's thinking about going to college but doesn't know anyone who has ever gone past high school may stop by to talk it over. Students tell us, "It's different from going to see a guidance counselor; it's more like talking to a friend." At the family center, students

"What happened in school today?"

Steve Constantino, a former high school principal, describes a typical scenario at his house:

Everyone is home for dinner, for the first time in three months. Dad the educator is trying to engage the kids.

Dad: "What did you do in school today?"

Answer: "Nothing."

Dad: "Any homework tonight?"

Answer: "No."

Steve's comment: "We have to ask better questions of our children. What hope is there if even I as an educator can't ask better questions than that? We must have a mechanism to equip parents to ask better questions."

feel free to talk about their fears and admit what they don't know. It's a continuing conversation, not a meeting.

Yes, students in middle and high school tend to want to be more independent. But they say they want their parents to be able to step in and help them if they're feeling threatened or troubled. When they need to go to a safe place, they want to know where it is.

High school parents need a place to go, too. They often want to talk with someone who's both friendly and knowledgeable, someone they can confide in and who can help them. Dealing with teenagers is challenging; the family center is a safe place to get advice, support, and information.

The connecting component, placing children's education at the center, brings the school community together. Parents and staff rally around a goal that is meaningful and important to both. When school staff show parents that they are truly committed to educating their children, parents more readily become loyal advocates of the school. When they work together as *equal* partners in educating children, parents and teachers build trust and understanding. This focus on the children is, in the final

Developing
Relationships

• • •

73

analysis, what keeps parents connected, involved, and feeling like important members of the school community.

The next chapter, "Linking to Learning," discusses in more detail how a school's family involvement program can be retooled to improve student achievement. It takes the ideas about connecting families to what their children are learning, and applies them to specific activities and programs some schools commonly use to engage parents.

Checklist

How Family-Friendly Is Your School?

WELCOMING ENVIRONMENT

1. Friendly signs inside and out welcome families and visitors and explain how to get around the building.

☐ *Already doing this* ☐ *Could do this easily* ☐ *This will take time* ☐ *This will be hard*

2. The school has standards of welcoming behavior that apply to all staff, including bus drivers, security guards, custodians, and cafeteria workers.

☐ *Already doing this* ☐ *Could do this easily* ☐ *This will take time* ☐ *This will be hard*

3. Front office staff are friendly—recognize visitors right away, provide information easily, and answer the phone in a way that makes people glad they have called.

☐ *Already doing this* ☐ *Could do this easily* ☐ *This will take time* ☐ *This will be hard*

4. There is a comfortable family resource room stocked with books, games, and educational information that families can borrow and where parents can meet.

☐ *Already doing this* ☐ *Could do this easily* ☐ *This will take time* ☐ *This will be hard*

5. Current student work is displayed throughout the building. Exhibits clearly explain the purpose of the work and the high standards it is to meet.

    ☐ *Already doing this*   ☐ *Could do this easily*   ☐ *This will take time*   ☐ *This will be hard*

6. All programs and activities for families focus on student achievement—they help families understand what their children are learning and promote high standards.

    ☐ *Already doing this*   ☐ *Could do this easily*   ☐ *This will take time*   ☐ *This will be hard*

7. Special workshops, learning kits, and other activities show families how to help their children at home—and respond to what families say they want to know about.

    ☐ *Already doing this*   ☐ *Could do this easily*   ☐ *This will take time*   ☐ *This will be hard*

8. The school reports to parents about student progress and how teachers, parents, and community members can work together to make improvements.

    ☐ *Already doing this*   ☐ *Could do this easily*   ☐ *This will take time*   ☐ *This will be hard*

STRONG RELATIONSHIPS BETWEEN TEACHERS AND FAMILIES

9. A "joining process" welcomes families to the school, offers tours, makes bilingual speakers available, and introduces them to staff and other families.

    ☐ *Already doing this*   ☐ *Could do this easily*   ☐ *This will take time*   ☐ *This will be hard*

10. Teachers and families have frequent opportunities to meet face-to-face and get to know each other—class meetings, breakfasts, home visits, class observations.

☐ *Already doing this*　☐ *Could do this easily*　☐ *This will take time*　☐ *This will be hard*

11. Teachers or advisors make personal contact with each family at least once a month.

☐ *Already doing this*　☐ *Could do this easily*　☐ *This will take time*　☐ *This will be hard*

12. A family liaison helps teachers connect to families and bridge barriers of language and culture.

☐ *Already doing this*　☐ *Could do this easily*　☐ *This will take time*　☐ *This will be hard*

DEVELOPING FAMILIES' SELF-CONFIDENCE AND POWER

13. Families are involved in planning how they would like to be involved at the school.

☐ *Already doing this*　☐ *Could do this easily*　☐ *This will take time*　☐ *This will be hard*

14. School committees and the PTA/PTO reflect the diversity of the school community and actively recruit and welcome families from all backgrounds.

☐ *Already doing this*　☐ *Could do this easily*　☐ *This will take time*　☐ *This will be hard*

15. The school is open and accessible—it is easy for parents to meet with the principal, talk to teachers and counselors, and bring up issues and concerns.

☐ *Already doing this*　☐ *Could do this easily*　☐ *This will take time*　☐ *This will be hard*

Developing
Relationships
· · ·

16. Parents develop school improvement projects and do action research—survey other families, observe in classrooms, review materials, and visit other schools and programs.

☐ *Already doing this*　☐ *Could do this easily*　☐ *This will take time*　☐ *This will be hard*

PROFESSIONAL DEVELOPMENT FOR FAMILIES AND STAFF

17. Families learn how the school system works and how to be an effective advocate for their child.

☐ *Already doing this*　☐ *Could do this easily*　☐ *This will take time*　☐ *This will be hard*

18. Teachers learn about effective approaches to working with families of diverse cultural backgrounds.

☐ *Already doing this*　☐ *Could do this easily*　☐ *This will take time*　☐ *This will be hard*

19. Families and staff have opportunities to learn together how to collaborate to improve student achievement.

☐ *Already doing this*　☐ *Could do this easily*　☐ *This will take time*　☐ *This will be hard*

20. The school reaches out to identify and draw in local community resources that can assist staff and families.

☐ *Already doing this*　☐ *Could do this easily*　☐ *This will take time*　☐ *This will be hard*

Which areas are you doing well in? Which ones will need more work?

_____

_____

_____

How are parents involved in making the school open, welcoming, and collaborative?

_____

_____

_____

What are your concerns?

_____

_____

_____

Reflection: What steps could you take to help your school become more family-friendly?

Right away:

_____

_____

Over the long term:

_____

_____

Chapter 5

Linking to Learning

How Will Involving Parents
Help Your Test Scores?

The point of this chapter is to help families support their children's learning, both at home and at school. To help their kids at home, parents need to know what's going on at school. For example, teachers often complain that parents don't bother to check their children's homework. But parents have told us, "We didn't know we were supposed to check homework. Tell us how to do it and what to look for. Explain what the teacher wants."

Engaging families in children's learning has a positive impact on student achievement.[1] Reading workshops and family math nights, home learning packets and Saturday academies, parent-run study centers and career portfolio nights can all help students do better in school. Studies show that families of students from preschool through high school are eager for this kind of information and will use it when they get home.

Yes, most schools offer programs like these. But consider all the other activities and events that schools put on for families—back-to-school nights, sock hops, PTA meetings, heritage festivals, winter concerts, ice cream socials, international dinners, and bingo. How closely are they connected to student learning? Clearly, the more a program is expressly designed to improve student achievement, the more impact it will have.

All the programs at your school should help families:

✦ Get a clear idea of what their children are learning and doing in class
✦ Promote high standards for student work
✦ Gain skills to help their children at home
✦ Understand what good teaching looks like
✦ Discuss how to improve student progress

Of course, schools should keep holding open houses and Fall Fairs. They're great relationship builders and they can be a lot of fun. We don't mean that every family activity should include a test-prep drill. Aim for balance. Almost any activity can include a link to learning. Here are some examples of how to give traditional programs a focus on achievement that your action team can consider:

Back-to-school night. Adopt an achievement-for-all theme such as "Reach for the Stars." Demonstrate lessons to show how teachers use high standards in the classroom and engage students at all learning levels. Brainstorm ideas parents can use at home.

School grounds. If the PTA or parent group wants to plant trees or a community garden, involve science teachers and their classes. Ask students to research plants that will thrive in your soil and climate, and to find out how to care for them.

Book fair. Announce a school-wide reading club. Set a high goal for the whole school, say, reading 100,000-plus books over the year. Ask students to calculate how many books students, parents, and teachers need to read per month to meet the goal.

Family fun night. If you're building kites, students can give a talk on the aerodynamics of kites and construct a scoring guide for a high-flying kite. Explain how teachers use scoring guides in the classroom.

Think before offering parenting classes

When planning programs for families, school staff often suggest workshops on parenting. Many parents are eager for information about how to help their children and keep them safe. But when offered "parenting" classes, families may feel insulted. We often hear parents say: "They think we're not doing a good job! I don't want someone telling me how to raise *my* kids."

"Parenting" tends to be a middle-class term. If parents want a workshop about how to talk to their teenagers, keep their kids from fighting, get them to go to bed on time, or be more responsible, respond to that request. We recommend, however, that you call it something other than "parenting," unless the parents you want to reach use that term first.

Parent group meetings. Spend less time on business meetings and more on showcasing student work. Invite student authors to give talks about their books. Ask a chemistry class to report on an experiment and explain what they learned. Sponsor a state-of-the-school report to review student performance and discuss plans to improve it.

This chapter is organized into the following sections:

- ✦ Helping families understand what's happening in the classroom
- ✦ Putting student work front and center
- ✦ Communicating regularly with families about learning
- ✦ Putting learning at the center of parent-teacher conferences— and including students
- ✦ Using student achievement data to design programs for families
- ✦ Collaborating with community organizations

Linking to

Learning

· · ·

All the activities we suggest in this chapter and throughout the book can take place in the community as well as in the school. Go where your families hang out: community centers, supermarkets, nail salons, churches, Laundromats, recreation facilities, parks, and families' front porches.

Helping Families Understand What's Happening in the Classroom

The ways that teachers teach and students learn have changed immensely in the past twenty years. When today's parents were last in

TIPS FOR LINKING TO LEARNING

Do more	Do less
• Displaying student work, along with scoring guides to rate levels of performance	• Featuring teacher-made bulletin boards with themes such as "Autumn Colors"
• Contacting families regularly about student progress, through Friday folders, notes, and phone calls	• Calling home only when students misbehave or are in trouble
• Holding math, literacy, and health nights, and family-questions-about-school events	• Offering parenting classes
• Offering student-led family conferences, where students discuss their work and assess its quality	• Focusing on student behavior and shortcomings at parent-teacher conferences
• Holding workshops for families on planning for college and information about college admission standards	• Hanging posters about drug abuse and teen pregnancy

Parents Are Hungry for Knowledge

A middle school principal in Los Angeles, Mary Lou Amato observes: "Often our parents did not get a good education in their country or here, but want their children to do well in school. They're just as hungry for education as their kids are. They're there because they want to learn. The school has a responsibility to build their capacity.

"As you're training them you're also working with their child. Help them be more self-confident; lead them to some education for themselves. They want ESL classes, either after school or on Saturdays. They want to learn to run meetings and speak in front of a group. Always give families something to take home to support learning, a book or learning kit—they really use them."

school, teachers stood in front of the class and student desks were lined up in rows. Every day, schools are adopting new approaches, new programs, and new terms—differentiated instruction, Success for All, criterion-referenced tests, Balanced Literacy, and text-to-text connections. How are parents supposed to know what these terms mean?

Parents and community members want to know about these changes. What do standards mean for their kids? How will students be assessed and what do their scores mean? How has teaching changed to help students measure up? Take advantage of their curiosity—let them experience what's different from when they were in school. Many schools have curriculum nights at which families learn more about math, science, and literacy. Here are some ideas for going a little deeper.

Classroom Visits

Classroom visits give parents a front-row seat on what happens at school. Parents may know something about standards, but they probably don't know what a standards-based classroom looks like. How do teachers structure lessons so that students do research, solve real-world problems, and pursue their own interests? What are critical thinking skills and how do teachers develop them?

Start the school year with "Check Out the Classroom" days and encourage families to visit throughout the year. For families who can't come during the day, demonstrate lessons at curriculum nights, book fairs, Saturday academies, and other family events. In middle and high schools, parents can "shadow" their students, following them from class to class during a morning or afternoon.

Here are five things to cover during a classroom visit:

1. Show how the room setup encourages learning. Why are desks grouped in clusters instead of in rows? How do beanbag chairs, soft cushions, and a quiet corner help students with different learning styles? What are the rocking chair and carpet for?

2. Explain the different learning centers. How do "word walls" (groups of words on the wall) and the classroom library develop literacy skills? What experiments are students doing in the science area? What are math manipulatives (items such as pattern blocks, coins, and bean counters) and how do students use them to master math? What's in the reference section?

3. Demonstrate a lesson that shows how students work together and critique each other's work. Model a classroom discussion and show how you draw all students into the conversation.

4. Use a scoring guide to show how standards are used in the classroom. If it's a research project, describe what students will learn and what you expect in "proficient" work. (A scoring guide, or rubric, describes what standards the teacher will use to grade an assignment. For example, a social studies essay requiring the student to draw conclusions from a table will get a 3 or an A if it draws clear, logical conclusions and backs them up with data from the table.)

5. Toward the end of the visit, suggest some ways parents can use what they've learned to talk to their children. Ask parents for their ideas.

Use music, dance, drama, and art to get parents' attention

Karen Parker Thompson, coordinator for family involvement and community resources in the Alexandria, Virginia, public schools, notes: "The arts let parents and students connect to education in fun ways. At a science workshop for middle school students, teachers, and families, we invited a woman who specializes in movement and drama. She had seventy-five parents and students moving around in circles to act out the solar system. A cluster of students was the sun; the others were planets, moons, and comets. They were having a great time. The kids enjoyed being with their parents and communicating about what they were learning. The rich parents and the low-income families were all just people learning together."

Class Meetings

Class meetings allow time for teachers and parents to learn from each other. They can be special events or part of open houses and back-to-school nights. Instead of discussing rules of behavior or filling out emergency forms, talk about your approach to teaching and ask families to brainstorm ways they can support their kids. Encourage discussions. Nuts-and-bolts information, such as class schedules and school supply lists, can be covered in handouts. Use the time to build relationships.

Class meetings that follow can cover specific subjects and raise expectations. Consider devoting one meeting each to showing how you teach reading, writing, and math. Explain an assignment and give parents their students' work. What standard did the assignment address? Show them the scoring guide you used and ask them to assess the work using the guide. Welcome hard questions: "What does this standard mean? How does this assignment reflect that standard? How do grades relate to standards?" Then talk about how parents can use scoring guides to discuss student work at home.

Linking to

Learning

• • •

A six-step agenda for a back-to-school night class meeting

Give parents name tags and ask them to sit at their child's seat. Then they can see the classroom from their child's perspective—and get to know more about their children's friends.

1. Ask parents to talk about their favorite teachers and what was special about them. Make a list of the main points.

2. Talk about why you became a teacher. Describe your qualifications and training to teach the class.

3. Express your vision of teaching. What kind of teacher are you? What is the role of students in your classroom? How will you encourage a love of learning? What skills and knowledge will your students gain over the year? Ask parents if this is different from when they were in school.

4. Discuss how you will help students who are struggling and challenge students who learn quickly. Describe your commitment to making sure that every student does well.

5. Do a mini-demonstration of a lesson you have taught in this class.

6. Explain that you will stay in touch with parents about student progress. When and how can parents contact you with questions or concerns?

Around midyear, ask parents what you think is going well in terms of their children's learning. Ask if their children are having any problems or other concerns. Compare this to your experience in the classroom. Finally, ask parents what you could do to help them work with their children.

Opening the Classroom to Latino Families

At McCoy Elementary School in Kansas City, Missouri, the number of Latino parents was growing, but not many were involved. The mostly white teachers worried that "these families aren't making education a high priority." According to the faculty, Latino families rarely came to school, and they pulled their children out for long trips to Mexico at odd times.

In a focus group, Latina mothers said they didn't realize their trips were a problem. No one at the school had said anything about it. They agreed to go during the summer or holiday breaks. If that was not possible, they would ask the teacher for their children's assignments to work on during the trip.

Switching the subject, the parents said they had noticed changes in the classrooms. "What are the carpets for? Why are the desks put together like tables? How do you teach reading in this country? It's not the same way that we were taught at home."

School staff were surprised that the parents had noticed. Earlier that year, they had adopted the Balanced Literacy program. Teachers were moving desks around, putting up word walls, doing read-alouds, and building classroom libraries. The principal arranged for parents to observe in classrooms, and asked the League of United Latin American Citizens (LULAC) to provide a translator.

Parents borrowed books from the school library so their children could read aloud to them in English. The school bought books in Spanish so that families could read to their children. Teachers signed up for training to do home visits, and bilingual parents agreed to translate. Did reading achievement go up? Of course.

In middle and high schools, parents can meet with a team of teachers or the students' advisors. Cover topics such as these:

- ✦ Interdisciplinary student projects that use writing in math and science in social studies
- ✦ Developing research and inquiry skills
- ✦ Coping with the homework monster
- ✦ Smart study skills
- ✦ What's in a grade—demystifying the ratings system
- ✦ What colleges are looking for

Preparing Parents to Work in the Classroom

Although volunteering in the classroom is a good way to see what students are learning, many parents don't feel confident taking on that task. Mary Lou Amato, a principal in Los Angeles, has this advice: "We had a big push to get parents involved in the classrooms and it didn't work. There were language issues, and parents felt they lacked content knowledge. Then parents came up with an interesting idea: why can't we work in the parent center to support the teachers? This was a big stepping-stone to getting parents into the classroom. The Open Court reading program has take-home books and other things that need to be put together. Parents were proud to do that and bring them to the teacher. They started reading things. They felt productive and that they were doing something important. Then they were ready to go into the classroom."

By the time students are in middle and high school, many of their mothers are working full time. Instead of volunteering in classrooms during the day, parents can run a student study center after school. Teachers can help parents develop the program and learning materials such as practice sheets and homework organization tools. Parents can also attend professional development classes to upgrade their teaching skills. Here are some services such parent-run centers can offer:

- ✦ Tutoring in various subjects
- ✦ Organization and study skills
- ✦ Test proctoring to help students make up missed exams
- ✦ English as a Second Language
- ✦ Test-taking skills
- ✦ Writing college essays

PALs—Parent Academic Liaisons

San Diego may be the only school district in the country to employ certified teachers as parent liaisons. The Parent Academic Liaison (PAL) program places experienced teachers at high-need elementary schools on special assignment.

According to PAL program coordinator Melissa Whipple, the advantage of this approach is that teachers have inside knowledge about how the system works and how to advocate for students. They also can explain the school's academic program to parents and offer specific ways for parents to support teaching and learning at home and at school. Adding to the classroom experience they bring to the job, PALs get training and support in developing research-supported programs to involve families.

Whipple adds, "We would really like to train administrators, too, since their lack of understanding in this area is one of the biggest obstacles to authentic parent involvement. They don't know what they don't know."

PALs have three major areas of responsibility, all aimed at improving student achievement:

1. School staff. PALs meet regularly with the principal, teachers, counselors, and other staff to reinforce the value of parent involvement, offer ways to establish and maintain trusting relationships, and identify student needs. They also work with staff to develop ways for the school to work with families to enable them to support their children as more powerful learners.

2. High-need students. PALs work with staff to identify students needing special learning resources (such as tutoring, mentoring, and after-school programs). They coordinate school, district, and community resources to provide supports that target students' needs.

3. Parent empowerment. PALs provide regular workshops for parents on the curriculum, the home learning environment, child development, and parenting. They also organize and train volunteers, recruit for other parent education programs, and coach parents on being leaders and advocates.

(continued)

PALs *(continued)*

Using the framework for parent involvement developed by Joyce Epstein and the National Network of Partnership Schools (see Chapter 10), the PALs have organized and put into place a comprehensive parent involvement program at the schools. "One of my greatest successes was parent workshops . . . that taught strategies, games, and information to help parents support their children's academic progress at home," said Nick Voinov, the PAL at Carver Elementary School. "Every week we had ongoing academic workshops that focused directly on what the kids were learning at school. Parents commented often how it was beneficial to have the opportunity to learn how to support their kids."[2]

Putting Student Work Front and Center

How transparent is your school? How much can parents and visitors find out about what children are learning and doing just by walking around the building? Is there clear evidence that all students are expected to learn at a high level? Posting student work in the hallways and classrooms is a great way to get this information across. Make it clear what the assignment was, what students were supposed to learn from it, and what standards students were expected to meet. Include a scoring guide so that parents can rate the quality of the work. Change the displays often.

Show student work out in the community, too. This can change the way people in the area perceive students, especially teenagers. ("Wow, these kids are really using their heads. Did you see that clinic they designed?") Arrange for students to show and discuss their projects in shopping malls, community centers, public libraries, church meeting rooms, and government buildings. Having an audience is a powerful incentive for students to do their best work. A well-informed community will support its public schools.

Exhibiting Work at School Events

At Curriculum Night, be sure that families can see good work for their students' age and grade level. (Good means "proficient," not "basic" or even "high basic.") At Diversity Night, feature student-made exhibits about the different cultures represented at the school. At the book fair, show books that students have "published," and ask them to read from their works. At the March PTA meeting, include a take-the-test activity, where parents try their hand at questions on the state tests and look at student responses. Discuss how the test questions (and what students must know to answer them) are different from the ones parents took when they were in school.

Students can be involved in planning events, such as an ice cream social or a luncheon to honor volunteers. In middle and high school, organizing an event can be a class project. Students can divide up the tasks, such as getting estimates for food costs, compiling an address list, setting the agenda, and recruiting help. At the event, ask students to report on what they did—and what they learned from it.

Ways to Use Portfolios

- At the parent-teacher conference, ask students to show their best work and assess its quality. Is it proficient? How could it be better? How can you use the skills you learned?

- In middle and high schools, hold regular exhibitions and invite parents, community members, and other students. Put students in charge of explaining and defending their best work to an audience.

- Train parents to help assess student portfolios, especially if your state uses portfolios as part of its assessment system.

Using Portfolios

A portfolio is a collection of a student's work. It may be the best pieces across different subjects or a variety of examples from one subject, such as writing or science. Sometimes the portfolio may show how a project developed—first draft, revisions, and the final piece. When students build portfolios, they take charge of their work. Their papers, projects, and assignments become products that demonstrate what they've learned and

Linking to

Learning

· · ·

93

Teacher outreach to parents pays off

In a study of Title I elementary schools, researchers found that teacher outreach to parents improved student progress in both reading and math. When teachers did these three things, student performance improved at a 40–50 percent higher rate:

1. Met face-to-face with each family in their class at the beginning of the year
2. Sent families materials each week on ways to help their children at home
3. Telephoned routinely with news about how their children were doing, not just when they were acting up or having problems[3]

accomplished. It's not just a piece of paper that teachers grade and no one else ever sees.

Whenever showing student work, try to get this information across:

1. What are students learning? Why is it important to learn this? How will they use it?
2. How are we helping students do work that meets high standards?
3. What does good work for your child's age and grade level look like?
4. How many students are working at a proficient level? How do we know?
5. What is the school doing to improve achievement? What can families do?

Communicating Regularly with Families About Learning

Look closely at how your school communicates with families. When families can work closely with teachers, their children adjust to school better, attend more regularly, and stay in school longer. They also earn higher grades and test scores. In addition, families are far more likely to be satisfied with their children's school (and school district) when they feel it is easy to be partners with their children's teachers.[4]

Full-Circle Conversations

To build a culture of accountability, parents and teachers should stay in constant touch about high-quality teaching and learning. An elementary school in Texas developed this five-step process:

1. On Mondays, teachers give students an assignment, along with a scoring guide to explain what level of work meets the standard.
2. Students work in groups or on their own, critiquing each other's papers.
3. Every Friday, students take home a folder of their work. Students explain how they did the assignment, using the scoring guide.
4. Parents ask their children how they could revise their work so that it would be at level four (the highest level), then write a note to the teacher. Comments about the teacher's assignment are welcomed and expected.
5. Teachers ask students to revise their work, and send it home with a final grade or rating.

TIP:

Prepare teachers to discuss standards with parents

A district in Los Angeles developed a curriculum for teachers to discuss student work with parents. At every grade level (K-12), teachers know how to have a conversation with parents around a standard. The teacher explains what the standard means, what's expected of the child, and how parents can help the child meet the standard.

School Newsletters

Think about how newsletter articles could give parents better information about what students are learning, how well they are doing, and what parents can do to help them. Here are some examples of newsletter entries from our files, and how they could be rewritten to focus more on learning.

Standard newsletter article	Linked to learning
Next Thursday, a noted naturalist, photographer, and lecturer will make a presentation, "Primate Safari," at the library.	**Add:** *Students are learning that plants and animals have features that help them live in different settings. Ask your children what they noticed about the animals. How do tusks, claws, body shape, and color help animals hide, find food, and protect themselves?*
The Gift of Reading program helps to build our school's library collection. Please visit the Bookstore, where books can be "adopted." Your name and a message will be inscribed on the bookplate, and your child will have the first check-out privilege.	**Add:** *This year we are working hard to raise students' reading skills. As our school report card shows, only one in five sixth graders is proficient in reading. To become a good reader, every student should read at least twenty-five books a year. You will be getting a collection of tips on helping your child read. We welcome your ideas!*
Students in the Nutrition and Wellness Class created displays called Wellness Corners. Each student focused on some aspects of teen wellness (physical, mental, emotional, and social health).	**Add:** *To create the displays, students applied current research on health to develop a personal fitness plan. Ask your student to explain his or her personal standards for healthy behavior, including nutrition, rest, and physical activity, and how these standards fit into the plan.*

Family Learning Activities

Even events that seem to be linked directly to learning (such as family reading nights or a science expo) could have a closer focus on achievement. A useful sequence of activities goes something like this:

- ✦ Explain what skills students are learning in class.
- ✦ Demonstrate a learning activity for parents and explain how the activity will develop those skills. Ask parents to act out the parts.
- ✦ Give materials to each family, offering advice as they use them.
- ✦ Help parents assess children's progress on the activity and steer children to the next steps.
- ✦ Lend materials to use at home.

In middle and high school, workshops in which parents and students focus on developing math, science, or writing skills can help students prepare for state tests. Parents and students work on specific tasks, guided by teachers, then take materials to use at home. At the end of the series, students and parents "take the test" using sample questions to assess their progress.

After assessing your school's programs (see the checklist at the end of this chapter), you may decide to offer more opportunities for families to learn about how to help their children. There are many good programs you can adopt to engage parents in improving children's skills. One of the most popular and widely used is TIPS (Teachers Involve Parents in Schoolwork), which is available through the National Network of Partnership Schools at Johns Hopkins University. (See Chapter 10 for more information.)

What's the connection?

When linking their newsletters and flyers to learning, schools often realize that activities they schedule year after year aren't directly related to what students are actually doing in class.

Linking to
Learning

• • •

Put Learning at the Center of Parent-Teacher Conferences—and Include Students

For many families, parent-teacher conferences are often their only chance to meet face-to-face with teachers. At their worst, these encounters are formal and awkward, with little real exchange of information. Many teachers dread them as much as parents do. At their best, a conference is one step in an extended conversation between people who know each other well. Both teachers and parents should be prepared and know what to ask each other. (See the Conference Checklist in Chapter 11.)

"In our district, students have to pass the high school entrance test at the end of eighth grade. In the fall and again in the spring, we had parent-child workshops for eighth graders at risk of not passing. Each workshop series was five sessions. Parents looked at the data on their students—their attendance, scores, and grades—with counselors and a parent trainer, and talked about how to help them. We made home visits to parents who were not coming, and attendance went up. Since we've done these workshops, we have not had to retain one child in the past two years."

(Mary Lou Amato, middle school principal, Los Angeles)

Prepare Parents to Ask About Academics

A middle school principal offers this advice: "Give parents workshops about asking good questions at conferences and meetings with teachers. Have them practice and do role-plays. They should not be asking 'How is my child behaving?' but 'At what level is he reading?'

"Next, they should ask: 'Show me level-four work so I can compare it to my child's work.' Questions focused on academics—this is what's going to drive better instruction at the school."

Develop an education checkup card for parents to bring with them. List questions that parents can ask (and—just as important—questions that teachers are expecting):

+ Is my child performing at a proficient level (up to standard) in basic skills? If not, is my child above or below? (*If it's below, ask:* What is your plan for helping my child catch up? How can I help?)
+ What do my child's test scores show? What are his/her strengths and weaknesses?
+ Can we go over some examples of my child's work? Will you explain your grading standards?
+ Does my child need extra help in any area (including adjusting to school)? What do you recommend? How can we work together to help my child?

BRIGHT IDEA

Children lead conferences in elementary school

Tom Delgado, an elementary school principal in Los Angeles, says, "We find that student-led conferences work even in a K-5 setting. Children take the lead and bring their parents to the teacher or a station. We tried it out on a volunteer basis, as teachers felt comfortable. We videotaped both types of conferences and showed them to teachers. The teachers sold it to their colleagues. We trained volunteers to be parent surrogates, so that no student is left in the lurch if a parent misses the appointment."

+ Does my child do all the assigned work, including homework?
+ Does my child seem to like school and get along with classmates?
+ Have you noticed any changes in my child over the year?

Include Students

Even though it's called a parent-teacher conference, the meeting is all about the student. Why should the central person be excluded? Students do better in school when they feel in charge and accountable for the quality of their work. Even in elementary school, students can benefit from being at the conference. In middle and high school, it is essential.

Student-led conferences generally require more preparation, especially by students. Essentially, the responsibility for doing quality work is transferred from the teacher to the student. Instead of being talked about, students discuss and defend a portfolio of work that demonstrates their progress.

Here is a useful two-part format for a student-led conference. In part one, the student is the presenter. Students begin by assessing their progress and presenting a piece of work as evidence. Teachers guide the process, encouraging students to stay on task and prompting them if they stumble. Parents are the audience and ask questions, such as: "How do you know this work is up to standard for your grade level? What did you learn from doing this work? Why is it important to learn that? Do you think you did the very best you could? What are you going to work on now?" In part two, teachers share grade and test score information and respond to

Parents Take the Lead: Organizing Student-Led Conferences

At Conway Middle School in Louisville, Kentucky, only 20 percent of families had attended the school's optional conferences. Many families had never been inside the school. The principal presented the idea of student-led conferences to a group of parent leaders, and the parents decided to take it on. These are the steps the parents took:

1. Met with the school council and teachers to win their support.

2. Created a committee of teachers and parents that developed a manual for parents, students, and teachers, outlining how teachers and students should prepare for the conferences.

3. Addressed barriers to parent attendance.

- Organized an "information fair" two weeks before the conferences, so families could learn about the new conferences and other school programs. This increased families' comfort level to meet with teachers.

- Arranged transportation and child care, and lined up "surrogate parents" for children whose parents could not come.

At the first conference, over 90 percent of the school's families attended. (For information about the Conway handbook on student-led conferences, see Chapter 10.)

parents' questions. The conference ends with a discussion about how to support the student.

Using Student Achievement Data to Design Programs for Families

There is a bright side to all the testing that's now required in schools—the results are a goldmine of information. Looking at the data, school staff and parents can see how students fare from year to year in the school. Student performance can be broken down by subgroups: boys and girls, low-income and middle-class, limited English-speaking, migrant and nonmigrant. The data can show if there are achievement gaps between African American, Latino, Asian, Native American, and white students. They can also show how students are doing in different subjects, at all the grade levels, and across all programs (Title I, ESL, special needs, honors, gifted, magnet, and so on).

Use these data to:

✦ **Focus programs and activities for families on student skills.** If reading is weak, adopt literacy as a major theme. If girls lag in science, form a science club for girls and involve their mothers and other female family members. If low-income students need to boost math skills, use Title I funds to adopt a family math program. If college attendance is low (or students tend to leave after the first year), schedule workshops and activities about planning for college and finding financial aid, and organize family field trips to local colleges.

✦ **Target extra help for students.** Give parents information about how to work with their children at home or find a tutor or after-school program. When student test reports come back, help parents analyze the information and identify skill areas that still need work.

✦ **Engage families in school improvement.** Give parents clear reports on how the school as a whole is doing. Help them become comfortable with using data—such as the school report cards from the state or district. Ask for their ideas about how to improve achievement.

If you find information gaps, collect your own data. How much reading do students do outside of class? Do they use the local library, and, if so, how often? What are parents doing at home to help with homework? What kind of information from school would help them? What after-school programs do students attend and what do they offer?

Create a Family-School Compact for Achievement

The No Child Left Behind law requires every Title I school to develop a school-family compact or agreement. This tool would be useful at any

Five Steps for Focusing Your Compact on Learning

1. Look at your school's test data with parents. What are the areas of low achievement? Break down the data to find any gaps between different groups of students.

2. Set priorities for improvement and establish a goal for each one. For example, if reading scores are low across the board, then make improving reading skills a priority. Adopt a goal of moving all students out of the bottom quartile ("below basic") and moving more students into "proficient."

3. Ask parents, students, and school staff what they should do to meet the goals. Then ask each group to list what it wants the others to do.

4. Focus the compact on concerns that have come up in the discussions. For each area (e.g., homework, communication, rules of behavior), list what each group can do.

5. Draw up a first draft, then ask for comments. Revise it based on parents', teachers', and students' reactions.

school. (Chapter 7 also includes advice and ideas for compacts.) Teachers and parents both find compacts to be helpful in making clear what each group should do to encourage students. Students appreciate being treated like responsible people.

The compact should describe:

✦ How parents, school staff, and students will share the responsibility for improving student progress

✦ How the school and families will build a partnership to help children meet high standards and communicate regularly[7]

Here is an example of how to revise a compact so that it is clear about what is expected. The "old-style" compact on the right is an actual (and typical) example from our files.

Compact linked to learning	Old-style compact
This compact pledges our school community to increase student reading and math skills so that all students will be proficient by the end of third grade.	This compact will promote effective working relationships to improve student achievement.
PARENT'S PLEDGE: I WILL	**PARENT'S PLEDGE: I WILL**
• Monitor my child's progress and let the teacher know right away if I notice any problems	• Send my child to school every day
• Use reading and math materials the school sends home each week to help my child	• Keep in contact with school once a month
• Read to my child twenty minutes a day and keep a list of new words	• Support the school dress and discipline codes
• Limit TV to one hour a day and ask my child to write a report on our favorite program	• Be an active participant in my child's learning process
	• Limit TV watching time

Compact linked to learning	Old-style compact
• Help my child see how to use reading and math to pursue interests and goals	

STUDENT'S PLEDGE: I WILL

• Ask for help from my teacher and family if I am having trouble doing my work	• Complete my classwork
• Read on my own and with my family every day	• Come to school prepared to learn
• Work on my math and reading skills at home, using the materials my teacher sends home	• Respect adults, myself, and other students
• Write down assignments, do my homework every day, and turn it in when it's due	• Obey school rules
• Write a report about my favorite TV program	• Complete my homework

TEACHER'S PLEDGE: I WILL

• Build a relationship with every family in my class	• Have high expectations for all students
• Keep families informed of their children's progress and needs in each subject	• Develop a classroom climate that is comfortable for all students
• Make sure every student gets the help he/she needs as soon as it's needed	• Develop proficient learners
• Send home learning materials in math and reading	• Enforce rules fairly and consistently
	• Provide the books and necessary supplies for education

Compact linked to learning	Old-style compact
• Explain my approach to teaching, expectations, and grading to students and their families • Work on my reading and math strategies so that I can reach all children • Make sure students understand assignments and what they'll learn from them	

Use the compact through the year. For example, refer to the compact at parent-teacher conferences and other meetings. Discuss how each side is doing in sticking to the pledges. Ask if other measures are needed. Revisit the compact every year, asking families, students, teachers, and other school staff how they think it could be better. Update it using the most recent data.

Collaborating with Community Organizations

Many community groups offer after-school programs for students, but they may not be linked to the school's curriculum. Do the program staff know what's being covered in their students' classes? Do they know what the state standards expect children to know and be able to do at different grade levels? Are they familiar with the textbooks the school is using, the books students are reading, and the math or science projects they're doing?

If not, community tutoring programs in reading or math may use a different approach than the school does. Tutors and mentors may not have information about their students' skill levels. The homework center at the housing complex may not have access to the students' assignments. How can schools collaborate with these programs to strengthen students' skills?

Here are some steps schools can take to be partners with after-school programs:

- ✦ Encourage after-school program staff and teachers to observe each other at work, and share ideas and information about the students.
- ✦ Invite program staff to attend professional development sessions to update and build their teaching skills.
- ✦ Inform program staff about the school's curriculum and learning programs (especially math and reading).
- ✦ Exchange textbooks, assignments, and learning materials.
- ✦ Share the school's data on student achievement and other outcomes.

For more ideas on collaborating with community groups, see Chapter 8, "Sharing Power."

Linking programs and activities to what students are learning should be a basic strategy in any school's improvement plan. The most important factors in improving student achievement are the quality of the school's academic program, a strong focus on student learning, high expectations for students, and the use of data to identify areas of weakness. Building in parent involvement will make your improvement plan more effective—and the benefits to students will last longer.

In the next chapter, we will discuss how differences of culture, race, and class can create powerful barriers to engaging parents, and what to do about this.

How Closely Is Your School's Parent Involvement Program Linked to Student Learning?

LEARNING WHAT STUDENTS ARE DOING IN CLASS

1. Student work is posted in school hallways and in public places in the community and is rotated often.

   ☐ *Already doing this*   ☐ *Could do this easily*   ☐ *This will take time*   ☐ *This will be hard*

2. Exhibits of student work show how to recognize high-level work at different grade levels. The assignments are challenging and the student work is not all the same.

   ☐ *Already doing this*   ☐ *Could do this easily*   ☐ *This will take time*   ☐ *This will be hard*

3. Families can regularly observe in the classroom and/or see teaching demonstrations.

   ☐ *Already doing this*   ☐ *Could do this easily*   ☐ *This will take time*   ☐ *This will be hard*

4. At parent-teacher conferences, students are present and discuss the quality of their work.

   ☐ *Already doing this*   ☐ *Could do this easily*   ☐ *This will take time*   ☐ *This will be hard*

5. Articles in the school newsletter and on the Web site discuss what students are doing in class and include tips on helping at home.

☐ *Already doing this*   ☐ *Could do this easily*   ☐ *This will take time*   ☐ *This will be hard*

6. A regular feature describes interesting approaches that teachers are using in class.

☐ *Already doing this*   ☐ *Could do this easily*   ☐ *This will take time*   ☐ *This will be hard*

7. The articles use data about the school, such as attendance rates and test results, and describe how the school is working to make improvements.

☐ *Already doing this*   ☐ *Could do this easily*   ☐ *This will take time*   ☐ *This will be hard*

8. The school offers regular workshops and other information sessions that help families understand how children learn and are being taught. The topics are suggested by families.

☐ *Already doing this*   ☐ *Could do this easily*   ☐ *This will take time*   ☐ *This will be hard*

9. Families regularly receive information and materials to help their children at home.

☐ *Already doing this*   ☐ *Could do this easily*   ☐ *This will take time*   ☐ *This will be hard*

USING STUDENT ACHIEVEMENT DATA TO DESIGN PROGRAMS

10. Programs and activities for families are focused on skills and subjects that students need to strengthen.

☐ *Already doing this* ☐ *Could do this easily* ☐ *This will take time* ☐ *This will be hard*

11. Student achievement data are shared with families in ways that solicit their ideas about how to improve achievement.

☐ *Already doing this* ☐ *Could do this easily* ☐ *This will take time* ☐ *This will be hard*

12. School staff and parents collaborate to collect other data about learning opportunities for students, such as community programs and resources.

☐ *Already doing this* ☐ *Could do this easily* ☐ *This will take time* ☐ *This will be hard*

COLLABORATING WITH COMMUNITY LEARNING PROGRAMS

13. School staff collaborate with community-based after-school programs and exchange ideas and information with program staff.

☐ *Already doing this* ☐ *Could do this easily* ☐ *This will take time* ☐ *This will be hard*

14. School shares curriculum, textbooks, assignments, and learning materials with community after-school programs.

☐ *Already doing this* ☐ *Could do this easily* ☐ *This will take time* ☐ *This will be hard*

15. After-school program staff can attend professional development at school. Staff development is also open to parents.

☐ *Already doing this* ☐ *Could do this easily* ☐ *This will take time* ☐ *This will be hard*

Which areas do you want to focus on first?

_____

_____

_____

How are parents and the parent organization involved in linking family involvement activities and programs to improving student achievement?

_____

_____

_____

What are your concerns?

_____

_____

_____

Reflection: What steps could you take to help your programs be better linked to learning?

Right away:

_____

_____

Over the long term:

_____

_____

_____

Chapter 6

Addressing Differences

How Can You Deal with Issues of Race, Class, and Culture?

Students from every country in the world go to school in America. In almost any urban area, in small towns, and in rural areas, we find an amazing variety of what we call "diversity." Diversity brings rich resources and opportunities for schools and communities, but it also can bring conflicts and misunderstandings. The reality is that diversity comes to school daily, and we need to be prepared for it.

Consider three examples from a single metro area. In one school, students speak twenty-nine languages, come from forty different countries, and have parents who are college professors, taxi drivers, hotel maids, office workers, business owners, and construction workers. In another school, the mostly African American and Latino students live in low-income neighborhoods near the school, while their middle-class white and African American teachers commute from suburbs an hour away. A third school is all white but has great economic and social diversity.

Its students live in neighborhoods that run the gamut from country-club estates to garden apartments and trailer parks.

We know that differences of race, language, income, religion, sexual orientation, occupation, ethnicity, class, disability, culture, and nationality create huge challenges in schools. Long-term residents sometimes resent the newcomers and make them feel unwelcome. Teachers complain in the lounge that they can't even pronounce their students' names. Students separate themselves into warring cliques, leaving teachers wondering how to make connections among them. White, middle-class PTA leaders wonder why no one comes to meetings anymore.

> "The diversity in our school district is our greatest strength and our greatest challenge. Our city is a gateway to the U.S. Watch a crisis unfolding in the world, wait a few months, and the refugees appear at our schools. Each one of these students has added amazing value to my class and school."
>
> *(Cathy David, teacher, principal, and district administrator, Alexandria, Virginia)*

Many teachers lack the training to address differences—or to examine their assumptions about the implications of these differences. While some schools have figured out how to use their diversity as a powerful teaching tool, many feel at a loss about how to do that. Principals, parents, teachers, and community members have told us they face three major challenges:

1. How do we improve student performance in a school with huge and constantly changing cultural diversity?
2. How can we address racial tensions and bias, including some educators' low expectations of low-income families and children of color (especially African American and Latino children)?
3. How do we deal with differences of class, which no one wants to talk about, or even admit exist?

This is a big topic and can't possibly be covered in a single chapter, so here we will discuss a few key ideas to get your action team started. The

"You have to have compassion for all the people who walk through that door, because some bring with them that little person inside themselves who was hurt in school. That's a legitimate hurt and can cause fear about how you will treat their child. We are strangers to them and they give us their most precious possessions. Of course, they wonder if we will keep their children safe and give them what they need to prepare them for life. I experienced this firsthand because my son was ill and nearly died. The first day I had to bring him back to school, I was very worried and fearful about his well-being."

(Mary Ledoux, principal, Brooksville Elementary School, Brooksville, Florida)

checklist and references at the end of this chapter and the resources and tools in Chapter 10 and Chapter 11 can take you a little further. Your own hard work will, we hope, take you the rest of the way.

We hear a lot of complaints about parents: "Those parents don't teach their children how to behave." "They're working so many jobs they don't have time to help their kids." "They're not even trying to learn English." "They don't value education the way we do." Do any of these remarks sound familiar?

We need to examine our assumptions about families. Do we expect all parents to respond the same way that middle-class parents do? When they don't come to events at school, we may think, "They don't care" or "They don't value education." Instead, we need to focus on ways to draw parents into the school and make them feel valued and welcome. If you think your staff may not be ready to move in this direction, take another look at Chapter 3, "Ready, Set, Go!"

We suggest that your team start with this premise: *All families, no matter what their income, race, education, language, or culture, want their children to do well in school—and can make an important contribution to their children's learning.* Even if your experience seems to cast doubt on this, thirty years of research bears it out. Let us begin in this spirit.

Addressing

Differences

. . .

RESEARCH BRIEF:
How high-performing schools engage Hispanic families

Jay Scribner, Michelle Young, and Anna Pedroza have studied high-performing His-panic schools in the Texas borderlands. They found that these schools share three key practices in building on their families' culture:

1. UNDERSTANDING CULTURAL VALUES. Hispanic families see their involvement as a way to support their children's total well-being. Informal activities at home tend to be more important to Hispanic parents than meetings, workshops, and committees at school.

2. BUILDING ON THE STRENGTH OF THE EXTENDED FAMILY. Parents like being treated as members of the school family. Hispanic mothers tend to view all children in their neighborhood as their own and often invite trusted teachers to family celebrations.

3. MAKING A PERSONAL COMMITMENT TO LEARN ABOUT HISPANIC CULTURE. These schools invited families to share their cultural values, stories, and traditions with teachers and in class. They hired bilingual school staff, learned Spanish, and extended invita-tions to families in Spanish. They also set up a family center where families could meet and talk in their language.[1]

Improving Student Performance in Culturally Diverse Schools

How do you improve student performance in a school with huge and constantly changing cultural diversity?

Recognizing, Learning About, and Affirming All Cultures in the School

Begin by finding out more about all the cultures in your school. Ask the district office for information about the countries and cultures your students come from. Invite speakers from those communities to talk to the faculty. Find out what multicultural professional development is available from the district, local universities, or local organizations.

As part of a "joining process" to welcome parents into your school (see Chapter 4), consider a personal talk with each family. A survey or interview process can be a useful project for the family-school coordinator and the PTA or parent group. Be sure to ask about the families' cultural background, the ways they would like to be involved, and their ideas and concerns. Community and religious groups also can help to do this. If your district has a parent involvement office, it may have developed a survey that you can use. (See the Parent Review and Family Welcome Questionnaire in Chapter 11.)

In invitations to come to school, make it clear in several languages that all family members are welcome. An important cultural difference is the way people perceive participation in events and meetings. "Welcome" should be addressed to the whole family, including young children, aunts, nephews, grandparents, cousins, and close friends and neighbors who act like family members.

When Cathy David got the job of opening Samuel Tucker Elementary School, the first new school in Alexandria, Virginia, in thirty years, her top priority was addressing the vast diversity of the school community. "My staff had to know that success must be the *only* option for the children we serve," she said. "We started with our hopes and dreams for the

EXAMPLE:

Hmong New Year Community Celebration

Each December, Como Park Elementary School in St. Paul, Minnesota, celebrates Hmong New Year. The children perform Hmong songs, dances, and a play. Everyone enjoys a feast of traditional foods and an exhibit of Hmong artwork. For the festivities, all students learn Hmong songs and dances, and families of all cultures prepare their traditional foods. Focusing on one culture allows the whole community to learn about Hmong people and the value of diversity. A strong publicity campaign and enticing program draw over five hundred people.[2]

Learn how to pronounce students' names

"I have heard colleagues make fun of children's names, questioning why they should be burdened with having to pronounce or spell such 'foreign' names," says Debbie Bambino, a teacher in Philadelphia. "This example speaks volumes to me. If I can't be bothered to respect your name, or your child's name, how can you expect me to respect you?"

The entire staff at Samuel Tucker Elementary School in Alexandria, Virginia, understand that knowing how to pronounce students' names correctly is critical to making each child feel respected and valued at school. Teachers print their class lists and write each child's name phonetically next to the actual spelling on the class list. To do this, teachers ask each student how to pronounce his or her name correctly, so the whole class can learn each other's names in the process. The school office then makes copies for the principal, counselors, and office staff.

school, writing them down on puzzle pieces that together made up a picture of the new building. We turned those dreams into three goals, and one was to build a partnership with families."

To do this, David knew she must have a fully committed teaching staff. "I asked each teacher to join a professional learning community (PLC) to build capacity in areas that would help us reach our goals. This really strengthened teamwork and collaboration in the building. The multicultural PLC realized that we had to learn more about the families' cultures, and gathered information, contacted embassies, and lined up guest speakers." David adds, "That was not enough. We realized that we also must know our families individually. You can't assume that all families from Ghana or Sudan think, act, and feel the same way about everything."

To help Tucker families understand the education system in Virginia, the school leadership team changed the standard lineup of activities for families. Back-to-school night celebrated the family-school partnership. Parents were treated to a video presentation featuring the highlights of

Welcoming Immigrant Families

When a new plant in a small Iowa town attracted a flood of workers from Mexico, school principals took the lead in integrating the new families into the community. Here are four things they did to put out a big welcome mat:

1. Visiting every new family. This was done by school staff, sometimes the principal.

2. Working with the human resources director of the packing plant, the major employer, to coordinate important school programs with parents' shift schedules.

3. Offering language skills and other classes for parents at a school site. A local community college and elementary schools provided the instructors.

4. Publicizing school board meetings in printed notices and on radio stations in multiple languages.

those first days of school. To make sure parents could understand, David bought translation headsets and arranged for interpreters at all family events. Other changes include:

+ Grade-level curriculum nights held each October educated parents about academic standards and accountability measures. Notices in English and Spanish were sent home and personal contacts encouraged more reluctant parents to attend. Babysitting was provided.
+ Instead of holding business meetings, the PTA offered "subject nights" that involved fun learning activities: family reading, physical education, math, and heritage night.
+ At all events, David talked about standards and accountability, then about what students must know by the end of the year. There was time for teachers to chime in and for parents to ask questions.

- Parent-teacher conferences were scheduled from 1:00 to 8:00 P.M. To avoid students' having to translate for their parents, there were translation stations for every language. The custodian, who is from Ghana and speaks Twi, was one of the translators.

"This was great for the PTA—it really brought out parents," David comments. "We would have four hundred family members at these nights."

Connecting Families' Cultures to What Students Are Learning

Parents and children welcome opportunities to share learning experiences and connect them to their traditions at home. Conway Middle School in Louisville did a school-wide project on Africa. Students studied the geography, cultures, architecture, climate, and plants and animals, then created displays to show what they learned. African American families contributed their knowledge and materials, and all families turned out in huge numbers to view the exhibits. Field trips and computer lab sessions can offer similar opportunities.

The four pavilions at Josiah Quincy Upper School in Boston are critical to its Chinatown community. As principal Peter Bak-Fun Wong notes, "They are the essence of the combination of the Eastern and Western styles of education. The pavilions are for both students and families." There are pavilions for information (science, technology, and mathematics), pathfinding (individual expression and twenty-first-century issues), and renewal (mental, emotional, and physical health). The fourth pavilion, culture, concentrates on world cultures, race, and ethnicity, symbolizing that school and family cannot exist without harmony in society.

"We have so many things in common. So we talk about the commonalities first. Then we talk about our diversity. A lot of people don't appreciate other cultures because they don't know or appreciate their own," Bak-Fun Wong observes. "We help to involve parents in the process by holding school meetings on Saturdays in different areas in the neighborhoods so they can actually attend."[3]

"We want more materials and books about Hispanic culture—this doesn't exist now in our school. What there is, is only about Mexico. In Honduras, we don't celebrate Cinco de Mayo."

(Parent, Alexandria public schools focus group)

Cultural Competence: Relating to People of a Different Background

A skill that soon may be required of job applicants everywhere is "cultural competence." This is the ability to relate and communicate effectively with people of a different culture, economic background, or language. According to the Council for Exceptional Children, culturally competent schools and classrooms look like this:

- Students are respected and responded to in warm and accepting ways.

- Students have opportunities to find connections between their lives and what they are studying.

- Students' knowledge, culture, and learning styles are considered and incorporated into class instruction.

- Teachers and school staff are familiar with their students' home cultures and know how to work in multicultural settings.[4]

Lessons and information about different cultures can enhance the curriculum. Here are a few ideas for your action team:

✦ Include all families' countries of origin in school geography lessons.

✦ Display students' research reports about the cultures represented in the school.

✦ Ask the librarian to supply literature about cultures in the school and have a reading period about them. Include these materials in classroom libraries.

✦ Show films about cultures represented in the school. Ask students to critique the films in writing assignments.

✦ Ask family members to tell traditional stories about their cultures and display children's drawings about the stories.

Kitchen Math Exchanges

Arlington, Virginia, was once a quiet, southern suburb, with middle-class whites on the north side, working-class African Americans and whites on the south side. Now it's home to all the DNA on the planet. To help connect families to what their children are learning, teachers at H. W. Barrett Elementary School enjoy meals with a diverse mix of families—all with a focus on math. The two-hour home visit starts in the kitchen, where family members show how they fix a dish from their home country. The teacher gives them ideas about how to use cooking to build math and English skills.

When all sit down to eat, the teacher gets to know the whole family and they talk about their history and experiences. If the teacher doesn't speak the home language, an interpreter comes along. After the meal, the teacher plays math games with the children so families learn how to use them. The games are a gift to the family. (Teachers receive $20 to buy the games.)

This "recipe" was successful with families of many backgrounds: Latino (Peruvian, Bolivian, Salvadoran, Nicaraguan, Honduran), Asian (Bangladeshi, Pakistani, Vietnamese, Cambodian), European (Bosnian), and African (Somali, Ethiopian). Program founder Rosa Briceno says, "Everyone has a kitchen, and a kitchen is a safe place for people of different ages and backgrounds to get together, share informally, and learn from each other. . . . The students glow with pride."[5]

Working with Community Members and Groups to Connect Families and the School

"Cultural brokers" are familiar with families' cultural backgrounds but also understand the culture of the school. They can help school staff and parents learn strategies for interacting with each other. A cultural broker reaches out to parents and brings them to the school, translates when they get there, and explains the families' values and traditions to educators. A school's parent liaisons (or family-school coordinators) should be able to act as cultural brokers.

Who else can act as cultural brokers and where can you find them? Some may be family members who help their relatives navigate the school terrain. Other members of the school community may also be cultural brokers, including school custodians, cafeteria workers, and aides. Faith-based and neighborhood organizations are another source. Their staff and volunteers are likely to know the languages and cultures of the community, as well as speak English and understand how the U.S. system works.[6]

The Parent Institute for Quality Education (PIQE) is a program in California with over 350,000 graduates, mostly recent immigrants. Instructors are recruited from the same backgrounds and life experiences as the immigrant families in the program. PIQE founder Vahac Mardirosian offers his take on a cultural broker: "Our instructors must have made it through college, but also remember what it's like to wash dishes in a restaurant. They must be able to explain how the system works and know how to shut up and listen."[7] The PIQE program is now available nationally through the National Council of La Raza, under the name Parents as Partners.

Recognizing and Supporting Different Forms of Parent Involvement

While some parents readily join the PTA and help organize bake sales, families from other cultures may have different traditions. John Diamond, a sociologist, made this observation about Asian families:

> People argue that the reason Asian students do so well is that they work harder and their parents are more invested in education. But if you look

Native American Day

Taking part in this activity got fourth graders at Hubbard Elementary School in Forsyth, Georgia, excited about studying Native Americans. Jim Sawgrass, a member of the Muskogee Creek Tribe, set up a Creek encampment behind the school. Students could see ways of life extending from when early migrating peoples came across the Alaskan land bridge to when Europeans began to colonize North America. Sawgrass talked about the different languages and housing used by various tribes, and demonstrated hunting weapons, from the early Clovis-point spear through the musket. Students had the chance to take part in sand painting, poetry, and Indian writing. Students and volunteers also sampled different Native American foods, such as beef jerky and dried fruit.[8]

at the traditional measures of educational participation, the group that is usually least engaged at the school site . . . are those Asian-American parents. They have a different model for how to be involved . . . so they make substantial investments in education in the home context . . . and use their social networks outside of school.[9]

Gerardo Lopez noticed something similar when he interviewed migrant workers with children who did well in school. These families saw themselves as *highly* involved in their children's learning, but they defined involvement as teaching their children the value of education through hard work. When taking young children to work with them in the fields, parents gave them *consejos* (advice) as to how limited their opportunities would be if they dropped out of school.[10]

African American families also may have a distinct approach to their children's education. Sherick Hughes has studied black families in North Carolina and found that they use their faith to help them understand the "hidden rules" of survival and success. Parents and grandparents tell their children stories of struggle and hope, of how even in the face of adversity members of their family were able to survive and succeed in an educational system that was not first designed to benefit black families.[11]

From a school point of view, these families do not *appear* to be involved. Because they may rarely interact with teachers or go to events at school, teachers may assume that they don't encourage learning at home. Diamond comments, "We can't go in with this single vision . . . of what parent involvement looks like or we miss the fact that all parents want to be involved. There just may be a different script for how they do it."[12]

Supporting Learning at Home

If given information and support, families will respond and use it to help their children. One way to find out what families are already doing at home is to conduct a survey. Teachers and students from St. Louis University developed a homework survey at Wyman Elementary School in St. Louis, Missouri. The school office mailed it home; over half the families responded. When the results were tallied, school staff marveled at how much parents were doing with their children at home, despite the fact that many worked long hours. (See the Homework Survey in Chapter 11.)

Addressing the Language Barrier

Offering translation and interpreters for meetings and other communications is critical. Your action team and school office staff can find translators among bilingual community members or neighborhood

Disabilities Are Another Form of Diversity

Joe Clifford, principal of West Hernando Middle School in Brooksville, Florida, is a twenty-nine-year veteran of public school teaching. In this rural district of 20,000 students, half of his 1,150 students are low-income. Many have special needs, including cognitive and kinesthetic disabilities. "Any discussion of 'diversity' must include special needs as well as race and ethnicity," he insists. "We must offer a fully inclusive environment. My advice to other principals is to prepare purposefully to bring a school to embrace inclusion." Clifford says that means they must make arrangements to "train staff appropriately," including how to create differentiated instructional plans.

Some Ways to Use the Information from a Homework Survey

- Send home a schedule that includes the amount of time the assignments should take, so that families know what to expect.

- Let families know if children have time built into the school day for doing homework. (Some children tell their parents that they've already done their work at school.)

- Offer workshops based on what families say they would like to learn. At Wyman, families said they would like skills for managing homework and information about the learning process.

- Give children homework that involves their families, using information from the survey about the families' preferences.

- Send home learning kits to help families that may not have materials or supplies such as rulers, construction paper, tape, and crayons.

and community groups, or even a student's older brother or sister more advanced in English. Naturally, people of different communities feel reassured when they see people who look and act like them.

Translate report cards and official documents, as well as notices and newsletters. Put notices about school events and activities on ethnic radio stations. Videotape classes with a voice-over in other languages, explaining what the teacher is doing. Distribute videos with tips for parents in families' languages.

Somali refugees are the second-largest English as a Second Language community in Eagen, Minnesota. To help Somali families feel comfortable with the school and connected to their children's education, a middle school teacher and staff members created a twenty-four-minute video in Somali. Watching the video, parents are led through a typical student's day as the students takes part in classes, congregates with friends at lunch,

BRIGHT IDEA

"One Hundred Easy Phrases"

To help administrators, secretaries, teachers, nurses, parent leaders, and others communicate with Spanish-speaking parents and students, Dr. Mary Urquidez in Wichita Falls, Texas, developed a simple program for learning Spanish. She selected one hundred easy conversational phrases to learn in Spanish. Each week, school staff learn five to ten phrases, then practice them in person, on the phone, and in e-mails. At the end of ten sessions, they have a vocabulary of more than five hundred words. The first session is greetings, expressions of courtesy, and farewells. Other sessions include telephone conversations, everyday phrases and directions, words of praise and encouragement, and basic communications with parents.

and hangs out by the lockers. Then the video explains school policies such as immunization and appointments, gives parents a tour of the school building, and describes athletic opportunities.

In Boston, many schools sponsor a "Pancake Breakfast Welcome" for families of students who are not native English-speakers. Held at the beginning of the year, the breakfast is an icebreaker. Parents don't have to stay; they can drop in, wave, and say hello to their child's teacher. The principal serves pancakes and talks with the families about what's on their minds.

"Our school has done a good job getting parents involved. The Spanish-speaking principal is always present at the meetings and uses translation headsets, which has really drawn the Hispanic community to our meetings."

(Parent, Alexandria, Virginia)

Parents as Authors

At Loreto Elementary School in Los Angeles, new immigrant parents created books and videos about their lives and experiences. They also wrote poems about their children and presented their work to their children. Fifth grade teachers met with families to create family books as gifts for the fifth grade graduates.[13]

Addressing Racial Tensions and Bias

How can we address racial tensions and bias, including some educators' low expectations of low-income families and children of color (especially African American and Latino children)? Researcher Vivian Johnson has noted that:

> Schools are very powerful places. What goes on (or fails to go on) in them greatly influences all children's futures. Parents and teachers are often uncertain in their relationships with each other. Each is concerned about the judgment of the other. Each feels vulnerable, exposed, unsafe and insecure. Even teachers feel this way when interacting with their own child's teachers.[14]

Race is a troublesome, often explosive topic in our society. Teachers worry about saying or doing the wrong thing and unintentionally offending students and parents. In many schools, there is a conversation going on, but it's not spoken. Instead, it plays out in people's minds, because they are afraid to speak.

Lisa Delpit calls this unspoken conversation the "silenced dialogue." Parents worry that if they say what they're thinking, teachers will be angry and "take it out on our kids." Teachers worry that if they speak what's on their minds, they will be labeled as "racist" or "insensitive." So the two groups circle each other, holding very different expectations about how teachers will use their power in the classroom.

As Delpit points out, many educators feel that their main goal is to help children become independent and find their own voice. This works when the children are part of the dominant culture and fully understand its rules. But parents from other cultures often want something else. They want to be sure that their children learn ways of speaking and interacting that will allow them success in the larger society.[15]

How do we deal with this? In this section, we will focus on three possibilities:

1. Using the power of the school to promote positive relations and open dialogue
2. Raising expectations for children and families
3. Getting to know the community and identifying its assets

The strategies discussed in the previous section on addressing diversity also apply to the issue of race—such as affirming all cultures (including African American history and traditions), connecting these cultures to what students are learning, and recognizing and affirming different forms of parent involvement.

Using the Power of School to Promote Positive Relations and Open Dialogue

The purpose of working with families is to build partnership in the care of children. In reaching out to each another, it is vital that both sides can clearly express their hopes and dreams for the children, as well as their expectations of each other. Working in partnership means listening to each other and maintaining an open dialogue between school staff and parents.

Listening and learning about racial experiences is important because each racial group has a unique experience in America. For example, the enslavement of African Americans is an uncomfortable subject that many prefer to avoid. When the curriculum does include slavery, slave resistance and the extraordinary accomplishments of African Americans in the face of continuing racism are often not covered. The existence of

Advice from a Principal:
Visit Your School's Neighborhoods

Mary Ledoux, principal of Brooksville Elementary School in Brooksville, Florida, says, "Principals can't simply rely on the data about demographics to tell them about the population of the school. They must do two things: make home visits and ride the school bus. Principals must meet parents in their own neighborhoods! Principals need to know the *reality* of their children's circumstances, not simply the data. Some children in my school have no running water and electricity. We usually want parents to come to us—we must learn that we must also go to them."

white privilege is also rarely acknowledged. The challenge for educators is to find ways to learn about and teach the dynamics of race in our society.

Glen Singleton challenges educators to have "courageous conversations" about race to understand its impact on the achievement gap between white students and students of color. An African American trainer and consultant, Singleton says, "The challenge is to focus the conversation on race, hold it there, and then deepen it." His training moves the discussion on race beyond the usual diversity topics to sharing racial experiences, including "whiteness." (For more information, see Chapter 10.)

Singleton's "color line experiment" helps educators appreciate the impact of race on everyday experience. Participants respond to a series of questions, each starting with "Because of my race or color . . ."

✦ If I should need to move, I can be pretty sure of renting/purchasing housing in an area I can afford and in which I would want to live.

✦ I can be pretty sure my neighbors in such a location will be neutral or pleasant to me.

✦ I can turn on the television or open the front page of the paper and see people of my race widely and positively represented.

✦ I am never asked to speak for all people of my racial group.

- When I am told about our national heritage or about "civilization," I am shown that people of my race made it what it is.
- I can be sure that if I need legal or medical help, my race will not work against me.
- I can comfortably avoid, ignore, or minimize the impact of racism on my life.

Participants rate each statement, based on their experience: 5 if the statement is "always true," 3 if it is "sometimes true," and 0 if the statement is "seldom true." After totaling scores, respondents form a "color line," with the lowest numbers on the right and the highest on the left. When people with highest numbers are asked to raise their hands, most of them are black, brown, and Latino. When people with lower numbers raise their hands, most of them are white. This reveals stark differences between people's daily experiences of race. Through the staff development that follows, discussions continue about differences in experiences based on race, and how those differences relate to the achievement gap.[16]

In their "courageous conversations," educators and parents can also examine the impact of labels. Being referred to as a "minority" makes people feel marginal. Why should students in a community where most students are not "white" (that is, European American) be considered a

---

EXAMPLE:

A Courageous Conversation about Race

To learn more about racism, parents have formed the Community Connections Book Group in Needham, Massachusetts. Ten parents from Boston, who send their kids to school in Needham through a voluntary busing system, meet regularly with ten parents from Needham. The group selects books that help them discuss how different their personal experiences are. These talks also have led them to discover just how much they all have in common—especially when it comes to what they want for their children. They are hoping to expand such book clubs to the thirty-two suburbs that have students from Boston in their schools.[17]

"minority"? Native Americans got here before any other group, and yet they've been treated as outsiders. African Americans' lineage here extends back four hundred years and includes explorers as well as enslaved ancestors who were not willing immigrants. The land that is now California and Texas was once part of Mexico, so who are the immigrants there?

Labels often create confusion when used to describe people, because the labels don't necessarily reflect how people see themselves. Labels also tend to take on negative meanings over time. To many, "minority" means "less than" the main group, and "immigrant" connotes someone "just off the boat" who doesn't "fit in." Instead of applying labels, ask people how they define themselves, and use the terms that they do.

Take Discussions of Race into the Classroom

In their article "A Pernicious Silence: Confronting Race in the Elementary Classroom," Lillian Polite and Elizabeth Saenger offer several suggestions:

✦ Read aloud good stories or books and have class discussions that explore different students' points of view. Noting that most authors don't specify race if a character is white, the authors suggest that teachers insert the word *white* or explain that the characters are white. This puts "white" on the same footing as "black."

✦ Clip stories about racism and discrimination from the newspaper and discuss them in class. Stories where black customers are mistreated, then complain and win a judgment, provide hope and vindication for African American students. They also open the eyes of European American children.

✦ Use "teachable moments," and don't let an incident pass without comment and discussion. If children tease an African American girl about her hair, use that as a way to talk about how hair is important to everyone and to compare differences in hair color, texture, and style.

✦ Don't ask children of color to be a spokesperson for members of their group, as in "Aisha, what do you have to say about this racial topic?" Introduce the question in a more general way and make sure that all students participate.[18]

Who Are "Minorities" and "Immigrants"—and How Do They Feel About This Label?

In Herndon, Virginia, a suburb of Washington, D.C., the majority (53 percent) of the population is Hispanic, Asian, African American, and Native American. At Floris Elementary School, the principal announced a "Principal's Coffee for Parents of Minority Students" to discuss how to increase parent involvement.

When parents came, they made it clear that they did not like being labeled "minority," voicing a concern about school labels raised by many people of color. Educators often use the term *minority* because it appears in federal and state laws, policies, and funding programs. It is also a not-so-subtle reminder of who is the majority (dominant) group.

It's not surprising that the Virginia families protested when the label was applied to them. The topic on the table was increasing parent involvement. They pointed out that low involvement is not only a "minority" problem but an issue for all parents. Every parent should be helped to be more comfortable with participating and speaking out, they said. After discussing reasons for low involvement, the group considered solutions. The chart below sums up their discussion.[19]

Causes of low involvement	Solutions
• Parents dislike being labeled "minority."	• Omitting labels and giving all parents a warm welcome and a safe place to raise their concerns.
• Parents with limited English feel intimidated: "We don't understand what's being communicated, so we don't attend."	• Offering an outreach program for non-English-speaking parents and inviting parents in their native language.
• Parents feel uncomfortable visiting the school.	• Holding small meetings with ESL parents and school staff, providing translators so parents can communicate their concerns.

(continued)

Causes of low involvement	Solutions
• Parents have trouble helping children at home because they don't understand how the subject is taught at school.	• Setting up parent visits to classrooms to observe teaching process and methods.
• Parents may use a different approach than a teacher to help a child learn	• More details in notes home about what parents can do. "Study math facts" is not enough.

Raising Expectations

Positive or negative teacher talk can become part of (and reflect) a school's "stream of beliefs," according to researchers in Chicago schools. John Diamond, Antonia Randolph, and James Spillane examined the beliefs, expectations, and practices that flow through a school, finding them to be "like a current that guides teacher expectations and sense of responsibility in a particular direction."

In one school that was 90 percent low-income and 100 percent African American, the stream of beliefs about its students and families was negative. Most teachers interviewed emphasized students' deficits, and about half the teachers believed that students' family backgrounds got in the way of their ability to teach them. These teachers resisted new methods for teaching and assigned students less challenging coursework, because they feared that students could not handle harder work. This research suggests that when teachers have negative perceptions about students' abilities, they feel less responsibility for their students' learning.

In contrast, leaders in another school with low-income African American students took steps to make its stream of beliefs more positive:

- School leaders created an environment in which teachers emphasized high standards, hard work, and meeting students' needs.
- Students' life circumstances were considered unacceptable as an excuse to reduce standards or teachers' accountability. This school affirmed positive aspects of African American culture and accomplishments of African Americans, to signal respect and high expectations for students.
- Recognizing the challenges faced by their students and families enhanced teachers' commitment and their sense of collective responsibility for students' learning.[20]

For more ideas about how your action team can address a negative stream of beliefs at your school, see Chapter 3, "Ready, Set, Go!" for suggestions about discussing staff attitudes and confronting negativity and bias. (Also look at the Attitude Check exercise in Chapter 11.)

"The questions that are at the heart of the dilemma of schooling for African Americans, and perhaps for any group for whom there is not a predictable or rational relationship between effort and reward, are these. . . . Why should one focus on learning in school if that learning doesn't, in reality or in one's imaginary community, have the capacity to affect, inform, or alter one's self-perception or one's status as a member of an oppressed group?

For African Americans, from slavery to the modern civil rights movement, the answers were these: You pursued learning because this is how you asserted yourself as a free person, how you claimed your humanity."

(Theresa Perry)[21]

RESEARCH BRIEF:
All Families Can Help at Home

Monitoring how children use their time, engaging in home learning activities, and expressing high expectations for their children have a greater effect on student achievement than does family income or structure. Reginald Clark's studies of what families do at home, across all backgrounds, have found that many high-achieving children live in single-parent households where the mother does not have a college education.[22]

Educators' lack of knowledge about families' circumstances and school experiences may also get in the way of engaging parents. As former principal Cathy David advises, "Make no assumptions about families. If they stay away from school events, we can't assume it's because they don't care or aren't motivated. Find out more about their circumstances." The Family Welcome Questionnaire in Chapter 11 will give you information about families' situations that can be used to contradict negative stereotypes about families.

Get to Know the Community and Identify Its Assets

For many reasons, such as immigration and racial discrimination, Latino and African American students often have white teachers. When schools are in low-income areas, teachers probably don't live there, shop in the neighborhood, attend local churches, or socialize with residents. Driving to work, they may see boarded-up buildings, trash on the streets, and lots overgrown with weeds. They may think of crime and violence, unemployment and gangs, homeless people and crack houses. When they see the neighborhood in this way, they are likely to overlook its strengths and resources.

Local residents might describe their neighborhood in a very different way. What are their plans and dreams for how it could be better? Every neighborhood has assets—we need to learn about them. Community mapping is an excellent action research project for the PTA or parent group. It also offers a chance for school staff to ask for help from parents. Parents, residents, community organizations, and the local library know their neighborhood—ask them to show it to you!

> "Taking advice from a few community members is more useful than taking educators with master's degrees, putting them in a room, and saying, 'How are we going to help these people over there?'"
>
> (Karen Forys, superintendent, Northshore schools, Washington)[23]

Check It Out: Walking the Community

Bruce-Monroe Elementary School in Washington, D.C., sits on a cultural fault line in the Columbia Heights–Shaw community. A long-established African American neighborhood is now home to a growing number of Central American and Vietnamese families.

To build relationships among families, staff, and community members, the PTA organized a "Community Walk." Parents and support staff who live in the neighborhood teamed up with community residents to plan and lead the walk. They got help from the Tellin' Stories Project, a community group that works to bridge cultural differences.

Just before school started in early September, families, teachers, children, administrators, custodians, kitchen workers, and front office staff gathered in the school's all-purpose room. After a welcome by the principal and PTA leaders, parents explained the route and what they would see on the way. Leading the tour were parents and the school custodian, a longtime neighborhood resident. Here are a few stops they made:

1. A new community food market, specializing in healthy foods and fresh vegetables.
2. An auto repair shop. A teacher remarked, "I could bring my car here and get it fixed while I'm at work."
3. The Blue Nile bookstore, offering books about African culture, history, and traditions. The owner said he would like to talk to classes and share his knowledge.
4. A side street where houses are being renovated by new Latino resi-

Switching Places

What if you had to deal with one or more of these situations? How inclined would *you* be to come to an event at your school if you:

- Had three little children and no child care?

- Didn't have a car or change for the bus?

- Didn't speak English and were pretty sure there wouldn't be a translator?

- Had been ignored or treated rudely by the school secretary?

- Had a husband/partner who expects you to be at home in the evening?

- Did poorly in school yourself and think your child's problems are your fault?

- Had to work Monday nights when the PTA always has its meeting?

- Saw the PTA as a snobby in-crowd that ignores people who don't dress a certain way, speak English well, or live in a "nice" neighborhood?

Map Your Community's Assets

Make a list of neighborhood resources to support the school and enrich children's learning:

- Informal citizens' groups, from clubs to block organizations and tenant groups

- Organizations such as private businesses, churches and religious groups, Boys and Girls Clubs, and Neighborhood Houses

- Public institutions such as schools, community centers, libraries, recreation facilities, parks, and police and fire stations

- Social services such as day care centers, hospitals, clinics, counseling programs, and family resource centers

- Physical features, such as parks, vacant lots (these could become community gardens or playgrounds), and other landmarks

- Local radio stations, newsletters, and newspapers

dents. Two formerly vacant lots are now tiny parks, with play equipment.

5. A formerly run-down apartment building now owned and renovated by the tenants' association. A resident spoke to the group about his hopes for the neighborhood and told teachers about a special loan program for teachers.

After the walk, the group returned to school for lunch. During the meal they talked about what they had seen. Several teachers reflected that their view of the neighborhood had changed: "I had no idea there were so many nice houses around here." "Did you see those little parks and the kids playing in them?" "This neighborhood is really going up."

As Jody Kretzmann and John McKnight point out in their book *Building Communities from the Inside Out: A Path Toward Finding and Mobilizing a Community's Assets:*

Even the poorest neighborhood is a place where individuals and organizations represent resources upon which to rebuild. The key to neighborhood regeneration . . . is to locate all the available local assets, to begin connecting them with one another in ways that multiply their power and effectiveness. . . . Household by household, building by building, block by block . . . mapmakers will discover a vast and often surprising array of individual talents and productive skills, few of which are being mobilized for community-building purposes.[24]

Dealing with Class Differences

How do we deal with differences of class, which almost no one wants to talk about, or even admit exist?

The family-school relationship is strongly affected by what researchers call "cultural capital." Like financial capital, cultural capital gives people resources they can invest. These resources include knowing how schools are organized, having a sense of entitlement to talk with teachers, owning a car to drive to the school, and understanding the words that educators use.

White middle-class families fit right in. They usually share the same background and use the same vocabulary as teachers, and they understand the hidden rules of school life. They invest their cultural capital to help their children do well in reading and score high on tests. They are more

Many schools have networks of parents, teachers and even children that control—typically through behind-the-scenes activities like volunteering, fund-raising, and phone trees—the classroom and school community. These networks may be so entrenched that those involved may take them for granted, not recognizing their influence. However, their existence can create an atmosphere of "insiders" and "outsiders" that can lead to feelings of resentment by those not included, especially if those excluded . . . are from minority groups and those included are from the majority group.

Teachers need to make themselves aware of such hidden networks, and they need to make them explicit. If these networks can benefit anyone, then they can benefit everyone, and the school can become a more just place.

(Polite and Saenger)[25]

likely to have child care and a car to drive to school than lower-income families. All these advantages give them authority and influence over others, which means, in short, that they have more power.

In their case study of a midwestern elementary school, Annette Lareau and Erin Horvat found that middle-class white families had a real advantage. Their social and cultural background gave them skills and assets that allowed them to work more easily with the school than low-income African American families. (Middle-class black families fared somewhat better, but only as well as working-class white families. Neither group fared as well as middle-class white families, because they didn't have as much power.) Even though school staff said that they welcomed all families, they recognized only a narrow band of behaviors as acceptable.

For example, African American parents questioned teachers' views of their children, asked teachers to pay more attention to Black History Month, and insisted that their children be moved up to higher-level reading groups. The mostly white staff found such actions to be "unacceptable" and "destructive." This disconnect between low-income African American parents and school staff had a negative effect on the families' relationship with the schools. The researchers concluded that differences in cultural capital, and how schools value and react to families' assets and behavior, both create and reinforce inequality.[26]

What happens at your school to parents and family members who don't have the resources that school staff think are important? How are they treated in the front office? Where do they sit—and who greets them—at PTA and other parent meetings? How do teachers act toward them at parent-teacher conferences? What happens if they complain when their children are assigned to lower-level programs and not to the gifted or honors programs?

Responding to Unequal Resources

How might school staff respond to families who don't seem to have middle-class advantages? First, identify and draw on resources they do have. You may be astonished at what you find. Every family has something to contribute to the school. They can listen to children read, design and sew costumes for a school play, organize meetings in their neighborhood, set up a clothing exchange, give music and art lessons, and demonstrate carpentry and computer skills. Every family should feel their contribu-

"The sting of remarks in faculty rooms"

Debbie Bambino, a middle grades teacher in Philadelphia, came from a working-class family, married young, and then decided to become a teacher. She offered this personal account during an online focus group.

Because I became a teacher in my mid-30's, I had the advantage of having felt the class bias of many school personnel toward blue-collar parents when my children were young. When a group of us parents asked questions about content and program at our children's school, our motives were suspect. We were treated like we had some nerve questioning professionals. Teachers may resent being questioned by middle class parents, but it's usually not blatant.

As a teacher, I have also felt the sting of remarks in faculty rooms when teachers talk about the age of our students' parents, assuming that all young parents are negligent. I had teenage parents. Any assumption that I was neglected would have been wrong, but it still was painful.

When parents, based on their experiences, encourage their children to stand up for themselves and fight back, they are written off as barbaric. I was taught to fight back as a child. A little investigation and trust-building would go a long way in this area.

I know that I have to continually reflect on my practice toward others who are different from me, to make sure that I am not making assumptions, or devaluing their experience in any way. If as faculties, we don't even acknowledge the possibility that difference is an issue, or that we might be biased, I don't see how we can build partnerships or trust with our students and their families.[27]

What Help Would Families Like from the School?

In surveys and interviews, families often make these suggestions:

- Lend books, computers, and other learning materials

- Offer after-school programs and workshops on how to help children at home

- Reach out—visit us at home and in community centers

- Hold events and activities at the most convenient times and days for working families

- Offer child care and transportation

- Take us on field trips and visits to college campuses

- Send home educational tapes we can watch on the VCR

tions are respected and valued. (See the Parent Review and the Family Welcome Questionnaire in Chapter 11.)

Make the Rules Together

Many issues that come up between families and school staff are about school rules, discipline, and the way people treat each other. If the school is reaching out to families and the community, these questions will come up in the course of normal adult conversation, rather than in hostile encounters between families and school staff. That's an important distinction, because it affects the development of trust, which is critical to healthy relationships. (For more about trust, see Chapter 4.)

"We think manners and morals are very important. The teachers here seem rude; they don't greet us at the door; they aren't polite. They say, 'Oh, it's okay' if our child is rude."

(Parent, Alexandria, Virginia)

Most families want schools to be a place where people treat each other courteously and where the rules are agreed on, well understood, and fairly enforced. Problems often arise around personal values about what is "appropriate" in dress, language, manners, body art, hairstyles, and religious expression. Making rules together about these matters is essential to maintaining trusting and respectful relationships in your school. (See the tool "Developing a Code of Conduct for Your School" in Chapter 11.)

Address Parent Group "Ins" and "Outs"

Even if school staff have taken steps to embrace all families, there may still be a parent clique that makes other parents feel excluded. There may also be deep-seated conflict in the community that no one knows what to do about. Parents who are not in the in-crowd often say they feel unwelcome, looked down upon, and "dissed"—even if they're the same ethnicity as the in-crowd.

One way to find out who feels left out is to do a school climate survey and break down the responses by class and culture. (See the sample School Climate Survey in Chapter 11.) Who says they feel welcome and who doesn't?

Even though the parent organization is supposed to bring parents into the school, it may have the opposite effect. In many places, the parent group is dominated by white, middle-class parents.

What Are the "Hidden Rules" of Your School?

Here are some possibilities:

- "Don't question our professional judgment about your child—we are the experts."

- "Parent involvement means coming to PTA meetings."

- "Be on time—don't you know it's rude to be late?"

- "Don't bring your kids with you when you volunteer—they'll get in the way."

- "Communicate clearly, both speaking and in writing—and in English."

- "Use proper grammar and complete sentences."

- "Dress appropriately (like me)."

- "Be polite and look at me when I'm talking to you."

How do families find out what these rules are? What happens at your school when a parent or family member breaks these rules? Are parents involved in making the rules?

Strategies PTA and Other Parent Groups Can Use to Bridge Diversity

- A fiesta for Latino families, with speeches by community group leaders in Spanish

- A barbecue at a housing complex where many Asian families live

- Get-togethers with the principal at local churches, mosques, and temples

- Hiring a local resident to act as a welcomer at a housing complex by visiting new families and introducing them to the school

- Leadership training seminars for families

- "Mini-PTAs" for Latino, African, and Asian families, connected to the main PTA but holding additional, separate meetings in their languages

- Community dialogue about changes in the racial and ethnic composition of the neighborhood.

They may not seem welcoming and friendly to parents of color or to parents who don't speak English or have the same style and manners. Your action team can work with the PTA/parent group to become more inclusive and reflect the diversity of your school.

One way to start is to convene parent and community leaders to talk about expanding participation in the parent organization. Consider these questions:

- ✦ Who are the parent group officers? Do they reflect the whole school community? How can parents from groups not represented be recruited to run for office?
- ✦ Who comes to meetings and where do they sit? Is there a greeter to welcome people as they come in? Does your group have a buddy system for new members?

- Is there a variety of activities that appeal to all kinds of families? Or do most meetings go by Robert's Rules of Order and feature committee reports?
- Are meeting times convenient for families who may work nights, have rotating shifts, or live across town?
- Does the group promote cross-cultural exchange? For example, icebreakers that bring people together? Small, diverse discussion groups? Rotating seating to break up cliques?

A Final Word

The topic of class and cultural differences is often avoided because it's daunting and complicated. Although we are deeply concerned about it, we are not experts in this field. We highly recommend in-depth professional development for school staff, especially if they're coping with students from forty countries who speak twenty-five languages, or with deep-seated racial and ethnic tensions in their community.

The following chapters on advocacy and sharing power offer specific advice for creating structures to give families access to important decision-making processes. Planning for their children's future and having a voice in school governance and community affairs not only signal respect for families of all backgrounds but also help them become full-fledged members of the community.

"Our PTA is an old-girls' network. They didn't want the participation. Hispanic parents came to one meeting, but they were observers."

(Parent, Alexandria, Virginia)

"PTA meetings should be widely announced and not held in the very cozy private office next to the principal's office. It sometimes seems like a private club."

(Parent, Alexandria, Virginia)

Checklist

How Well is Your School Bridging Racial, Class, and Cultural Differences?

PROMOTING UNDERSTANDING OF DIFFERENT CULTURES

1. The school's racial and cultural diversity is recognized and openly discussed in a constructive way at parent group and faculty meetings, school council meetings, and discussion groups that include staff and families.

    ☐ *Already doing this*   ☐ *Could do this easily*   ☐ *This will take time*   ☐ *This will be hard*

2. The school's curriculum reflects cultures of families, and there are books and materials about families' cultures in classrooms and the library/media center.

    ☐ *Already doing this*   ☐ *Could do this easily*   ☐ *This will take time*   ☐ *This will be hard*

3. Families' cultural traditions, values, and practices are discussed in class.

    ☐ *Already doing this*   ☐ *Could do this easily*   ☐ *This will take time*   ☐ *This will be hard*

4. Activities and events honor all the cultures in the school.

    ☐ *Already doing this*   ☐ *Could do this easily*   ☐ *This will take time*   ☐ *This will be hard*

RECOGNIZING AND ADDRESSING CLASS AND LANGUAGE DIFFERENCES

5. The PTA/PTO is not dominated by any one group of parents, and its officers reflect the school's diversity.

☐ *Already doing this*   ☐ *Could do this easily*   ☐ *This will take time*   ☐ *This will be hard*

6. Extra efforts are made to recruit and welcome all families, and families of all backgrounds are involved at the school.

☐ *Already doing this*   ☐ *Could do this easily*   ☐ *This will take time*   ☐ *This will be hard*

7. School activities and events are planned with parents and respond to their interests.

☐ *Already doing this*   ☐ *Could do this easily*   ☐ *This will take time*   ☐ *This will be hard*

8. Interpreters are available for all meetings and events, and report cards, newsletters, signs, and other communications are translated into the school's major languages.

☐ *Already doing this*   ☐ *Could do this easily*   ☐ *This will take time*   ☐ *This will be hard*

9. English-speaking staff and families make an effort to mix with families who speak other languages.

☐ *Already doing this*   ☐ *Could do this easily*   ☐ *This will take time*   ☐ *This will be hard*

ADDRESSING ISSUES OF RACE AND RACISM

10. School staff and families use books and stories about different groups' experiences, including African Americans, to stimulate discussions about their own backgrounds and values.

☐ *Already doing this*   ☐ *Could do this easily*   ☐ *This will take time*   ☐ *This will be hard*

11. Teachers and other staff use "teachable moments" and stories from local media to comment on and discuss racially motivated incidents.

☐ *Already doing this*   ☐ *Could do this easily*   ☐ *This will take time*   ☐ *This will be hard*

12. Professional development for staff explores negative attitudes, practices and expectations for students of color, and aims to create high standards, rigorous practice, and increased expectations for all students.

☐ *Already doing this*   ☐ *Could do this easily*   ☐ *This will take time*   ☐ *This will be hard*

WELCOMING AND RESPECTING ALL FAMILIES

13. Parents and teachers are surveyed about school climate, and school staff and parent group leaders follow up on the results.

☐ *Already doing this*   ☐ *Could do this easily*   ☐ *This will take time*   ☐ *This will be hard*

14. The school has a system for helping staff and students learn how to pronounce all students' first and last names correctly.

☐ *Already doing this*   ☐ *Could do this easily*   ☐ *This will take time*   ☐ *This will be hard*

15. Front office staff are warm and welcoming to all families and visitors and compliment family members on their contributions.

☐ *Already doing this*   ☐ *Could do this easily*   ☐ *This will take time*   ☐ *This will be hard*

Which areas are you doing well in? Which ones do you want to focus on improving first?

_____

_____

_____

How are parents and the parent organization involved in addressing differences?

_____

_____

_____

What are your concerns?

_____

_____

_____

Reflection: What steps could you take to address differences of culture, race, and class?

Right away:

_____

_____

Over the long term:

_____

_____

Chapter 7

Supporting Advocacy

*How Can "Problem Parents" Become
Partners You Can Work With?*

Parents who shout, "I'm gonna come up there and kick your butt," physically intimidate teachers, curse out loud in front of children, and threaten lawsuits over seating assignments create a climate of fear at a school. Then there are parents who demand that their child be put in the gifted program, barge into a classroom without notice to "observe," and bad-mouth teachers after spending a day in the school "helping out." These parents are every school's nightmare.

Let's be realistic: this is tough territory. How do you defuse angry parents who are probably carrying a load of emotional baggage that dates back to their own days in school? How can you handle high-powered professional parents who insist on having their way? While these seem like two different questions, their root is the same. These parents want to protect, help, or get a better deal for their children. They are trying to be advocates, but they don't know how to act constructively. This chapter is about how school leaders (including the parent organization) can help parents be better advocates for their children.

Parents like these take up a lot of staff time and energy. They color perceptions of all parents and pose a major challenge to already overburdened educators. We don't pretend to have easy answers to this problem. The approach we recommend has two parts.

First, recognize that parents have the right to influence what happens to their children in school. Be very clear that their requests will be treated with respect, as long as they are made in a civil manner.

Second, set up a proactive process for collaborating with families to monitor students' progress, address their difficulties, and plan for their future. Explain the process clearly and apply it fairly. The goal is to avoid a situation in which some families have (or seem to have) a lot of inside influence, while others have (or feel they have) little or none.

Parents have told us that they are more likely to be angry and lose control when they feel no one cares about their situation or will listen to them. Many—but not all—problems can be prevented by developing trusting relationships that welcome and honor families. Some ways that your action team can approach this are described in Chapter 4, "Developing Relationships." Adressing differences of culture, race, and class, and discussing those differences openly, may also head off problems, as discussed in Chapter 6.

This problem is one that confronts every teacher, but that needs to be resolved with school-wide strategies. In this chapter, we discuss four practices that your action team can promote to encourage and support parents to be constructive advocates for their children:

1. Work with families, teachers, and other staff so they can understand what it means to be an advocate, develop and use their advocacy skills, and learn how to resolve a problem.
2. Collaborate with families to monitor their children's progress, give them a voice in their children's placement or program, and figure out how to assist their children when they're struggling.
3. Give families and students the information and support they need to make smooth transitions to kindergarten, middle school, and high school, and from there to postsecondary education and a career.

4. Help families be actively involved in setting goals for their children's future, steering them toward higher-level programs, and planning for postsecondary education.

What do we mean by an advocate? Not everyone understands the term. An advocate is a person who speaks out for another. Children are vulnerable—very few know how to stand up for themselves, or even ask for help if they're in trouble. Although a teacher, counselor, or other staff member can step in (and we've all heard stories about how a person's life was turned around by a caring teacher), the students they help will soon be passing on to the next level.

An advocate must be in the child's life over the long haul—a person who knows the child well, talks to her/him often, and sees him/her every day; a person who believes in the child, wants him or her to soar, and can step in if he or she is falling behind. Who is this person, if not the child's parents, a guardian, or a close friend or family member?

What do parents (or people standing in as parents) do when they advocate for a student?

- ✦ Set high expectations and follow their children's progress—monitoring attendance, homework, grades, and test scores
- ✦ Help the student set goals and plan for the future
- ✦ Steer the student through the system, selecting courses and programs that match his or her goals
- ✦ Intervene if the student is under pressure, has a problem, or is being treated unfairly
- ✦ Get assistance when needed, such as tutoring, medical attention, or counseling
- ✦ Monitor the student's out-of-school time and make sure it is spent in constructive activities
- ✦ Line up other educational activities, such as sports, recreation, drama, and music lessons

It's in the school's interest to work with families in this way. Think how much easier it would be for educators if every child had an effective advocate. Our country has the most complex educational system in the world. Navigating it without consistent, caring guidance would be almost impossible for many students.

RESEARCH BRIEF:
Power Is Positive

The more that parents feel that they have the power to influence their children's future positively, the better their children tend to do in school. This is called "efficacy"—the power to have an effect. Researchers Lee Shumow and Richard Lomax found that parents with a high sense of efficacy are more likely to monitor their children and be involved in school. As a result, their children tend to do better in school and feel happier, safer, and more stable.[1]

Some readers may not want to hear this, but children actually do better when their parents *are* pushy—if they're not overly offensive about it. In fact, being pushy is part of a parent's job description. Researchers use the term *press*, as in "press for success," and have found that such pressure, when judiciously applied, is a key factor in student achievement.

Let's agree that it's okay for parents to press the school and their children for better performance—to a point. When is that behavior going too far? We recommend that your action team discuss this question with parents and teachers and come to a mutual agreement on what's productive and what's not. The examples in the chart below reflect our discussions with parents and educators on this topic.

"Teachers *need* parents to know how to 'press for success'—both with their children and with their children's teachers. Asking good questions and showing genuine interest in student performance communicates a sense of urgency and shared responsibility for student progress. This can reenergize teachers and keep them from becoming complacent or lackadaisical about student progress."

(Melissa Whipple, coordinator,
Parent Academic Liaison program, San Diego)

What's good advocacy?	What's over the line?
• Requesting a certain teacher, with the particular needs of their child in mind	• Applying political pressure to get "the best teachers" for their own child
• Questioning a student's placement in a program, such as a remedial program	• Pushing for an award, honor, or position that their child has not earned
• Requesting that a student be moved to a higher-level group, program, or class, with extra support to succeed	• Demanding that a student's grade or test score be changed without a well-documented reason
• Talking to the principal or administrator about problems with a teacher, policy, or program	• Yelling at or threatening teachers and/or school staff with physical harm
• Suggesting that curriculum or instruction be modified to meet a special need	• Doing their child's homework or writing their college essays
• Questioning discipline policy or methods and requesting a hearing with an impartial advocate	• Refusing to accept a teacher's word or criticizing classroom discipline in front of their child
• Requesting that their child be excused from reading a book or doing a project that is offensive to the family's culture or religion	• Demanding that certain books be removed from the school library

Helping Families Understand and Use Advocacy to Resolve Problems

Being a capable advocate requires a special set of skills. You have to know how the system works, how to be both polite and persistent, and how to hold your ground. Many parents don't understand this role or how to play it in the school system. Many schools don't encourage parents to be advocates, perhaps fearing an onslaught of "pushy parents."

It's important to keep in mind that an advocate is not an adversary. If parents don't feel they may approach teachers or question decisions made by school staff, how can they be effective advocates for their children? What should families know to be effective advocates?

Parents Have to Understand How the School Works

What programs does it offer? What do the people who work there actually do? Who decides what program a child is placed in or assigns a child to a particular teacher? Where do you go if your child is having problems or you have other concerns? For many parents, what the school social worker and counselors do is a mystery. They may not understand the purpose of an assistant principal or the reading specialists. We can't assume that families will get this information through the grapevine.

Consider these five ideas for introducing your families to the school:

1. Hold an orientation at the start of the year and introduce the entire school staff, including custodians. Give families a chance to meet them personally.
2. Put a diagram or chart of the school's organization in the school handbook. Explain how and when parents can contact the principal, teachers, counselors, and other staff. Let them know, step by step, how to resolve an issue or concern.
3. Run a regular "who's who" column in the school newspaper.
4. Publish a catalog of all the programs in the school. Describe how to apply and who is eligible. Include Title I, special education, gifted and honors programs, and vocational and career education.
5. Post information on the school Web site about school staff, with their pictures and what they do. (While you're at it, include the information in points 2, 3, and 4.) Add a section on the school district—the superintendent, school board (identify your area's representative), and key district staff, plus a link to the district Web site. Include a list of district-level and school-level committees that parents can join.

Families also need information about the curriculum and the state's standards:

Instead of an orientation night, offer a six-week orientation program for kindergarten and preschool parents before their kids start school

"Parents can get overwhelmed with too much information. Space it out. Hold the meetings at the preschool and kindergarten sites. For each meeting, invite two key staff members from the school to explain what they do. For example, the librarian may talk about how children check out books, bring examples of some books for that age group, and talk about public libraries in the area. The attendance clerk can talk about what to do when your child is absent or tardy, and the importance of being on time for school. For the last session, take parents on a tour of the school and say 'hi' to the people they've met," advises Karen Parker Thompson, coordinator for family involvement and community resources in the Alexandria, Virginia, public schools.

+ What should their children know and be able to do at each grade level?
+ How are a student's report card grades connected to standards?
+ What does the state test measure and how are the results used?
+ What is a portfolio and how is it used to assess students? What is a rubric?

Curriculum nights, family learning activities, interactive learning kits, and exhibitions of student work are opportunities to introduce these concepts. (For more information about linking your family involvement program to student achievement, see Chapter 5.)

Today's teaching methods look different from when most parents were in school. Students often sit at tables, not in rows. They may be working in groups on projects rather than reading textbooks to themselves. They learn math through manipulatives and hands-on activities, not by filling out drill sheets. In many classes, students are expected to use original sources and do more critical thinking, not just repeat what the textbook says. Parents want to know how the school teaches students to read and do math, and what is meant by "interdisciplinary approach."

If parents understand these changes, they will be better prepared—and more likely—to talk about school with their children and help them at home.

IN THE NEWS:

African American Parents Tackle the Gap

Many low-income and African American parents think that only white, middle-class parents have the time and know-how to navigate a school system. As Aisha Tomlinson, a single mother in Harlem, says, "I only went to the school when I was called. Now, I go to the PTA meetings because I want to know what's happening."

This kind of change is the aim of a new effort launched in 2003 by African American academics, social workers, and the College Board. They want black parents, no matter what their income, to match the involvement of well-to-do white parents.

This initiative is part of a wider movement to close the achievement gap between white students and students of color. "What we are trying to do in the black community and Latino community is to build a commitment to intellect," said Edmund Gordon, a retired psychology professor at Yale University and a leader of the Harlem campaign.

Although poverty, poor teaching, and racism also contribute to the gap, Ron Ferguson, director of the Achievement Gap Initiative at Harvard, says that some middle-class black families lean too much on schools to educate their children. According to his research, fewer college-educated black parents read to their children daily, compared with white parents who are college graduates. White parents also have more books at home and are more likely to discuss science or nature with their children.

In Harlem, the initiative has launched a public awareness campaign to get this message across to African American mothers and fathers: "You have to advocate the way affluent parents do—or your child isn't going to make it. The school alone can't guarantee success." Researchers are spreading the message in churches and from door to door, and it will be preached during the summer at parent conferences.[2]

(Boston Globe, 2005)

Parents Need to Know How to Resolve Problems That Their Children Are Having in School

Your problem-solving process should answer these questions:

- What is the chain of command—whom should parents contact if there's a problem?
- Where do they go next if the problem isn't settled at that level?
- How can they work with teachers to define and solve problems and ensure that students' rights, opinions, and needs are respected?

Both parents and teachers may need professional development to build their relationship skills. They need to know about community services that can help, such as tutoring, mentoring, recreation, counseling, and health care. School district staff can help by publishing a list of community contacts, to be posted at the school and/or in the district office, for information and assistance.

When students are in high school, they often prefer to work on behavior issues with teachers or counselors on their own before their parents are called about it. Kathleen Cushman, author of *Fires in the Bathroom*, cautions that students "may have conflicts at home that could be made worse by a call from a teacher." To forge successful relationships with families, teachers must understand their students' home situation to assess how and when to include parents in the discussion. (See the Parent Review and the Family Welcome Questionnaire in Chapter 11. Cushman's book includes student surveys that ask who to contact at home.)[3]

Be proactive. Identify groups of students who may need extra help and reach out to their families. If, for example, a group of first graders did not attend preschool, invite their parents to a workshop series on supporting reading skills at home. Or if the science scores of African American and Latino girls are lagging, develop a special four-week program on family science activities to show parents how to help raise their academic achievement. Karen Parker Thompson offers a tip: "A project like this might interest some of the 'overinvolved parents' in coordinating a program and working with eight to ten of those families."

Give Parents Strategies to Help Their Children

Kris Amundson writes an advice column in *Ideas Staff Can Use,* published by the Parent Institute. She gave this advice to a teacher who wrote about an aggressive fourth grade boy whose mother does not see the problem: "Help this mother recognize that her son's aggressiveness is a problem for you, the other children in your class—and most of all, for her child." She advised the teacher to work with the mother by:

- Allowing her to observe her son's behavior in the classroom.

- Helping the mother and son make a list of positive ways he could act when he's angry.

- Developing a signal that the boy can give in class if he's starting to feel angry. Let his mom know that the teacher will let him take a short time out to get himself under control. She might try the same thing at home.

- Asking the mother to eliminate violent TV programs and video games and to monitor the child's media activities.

- Asking the mother to encourage her son to run and play outside. Explain that exercise will help reduce her son's aggression by channeling it to a healthy outlet.[4]

For more information about the Parent Institute, see Chapter 10.

When she prepares teachers to work with parents, Melissa Whipple, a veteran teacher in San Diego, quotes Robert Frost: "Education is the ability to listen to almost anything without losing your temper or your self-confidence." She cautions teachers "to be sensitive and take the time to respond when things first come up. That way you'll minimize big problems, or even keep them from occurring." Whipple continues, "I always tell them that the five most dangerous words in the English language are 'Maybe it will go away.' It might—but not likely. More likely it will get bigger and more difficult to handle."

Families Need Opportunities to Identify and Help Solve Problems That Affect Many or All Students

How can a school work with families to develop and use their advocacy skills for their own and other children? As we discussed in the previous chapter, a family's income and education will affect their ability to navigate the system. Middle-class families tend to be well established and have networks of contacts they can use to get information and support. They also know how the system works—and how to make it work for their children. When African American and other parents of color try to push the system, school staff are sometimes not as receptive.

A PRINCIPAL'S STORY:

It Takes More Than a Process to Settle a Problem

Cathy David, a principal in Alexandria, Virginia, recounts:

All semester, staff at Barrett Elementary School had been struggling with a child who had extreme difficulty controlling his behavior. His mother was angry and unpleasant to deal with. It was a difficult situation all the way around.

One day, I was meeting with the teacher and the parent when suddenly the mother exploded with anger and foul language. I stopped the conference, saying, "We want to help, but we can't do it like this. Let's meet again when your words are not controlled by your anger."

About ten minutes later, the student's mom came back into my office in tears, saying, "I'm sorry, this is not the way I want to be, but I failed school here, and no one liked me. I don't want this to happen to my kid."

I suggested that we take a walk outside, away from the school environment with so many tough associations. We walked awhile, then sat on a bench and talked. Together, we imagined a different situation for her child. After that we worked to make it happen. Sure, we still had troubles, but it went much better after we understood each other.

Advice from a Principal:
You are "the System"

"Parents from poverty don't know how to access the system," points out Ralph Spezio, an elementary school principal in Rochester, New York. "Show them how. Train parents—bring in activists as trainers on how to engage the system. Create leaders. No hiding. Have your desk near the entrance. Face your desk toward the parents. No fancy appointments. Don't be too busy for parents."[5]

Leadership training programs can help families of all backgrounds learn and practice the skills they need to be advocates and problem solvers. Many nonprofit organizations have developed such programs, and many of these train parents and community members to become trainers themselves. Action Alliance for Children describes nine such programs in its useful guide, *Pathways to Parent Leadership*.[6]

The Right Question Project (RQP) is a good example. When meeting with people who have power, parents can feel intimidated and confused. RQP trains parents about how to get the information they need to solve problems. Guided by facilitators—often RQP graduates—parents learn how to focus on what they want, and how to ask for it. (For more information about RQP, see Chapter 10.)

At RQP workshops, parents brainstorm ideas, set priorities, and reformulate questions. Then they develop an action agenda. In this process, they learn to think through an issue in a logical way. After finishing the program, parents often go on to get more education and become active in their schools and communities. The basic training works like this:

1. Parents are given an issue to discuss, such as reading and understanding a form letter explaining what school their child will attend.

2. In small groups, parents develop questions to ask. "Who made this decision? How is school assignment decided? Is this a good school?" Parents are encouraged to be objective and open.

3. Parents narrow down their list of questions to the three most important.
4. Parents meet again in small groups to refine the questions.
5. The whole group decides on a few questions that reflect their deepest concerns, such as, "How qualified are the teachers at this school? What if I'm not satisfied with this school? How can I go about changing this decision?"

The Commonwealth Institute for Parent Leadership (CIPL) in Kentucky has trained parent leaders across the state to work with schools to improve student achievement. This ambitious program is designed to help parents be advocates for their own children, as well as for better education for all children. The CIPL curriculum provides a useful three-part framework on how to work effectively with educators and other parents. (For more information about CIPL, go to Chapter 10.)

1. **Improving student achievement.** Parents learn to design and carry out projects that will have an impact on student achievement.

    • What is the state standards-based system, and how does it work? Where are the access points for parents to speak out and influence decisions?
    • Are there achievement gaps between groups of students? How do we use student achievement data to drive improvement?
    • How do children learn? Consider new approaches to improve student learning; look at student work in the light of standards; develop effective teaching practices.

2. **Increasing parent involvement.** Parents learn how to engage other parents, especially parents who are not involved at school and whose children may be struggling.

    • Connect with families of all backgrounds—reach out and learn what skills and experiences they can offer.

Dealing with Angry Parents

Karen Parker Thompson, coordinator for family involvement in the Alexandria, Virginia, public schools, has a lot of experience working in the community. "Many African American parents are really angry. I feel they mistrust the school system because they, their parents, and maybe even their grandparents have had a long history of dealing with racism in education, starting back to when schools first integrated in Alexandria.

"I remember going to an all-black school in Florida. There were teachers all around who looked just like me. It was an awesome experience! Teachers really seemed to care. They challenged me and believed in my ability to learn. When the schools became integrated, no one seemed to want us there. You don't forget those feelings. I'm sure that our parents remember those feelings. They don't trust the schools because of their past experiences and want to protect their children from going through the same ordeals.

"One way to build trust is to talk to parents about their experiences, what they remember and what they and their families went through. Use their stories as part of the learning experience—yours and theirs.

"We can turn anger and frustration into positives. Listen to African American parents. Provide opportunities to build relationships. Find out what they think about your school's climate, policies, and curriculum. Discover the strengths of your African American families and use them to increase the academic success for students in your school. Create parent leaders working with your school instead of standing on the outside of your school.

"In a mostly Latino school in my district, African American parents feel left out. So working with the principal and family involvement coordinator, who are both Latina, we are forming a principal's advisory committee for African American student achievement. It's important to make our African American families feel safe in our school and to make them leaders. We plan to provide dinner, child care, and transportation, invite a spoken-word performance artist to get people laughing and talking together, then start conversations about African American student achievement in the school.

"Don't start with parenting workshops! Build relationships, try new ideas, develop trust, and listen. Never give up."

- Run effective meetings, using group process, identifying common goals, resolving conflict, and developing an action plan.
- Facilitate a constructive dialogue between parents and teachers.

3. **Having a lasting impact.** Parents learn how to help themselves and other families become powerful advocates for higher achievement for all students.

- Who has power? How can parents have a voice in decisions?
- Learn ways to get a project or program adopted by the school and into the school improvement plan.
- Find local or state sources of funding and get a grant.

If your school does not have the funds to bring in a nationally recognized program, it is still possible to offer workshops that cover the information and skills listed above. As we discuss in Chapter 8, local community groups can be an important resource.

Wait a Minute—What Can We Do About the Pushy Parents?

"Power parents" are well educated and have lots of know-how. Instead of avoiding them, direct their energies and talents to help students and families in their school. Karen Parker Thompson offers this advice: "Does your school need a parent liaison, but you don't have funding? Maybe the 'power parents' can help write a proposal. Do you need someone to help organize after-school tutoring or recruit volunteers? Maybe they belong to an active religious congregation or community group that would offer some time. Does your social worker need someone to organize a winter coat drive or orient new families to the city? Maybe they and their friends can pitch in. These parents make active, energetic action team members."

Collaborate Closely with Parents

At the beginning of this chapter, we posed a key question: if parents don't feel they may approach teachers or question decisions made

How Can Schools Defend Themselves Against Unreasonable Demands?

Take the time to develop written policies and explain them clearly to families. Be sure to cover standards for grades, awards, and admission to programs. For example, scoring guides or rubrics for all major projects should spell out what's expected for a top grade. Any questions about the grade can be referred back to the rubric. Complaints about school staff and questions about discipline policies should be handled the same way. Be clear how the complaint process works, and spell out the discipline policy carefully. The less arbitrary these decisions, the easier they are to defend.

by school staff, how can they be effective advocates for their children? Advocacy requires reciprocity—to be heard when they speak out, parents need someone who is listening. Give parents a voice in their children's placement or program and regular updates on their progress, and work with them to resolve problems.

Programs That Promote Family Advocacy

One way to make sure that a student succeeds is to establish a close collaboration between a teacher (or other staff member) and the student's family. It's not enough to have parent-teacher conferences once or twice a year, send occasional notes home, and meet casually at an open house or PTA meeting. Instead, we mean the steady, intentional practice of face-to-face meetings, phone calls, notes, and e-mails with each family—and not just when there are problems. *We strongly recommend that this be spelled out in your school's policy, so that this is standard practice for every student in your school, starting with those most at risk.*

Kansas City, Kansas, an urban district with twenty-one thousand students, was first in the country to adopt a Family Advocacy System, a feature of the First Things First school reform program. The family advocate is a teacher, administrator, or other staff member. Each family advocate works with fifteen to seventeen students and their families, meeting regularly and making clear how each party can support a student's success. (For more information about First Things First, go to Chapter 10.)

To win teachers over, the district agreed to offer additional training and staff support, as well as translators for ESL families. The school schedule was restructured to allow time during the day for advisory activities. Family advocates learn how to engage students and families in setting goals and identifying action steps for each person to help the student achieve the goals. Advocates are responsible for:

+ Checking in with every student individually once a week
+ Meeting weekly with their students as a group
+ Meeting in person twice a year with every student and family together
+ Communicating at least monthly with every family through phone calls, e-mails, or notes home to keep families up to date
+ Working with other staff to support the student's goals, head off problems, and deal with challenges that arise

Recent evaluations show that test scores and other student outcomes have risen steadily since the First Things First reform program was adopted. The graduation rate for the district's four nonselective high schools climbed from 48 percent in 2000 to 78 percent in 2004. (These gains stem from the whole program, of course, not just the Family Advocate System.)[7]

Short of adopting an entire program, an action team can take steps to help families monitor their children's progress and keep them on track. Here are three examples of promising practices:

+ **The parent review.** The parent review is a simple assessment process used by teachers and parents. During the review, teachers ask parents for information about their children: What

"I observed a parent presenting a review of a child and was really impressed. The way the parent described him, you got a picture of the whole person. I've learned that there is no one who understands your child better than you do. We parents are constantly assessing our children when we ask them how their day went, or whom they played with, or when we observe what activities they like best at home, how they play and the quality of their conversation."

(Parent, New York City)

Preparing Parent Advocates to Focus on the Main Thing: Achievement

To find out what they need to know about their children's program or placement, the Center for Law and Education recommends in *Urgent Message for Parents* that parents ask questions like these. Does your school encourage parents to ask these questions? Are your teachers and counselors ready to respond when parents ask them?[8]

1. **To find out if your child is in a high-level or lower-level program or class:**

   - What are the different programs in the school? Are there gifted, magnet, advanced, or honors programs for high-achieving students? What about remedial or regular classes—are they lower-level? Is the school tracked by classroom, with some classes at a lower level than others?

   - What level class is my child in? How many learning levels are there? Where does my child's program or placement fall?

   IF YOUR CHILD IS NOT IN A HIGHER-LEVEL CLASS:

   - Is my daughter learning the same things as the higher-level classes? If not, how will she meet the standards for proficient work? What does she need to do to move up to a higher-level class?

   - How will the school help my son catch up so he can learn higher-level skills as well as the basics? What can I do to help him? Where else can he get extra help?

   - If my daughter stays in this program, how will she learn the skills needed to do well in middle and high school? What should my daughter be studying now so that she will be able to go to a four-year college?

2. **To find out what your child is learning:**

   - Is my child's work at or above standards for her age?

(continued)

- Does my child understand what he must do to meet the standards?

- Are most students in the class above or below proficiency in meeting standards?

- What do the standards say the students should know and be able to do?

- What guidelines do you use for grading? How are they related to the standards?

3. To find out if your child is getting the help he or she may need:

- Is my son falling behind in any area? If so, what must be done to help him?

- Does my daughter have any problems with learning? Is she getting the help she needs?

- Is my child getting enough help to catch up quickly? Is it working?

- How can I help?

are their hobbies, interests, and special skills? Is there any specific history or situations that the teacher should be aware of? How should parent and teacher stay in touch about how the child is doing? (For a sample Parent Review, see Chapter 11.)

✦ **The personal learning plan.** Personal learning plans identify a student's strengths, areas to develop, and targets for improvement. In some schools, only students who are at risk of failing have such plans; in others, all students do. A teacher, the student, and a parent develop the plan together and refer to it though the year.

✦ Advocacy workshops for families (with corresponding information for teachers). Even if they have access to teachers, parents may not know how to make the most of that opportunity. Workshops can help them practice holding a productive conversation with a teacher and explore what to ask. Title I is a good source of support for such workshops. Of course, teachers and school staff need to be aware of (and prepared for) the questions that parents will be asking.

EXAMPLE:

Barren County Middle School, a School to Watch

For extending an inviting environment to parents and community members, Barren County Middle School has received the "Welcoming Schools" award from the Partnership for Kentucky Schools. It has also been named a "School to Watch" by the National Forum to Accelerate Middle-Grades Reform. The school offers:

- "Information on Demand"—a line for parents to call for information about their child's attendance, behavior, homework, and grades, using a PIN (personal identification number)

- A homework hotline for parents and students to access homework assignments

- Administrator and teacher e-mail addresses on its Web site

- A volunteer training program to screen and inform volunteers in areas ranging from student confidentiality to running the copying machine

- An information network run by parent volunteers, who are each assigned ten families to keep updated on school events, science fair deadlines, and test scores

As one parent said, "Parents are accepted as full partners in the school. We are welcomed with open arms. The principal and teachers know my name. BCMS reaches out in extraordinary ways to parents."[9] (For more information, see Chapter 10.)

Time is always a problem. Teachers may say they are too busy to build these collaborations with parents. Melissa Whipple says it's important to address the what's-in-it-for-me factor: "Teachers deserve to know how cultivating a two-way relationship with parents will help improve student behavior and performance. They need specific training and coaching about how to do this. Telling them to 'just do it' without training and support won't work."

In elementary school, parent advocacy should focus on making sure that students are learning at a proficient level. In middle and high school, the focus of advocacy should shift toward steering students toward graduation and postsecondary education. Planning for the future is covered later in this chapter.

STORY:

Creating Opportunities for Parents to Learn and Practice Advocacy Skills

Guadalupe Castro, a Parent Academic Liaison (PAL) in San Diego, tells this story about what happened at her school's first "Coffee with the Principal"—and what she did about it.

At the Coffee, the principal was explaining how to read the district test score information that parents get in the mail. When she asked if parents had any questions, a few started talking about the cleanliness of the school grounds and bathrooms and the cafeteria food.

I told them to save those questions to the end, because we were talking about something else at that moment. This triggered an angry response. Many parents started saying that the principal never listened to their concerns. More joined in, and some started pointing their finger and accusing the principal. I was right in the middle and I knew I had to do something.

First, I worked with the parents. At a workshop a short while later, I told them that yelling at the principal was not the best way to address their concerns. Some got angry and said I was on the principal's side. I told them that I was on the *children's* side—I just wanted to help them get their voices heard. When some threat-

(continued)

ened to write a letter to the district complaining about the principal and me, I offered to help them write it in a way that their concerns could be heard. That was the end of the letter.

I offered the parents a series of workshops on leadership. We covered all the basics:

- How to follow an agenda and ask questions related to the topic
- How to reach consensus
- How to work in small groups to discuss issues and possible solutions

We also adopted some techniques to flag concerns that are not on the immediate topic. If they have a "burning issue," parents can write their idea on a piece of paper and hand it in, or they can stick it on the poster board marked "parking lot" to be dealt with during the next break. We use these in all our meetings.

Second, I went to the principal and explained that parents want to see their own issues on the agendas. She agreed. Many times we had to bring other staff to answer to the parents. We used parents' "parking lot" and "burning issues" notes to plan the agendas, and also included the information that parents had asked for.

As a result, Principal's Coffees were better attended and parents felt validated. We were able to cover all items on the agenda. If we were not able to resolve their concerns, parents were willing to be part of the solution. We had more parents involved on the school site council, governance team, and other committees. We have lots of volunteers that were willing to help in any way. Many parents reported that now they felt comfortable talking to the principal about any issue.

Give Families and Students Information and Support to Make Smooth Transitions

When students feel comfortable at school, they are more likely to attend regularly and earn higher grades and test scores. Their comfort level drops when they move from one school to the next. Explaining what's expected, and giving students and their families a firsthand look at what's next, can help them get ready for the next level of education. So will making sure they are prepared academically and socially. At times of transition, we are more likely to be receptive to learning new information and changing our behavior.

Children who are ready for kindergarten tend to do well in school over the long term. Because they experience more success, they bond well to school and learn what they need to know to enter first grade. They are less likely to fall behind or tune out during elementary school. The same is true for middle and high school.

Remember, it's not just the student who makes the move, it's the whole family. Even a simple orientation program for students and families can

EXAMPLE:

Parent Advocates Help Students Make the Transition to Middle School

To help sixth graders make the switch to Noe Middle School in Louisville, Kentucky, two parent leaders worked with teachers, other parents, and the principal to develop a Transition Night. The first event, which attracted over a hundred parents, offered workshops on adolescent development, academic standards, and school safety. Lead teachers reported on the school's team organization and concept. Since then, the school has sponsored a Transition Night for each grade. PTA membership has doubled, and many more parents are active in the school. Students report that they like having parents in the building—and that they feel safer.[10]

have a positive impact on grades and attendance. A well-designed transition program should have these goals:

1. Students and families will be familiar with the new school staff and facilities.
2. School staff and families will know each other and develop relationships.
3. Students will feel safe and connected to the school—they will know other students, be able to find their way around the building, meet the teachers, and understand the program they'll be taking.
4. Families will feel welcome, know their way around, and know who to contact to discuss how their children are doing.

Consider these examples of transition practices and programs developed by other schools:

Visits to feeder schools. Teachers, administrators, and students visit the feeder schools (or preschool programs) to meet with families and younger students and answer their questions.

Tours of the "new" school. Students and families take a look at the building, often with student tour guides, and attend social events and information sessions about the school and its programs. Some middle and high schools have Web sites that offer virtual tours, a map of the building, and a section to answer frequently asked questions.

A "buddy system." Incoming students are assigned an older student "buddy" who takes them under their wing for a day or two. Some schools have a "spring sampler" program, where students spend a day at the next school, in the company of a buddy.

Home visits. Over the summer, some schools make home visits to families with children about to enter kindergarten, and to families who will be new to the school. The purpose of the visit is to welcome the families to the school community, make a personal connection, and leave behind some information about the school and its programs.

Neighborhood walks. On a spring weekend in good weather, the principal, teachers, and other school staff visit a neighborhood and walk the streets, greeting people and introducing themselves. Neighborhood walks right before school starts can be part of a before-school staff development program.

Letters and phone calls. Teachers send out letters or phone calls introducing themselves and welcoming new students to their class. They include reading lists, useful school supplies, information about summer programs, and a summary of what students will be learning the first month in school. After school starts, sending a quick note home saying, "Your child had a great day," or relating something nice the child did that first week, goes a long way toward building relationships.

RESEARCH BRIEF:
Support from Parents and Teachers Is Related to Higher Grades

Researchers Leslie Gutman and Carol Midgely asked low-income African American sixth graders what helped them make the change from elementary to middle school. The students mentioned three key influences:

- *Support from parents:* talking to them about school, checking their homework, attending events, and volunteering at school.
- *Support from their teachers:* taking time to help them if they don't understand a lesson or assignment, and being supportive rather than critical.
- *Feeling they "belong" at school:* being accepted, respected, and included at school.

Students who reported they had all three influences (or support from parents *plus* support from teachers or feeling they "belong") had higher grades than students who reported low support.[11] (The Search Institute, a nonprofit organization that promotes healthy communities, has created a framework of protective factors such as these. For more information, see Chapter 10.)

Help Families Be Actively Involved in Setting Goals for Their Children's Future

Kindergarten is not too early to start thinking about (and planning for) what a student will do after high school. Nearly all school districts have a myriad of special programs, magnet schools, and alternative schools. Many of these have themes such as the arts or science and technology. Within schools, there is a variety of programs and placements. These include gifted programs, "houses" or "teams" where a group of students is assigned to a specific group of teachers, schools within a school, and academic and career academies. Which one a student picks, or is assigned to, can have a major impact on that student's later options.

Waiting until high school to plan for college may be too late for many students. Unless they develop strong reading and math skills in elementary school, students probably won't be placed in high-level classes in middle school. Without those important middle school courses (such as first-year algebra and a foreign language), students will not qualify for the college prep program in high school. Many parents and students don't know this. Parents need to know whom they can work with to steer their children through this complicated system and choose the schools and programs that are the best fit.

When their children enter sixth grade, parents need to understand three things:

1. Courses that are required for college admission
2. What students should take each year to complete the requirements by the end of their senior year
3. How to navigate the process of applying for college or other postsecondary education programs—and how to pay for it

A policy report by the American College Testing (ACT) service describes programs that schools have adopted to assist families with college planning.[12] In sixth grade, teachers and counselors discuss middle school courses that will prepare students to take honors and AP classes in high school. Parents get lists of middle school courses and information about how they connect to high school courses. In workshops and other

College Planning Nights for Parents and Students

At Glenmary High School in Alberta, Canada, a rural area far from any colleges, an action team of parents and teachers organized special events for students and families, by grade.

Eleventh grade Career Portfolio Night. In advance, students researched a career that interested them, interviewed a professional in that field, and created a portfolio and personal career path. At the event, students displayed their portfolios and made presentations to their families, fellow students, and teachers.

Twelfth grade College Information Night. In advance, school counselors met with each senior and showed them how to investigate careers and financial aid online. Students also got a form on graduation requirements. At the event, students and families brought the graduation forms. Counselors profiled a few careers, showing the entrance requirements, courses, and average grades needed. Then students and parents went to the computer lab to complete an interest and skills inventory, which suggested career options they could explore on the Internet.[13]

meetings, counselors explain how parents can monitor their child's progress, such as by keeping an academic portfolio that contains examples of their students' work over time. Families learn how to develop a college finance plan, after a thorough review of college costs and expenses and sources of financial aid.

During the eighth grade year, counselors meet one-to-one with students and their parents to discuss academic goals, select the following year's courses, and review typical college admissions requirements. Parents can preview high school courses during open house gatherings and meetings with high school counselors.

At the high school level, another set of activities begins. Using test results, counselors confer with parents and use students' scores to select courses and programs that will allow students to develop the necessary academic skills. Teachers also use test results to suggest strategies parents can use to help improve their children's performance.

College planning handbooks developed by schools for students and parents cover:

✦ Postsecondary options, including college
✦ Tips for researching colleges and other postsecondary institutions
✦ Guidance on application procedures
✦ What to look for in a college visit
✦ Detailed time line for applying to college

At financial aid workshops, families get help from counselors to fill out forms and apply for scholarships and other aid. Representatives from local banks explain the student loan process.

Students of varied ethnic backgrounds and those from low-income families face more barriers to attending college than white middle-class students. They are more likely to go to college and prosper there if they have had support from their families and teachers, and tutoring and mentoring from organizations and older students from their own community. It's important for students and families to understand that there are more pathways to a BA degree than applying to a four-year college in the senior year for the following fall.

Aside from special activities and events, schools also can structure regular opportunities for parents, students, and teachers or advisors to track progress and plan for life after high school.

Advisory system. In middle and high schools, assigning an adult advisor for every student gives families a point of contact. It also gives students someone they can turn to for support. The family advocate system described earlier in the chapter is an example.

Study skills program. Programs such as AVID (Advancement Via Individual Determination) can help middle and high school students prepare for the demands of honors and advanced classes. The program is offered as a special class during the school day. Students practice note-taking and study skills and learn about the "hidden curriculum" of the school—what courses to take, which teachers to seek out, and the importance of tests. AVID programs have workshops for families to explain the program, and some organize family activities and tours of college campuses. This program also helps students develop connections to others with similar goals. (For more information, see Chapter 10.)

Student support team. When students enroll in the Met High School in Providence, Rhode Island, they are assigned a support team. (The Met is a model for the Gates Foundation's small-high-school initiative.) The team usually consists of three people: a parent (or someone acting as one); a teacher, counselor, or other advisor; and a community member who is the student's mentor. The team reviews the student's work regularly and holds the student accountable for its content and quality. It's the team's job to make sure the student gets through school successfully.

Individual graduation plans. Individual graduation plans help students with academic and career planning. In Kentucky, the state education agency offers folders and forms that can be downloaded by families and teachers. Folders include a four-year high school plan and space to record information about academic and career goals, interests and hobbies, school and community activities, and work experience. (For more information, see Chapter 10.)

Family conferences. The standard parent-teacher conference can be a tense, awkward encounter, especially if it's the only time during the year that parents and teachers see each other. In Chapter 5, we discuss the value of student-led conferences using portfolios of student work. In schools with advisory systems or student support teams, those meetings take the place of the standard conference, and they are part of a steady stream of communication. There is good advice on the Internet and elsewhere about how to have a successful conference, so we won't repeat it here. (See Chapter 11 for the Conference Checklist.)

Mother-daughter programs. Several districts offer these programs for Latino families. Girls enter the program in middle school and are followed through to high school graduation. Many will be the first in

Family Support Is Key to More Diversity in Advanced Classes

Annandale High School in Fairfax County, Virginia is a typical inner-ring suburb. Formerly an all-white middle- and working-class student population, it now looks like the United Nations. Once a school that retained its white middle-class families by offering gifted programs, it now offers a challenging program open to all students.

Program coordinator Erin Albright says that engaging parents in the decision to take the advanced program has been an important strategy in the program's success. She uses these approaches to build low-income and immigrant parent support for the advanced program:

- Parent information nights at the feeder middle schools. Information is tailored to families' backgrounds, including explaining how the U.S. education system works.

- Workshops and meetings in families' languages or with an interpreter. Start with the families' expectations for their children. What do they want for their children? How can they use this program to meet their goals?

- Planning for college, taking families' concerns in mind. Many families from overseas do not want their children to go far from home, or for their daughters to live in dormitories. Cost is a major concern, too. Options include attending community college for two years while living at home, then transferring to a four-year college.

- Using eighth grade parents' night, freshman orientation, and advanced program orientation to present high-level goals for students.

- Recruiting bilingual parents and students in the program to get the word out to other families.

- Working through the school's parent liaisons. They get the message across to families that advanced classes are open—and there is a person at the school they can talk to.[14]

their families to attend college. The program includes college field trips, mother-daughter conferences on the campus, tutoring, and mentoring. (For more information, see Chapter 10.)

Moving Beyond Tracking

When schools are rigidly structured to track students by "ability," access to challenging programs is limited. This puts students with less determined parents at risk. Students who take advanced classes in high school are more likely to go to college and stay there. Knowing this, many high schools are reversing policies of exclusion and encouraging low-income students of all backgrounds to enroll in higher-level classes.

A case in point is Annandale High School, in Fairfax County, Virginia, a suburb of Washington, D.C. Once wedded to the gifted-and-talented model, Annandale has adopted an honors approach. Students qualify for advanced programs based on motivation and performance in class, not on test scores. In 1995, the gifted English 9 class had eighteen students, of whom seventeen were white and one was African American. No Latino student had ever applied. Now there are over one hundred students in advanced English 9, and they represent the entire student population, which comes from ninety-two countries and speaks forty-five languages.

Students spend 70 percent of their waking hours outside school. How they spend that time and with whom they spend it have a big effect on how well they do in school. The job of monitoring their out-of-school activities falls mainly on their families. That, too, is a form of advocacy. When families can connect their children to sports, recreation, and education programs in the community, and to other responsible adults, they are guiding them toward a successful future. By creating a program to support parents as advocates, schools are strengthening the capacity of families to supervise and guide their children both in and out of school.

Supporting advocacy is a way to share power and responsibility with families. As parents develop advocacy skills in the school arena, they will be preparing to engage the larger system, which will serve both them and their children well over the long run. The next chapter explores opening up the school decision-making process to parents and community members in ways that will promote democracy, not just at school but in our society.

Checklist

How Well Does Your School Support Parents as Advocates?

EXPLAINING THE SCHOOL TO FAMILIES

1. The school handbook and Web site show how the school is organized and provide information for contacting school staff.

    ☐ *Already doing this*   ☐ *Could do this easily*   ☐ *This will take time*   ☐ *This will be hard*

2. All families get information about academic and after-school programs for students and how to apply for them.

    ☐ *Already doing this*   ☐ *Could do this easily*   ☐ *This will take time*   ☐ *This will be hard*

3. There is a clear written process for resolving complaints or problems, and all families know how to use it.

    ☐ *Already doing this*   ☐ *Could do this easily*   ☐ *This will take time*   ☐ *This will be hard*

CONFERRING WITH TEACHERS

4. Teachers contact each family at least once a month with an update on their child and send graded student work home for review once a week.

☐ *Already doing this*   ☐ *Could do this easily*   ☐ *This will take time*   ☐ *This will be hard*

5. Parents can easily contact teachers and other staff with information and questions about their children.

☐ *Already doing this*   ☐ *Could do this easily*   ☐ *This will take time*   ☐ *This will be hard*

6. If your school is a middle or high school, each family knows an adult in the school they can contact about their child.

☐ *Already doing this*   ☐ *Could do this easily*   ☐ *This will take time*   ☐ *This will be hard*

SUPPORTING ADVOCACY

7. At workshops and other information sessions, parents learn how to ask the right questions about their children's progress and placement.

☐ *Already doing this*   ☐ *Could do this easily*   ☐ *This will take time*   ☐ *This will be hard*

8. The school confers with families about which program is best for their children and gives them the information they need to make the best choice.

☐ *Already doing this*   ☐ *Could do this easily*   ☐ *This will take time*   ☐ *This will be hard*

9. The school actively recruits students for gifted and advanced programs and works with families to explain the program and obtain their support.

☐ *Already doing this*   ☐ *Could do this easily*   ☐ *This will take time*   ☐ *This will be hard*

10. Parents are part of the decision-making process about student placement in these programs.

☐ *Already doing this*   ☐ *Could do this easily*   ☐ *This will take time*   ☐ *This will be hard*

11. Counselors and teachers refer families to education and recreation programs in the community that can help their children.

☐ *Already doing this*   ☐ *Could do this easily*   ☐ *This will take time*   ☐ *This will be hard*

TRANSITION PROGRAMS

12. The school makes personal contact with all new families before the school year begins.

☐ *Already doing this*   ☐ *Could do this easily*   ☐ *This will take time*   ☐ *This will be hard*

13. Teachers and students visit preschool programs and feeder schools to talk about the school and answer questions.

☐ *Already doing this*   ☐ *Could do this easily*   ☐ *This will take time*   ☐ *This will be hard*

14. Special events for students and families welcome them to the school, give them a tour of the building, and connect them to "buddies" or mentors.

☐ *Already doing this*   ☐ *Could do this easily*   ☐ *This will take time*   ☐ *This will be hard*

PLANNING FOR THE FUTURE

15. If your school is an elementary school, school staff ask families about their goals for their children and discusses how the school can prepare them for that future.

☐ *Already doing this*   ☐ *Could do this easily*   ☐ *This will take time*   ☐ *This will be hard*

16. If your school is a middle school, all sixth-grade parents get information about what courses are required for college or other postsecondary education and what students should take in middle school to qualify for those courses in high school.

☐ *Already doing this* ☐ *Could do this easily* ☐ *This will take time* ☐ *This will be hard*

17. If your school is a high school, all ninth-grade families get a college or career planning handbook that contains an individual graduation plan and explains all the steps for applying to college. It also lists what courses are required for college admission.

☐ *Already doing this* ☐ *Could do this easily* ☐ *This will take time* ☐ *This will be hard*

Which areas are you doing well in? Which ones will need more work?

_____

_____

_____

How are parents involved in your school to promote constructive advocacy?

_____

_____

_____

What are your concerns?

_____

_____

Reflection: What steps could you take to develop a program to support parents as advocates?

Right away:

_____

_____

Over the long term:

_____

_____

Chapter 8

Sharing Power

Who's in Charge Here Anyway?

To be serious about partnership, a school also must be serious about following democratic practices. Supreme Court justice Louis Brandeis coined the term "laboratory of democracy," and that is what we think every school could be. Democracy is a way of living together that promotes fairness and social justice. The best way to get these ideas across is to make the lessons we teach in civics class come alive in our schools. In other words, we should practice what we teach.

In this chapter, we'll discuss three practices that we think schools (and school districts) must follow to become living examples of democracy:

1. Provide workable mechanisms for teachers, parents, and students to voice their ideas and concerns, and to take part in decision making.
2. Build a broad base of involvement by increasing families' political knowledge and skills, and their connections to other parents and people in the community.
3. Strengthen families' links with community organizations and resources.

Two other practices are critical to a democracy: respecting the rights of all members of the school community and collaborating with parents on decisions that affect their children. These topics are addressed in Chapter 6, "Addressing Differences," and in Chapter 7, "Supporting Advocacy."

If families, students, and other community residents can practice the "tools of democracy"—speak their concerns, take part in elections, and meet openly to make decisions—they will be actively learning how a democracy works.

Provide Workable Mechanisms for Teachers, Parents, and Students to Take Part in Decision Making

Partnership requires sharing power. The starting point for teachers and administrators is to see families as partners and not simply as clients or guests. All partners must have a voice in school affairs, including decisions about budgets, school programs and personnel, changes in curriculum and instruction, and student behavior.

One way for your action team to start is to hold a town meeting or a series of discussion groups to plan workable ways for teachers and other staff, parents, and students to express concerns and take part in decision making. (For information about forming an action team, see Chapter 3.) Ask all participants for their ideas about how to strengthen the school's links to families and community members. Offer other opportunities to invite suggestions such as homeroom discussions, parent association meetings, or surveys that older students or parents could design and administer. (Sources of surveys are listed in Chapter 10.)

Some important and widely used mechanisms that can foster democratic decision making, if they are implemented in a genuinely open spirit, are:

1. School councils and committees
2. Parent or parent-teacher associations
3. School action teams for planning and research, including an action team for partnerships
4. Parent-school compacts or contracts

Take Advantage of the Law

The No Child Left Behind Law applies to all schools, especially those funded under Title I. It provides several leverage points for parents to advance democratic practices in schools:

- **A school-family compact,** developed with and approved by parents. Bring parents and teachers together to discuss how they can work together more effectively to improve students' skills and put their ideas in the compact.

- **A written Title I parent involvement policy,** also developed with and approved by parents. Does the school need a new policy to help teachers and parents work better together? When and how may parents attend professional development? Observe in classrooms? Meet with the principal?

- **A report card on every school** explaining how the school and the district are performing. Prepare teachers to explain student test reports fully to parents. Have a "state of the school" meeting to discuss what the school is doing to improve student progress.

- **Options for parents** if their child's Title I school is not making adequate progress in improving student achievement. Parents may request to transfer their children to another school or they may decide to stay, become involved in improving the school, and receive extra services for their children.

TIP: To keep parents committed to the school and making it better, prepare them to take part in the school improvement committee.[1]

In a school community, action trumps talk. Teachers and parents tire easily of talk about democracy and participation if these values aren't reflected in the way things are done. In all the strategies we suggest, it is always important to put fairness first. Use open communication, negotiation, consultation, and compromise when seeking to solve school problems.

Preparing Parents to Become Effective Members of Councils and Committees

Many advisory committees and school site councils are not as effective as they could be. From the members' point of view, such committees are worth the effort only if administrators take them seriously. Here are a few ideas to make them work well.

- ✦ Give council and committee members staff support and resources to do their work—for example, access to computers, copy and fax machines, and telephones.
- ✦ Make sure they have important problems and issues to deal with—how to improve the achievement gap in math and raise reading scores, not just selecting a color to repaint the lunchroom or a theme for the annual awards ceremony.
- ✦ Give families honest and timely information about budgets, pol-

icies, and student achievement. Use test data to identify problem areas that need improvement.

✦ Make training available for participants (including teachers). Knowledge is power. The more that parents understand education issues, the more powerful and constructive partners they will be.

✦ Encourage parent associations and councils to reach out to families who have not been involved.

✦ Make sure that the councils and school officials take committee recommendations seriously.

Involving family and community members on councils and committees means that different points of view and opposing interests will be represented. This is the whole point, of course, but it means there will sometimes be conflict and disagreement. This is a good thing. Better decisions usually emerge from debate and compromise.

At Parkside Elementary School in Chicago, the principal proposed a budget that included four new professional positions. The local school council (LSC), which has a parent majority by law, believed that the funds would be better spent on programs that serve students.

Why did the school need a new computer teacher, the LSC asked, when the computer lab was used only for playing games? They also disputed the need for a "disciplinarian," a coordinator for the Title I program, and another "program coordinator." They felt it was not the best use of funds to add high-paying positions that were not clearly related to helping students.

The LSC turned for help to an intermediary organization, Parents United for Responsible Education (PURE). (For more information, see Chapter 10.) PURE staff worked with LSC members and district staff to amend the principal's plan. The changes that were finally negotiated redirected the budget to provide more services for students. These include a school psychologist to address students' behavioral issues, an upgraded and academically oriented computer lab and new textbooks, and an intervention program for eighth graders at risk of not graduating.[3]

Mary Lou Amato, a middle school principal in Los Angeles, offers this advice: "Prepare parents to take part in governance structures. Whenever possible, parents should train other parents. Create committees so they can learn about proposals and ask questions in advance of decision meetings. Insist that school staff and other council or committee members treat parents with respect." Amato offers these three tips:

- Give parents plenty of chances to speak up and ask questions.
- Translate all materials and proposals into their languages.
- Give parents time to think and talk about proposals before they go to a board for decision.

Amato adds this example from her own experience: "Every year I take the Title I budget to the parents for approval. A month before, I call for volunteers for the budget committee. We do a two-hour workshop and put the budget together. Then they present it to the other parents. Instead of me droning on for twenty minutes, the parents present the budget and the rationale for it. That's the kind of capacity building that I'm talking about."

The O'Hearn elementary school in Boston follows her advice. The school has a school council, or site committee, that governs the school and is open to any parent who wants to take part. In their guide, *Including Every Parent*, O'Hearn parents recommend five steps to empower parents, honor their insights, and harness their leadership skills:

1. **Welcome everyone.** At the first meeting, invite the whole school—parents, teachers, and school staff. Make it clear that everyone is welcome to attend all meetings, even if they are not voting members.

2. **Accommodate all parents.** Provide food and child care, vary the days and times of meetings, and offer translation.

3. **Discuss and settle on a protocol.** Decide who will be voting members and how long their terms will last. At the O'Hearn, each voting member has one vote, and a parent's vote carries the same weight as that of a teacher or the principal.

4. **Set and stick to clear, precise agendas.** Use meetings to address specific, pressing issues. Avoid broad, philosophical discussions.

5. **Facilitate, don't dictate.** Don't let a few people (even the

principal) dominate the discussion. Keep the conversation open and make sure everyone feels comfortable to speak.[4]

The O'Hearn school's success illustrates that both teachers and administrators have a great deal to learn from parents and other family members. Parents bring knowledge about their children, their culture and values, their understanding of the community, and their own interests and accomplishments. They also have constructive ideas about how to improve achievement.

In a democratic school, it's important to have more than a cadre of skilled parent leaders who represent the diversity of parent interests in the school. There should also be a broad base of involved families and community members to whom the leaders are accountable and from whom they draw their strength. All families in the school community should be offered a wide variety of possibilities for participation.

EXAMPLE:

Parents make a difference on school councils

In Kentucky, school councils select the school principal, interview candidates for other positions at the school, and write a comprehensive school improvement plan every year. At a high school in Ashland, Kentucky, the council was interviewing prospective math teachers. Teachers asked the candidates about their education philosophy and teaching experience.

A parent member pulled out a ninth grade math text, opened the book, and asked, "Please explain the problem on this page so that I can understand it." Only two of nine candidates did so satisfactorily— and one of them got the job.

Building the Leadership Capacity of Parent Associations

The National PTA has a long history as an advocate on issues such as kindergarten, child labor, parent education, and children's health and safety. The national organization, its state affiliates, and its thousands of local chapters have been strong allies of public schools. Joining this

Sharing

Power

· · ·

193

national organization gives a local parent group access to a network that offers training, information, and influence in state capitals and with the federal government.

Despite the PTA's historic role in state and national policy, local parent groups often shy away from decision making and advocacy. Where is your school's parent association? Does it play a leadership role, or does it follow a more traditional model?

There is no question that when PTAs and other parent groups include a solid cross section of a school's parent community, they can support

Leadership-style parent organization	Traditional-style parent organization
• Focuses on improving student achievement and helping families understand standards, tests, and performance data	• Focuses on fund-raising and recruiting volunteers to help in the lunchroom, office, and playground
• Varies times and places, such as meeting on weekends in an apartment complex community room	• Holds all meetings at school, on the same weeknight each month
• Plans the agenda based on issues important to parents, using parent surveys	• Meets with the principal to set the agenda
• Communicates parents' ideas and concerns to the principal and school staff	• Communicates the principal's message to other parents
• Features student work and performances at meetings and activities, and offers translation	• Follows Robert's Rules of Order and holds meetings in English only
• Invites the whole family and offers food, child care, and help with transportation	• Expects parents to feed their families, hire babysitters, and drive to the monthly meeting
• Presents concrete proposals for improvement to principal and local school board	• Holds an annual awards dinner with district staff and local officials

school improvement, provide a training ground for civic leadership, and build support for the public schools. Here are some steps that an action team can take so the parent group can develop into a more powerful and inclusive organization:

1. Use PTA/PTO meetings as a forum for discussing changes in school policy and improvements in student achievement.
2. Charge the parent association with conducting a school climate survey each year.
3. Give the parent group officers a seat on the school council and a voice in all major decisions affecting the school.
4. Ask the PTO/PTA to conduct focus groups in all communities served by the school to identify barriers to parent involvement and get ideas on how to address them.
5. Work with the parent group to research issues such as low student attendance, the need for child care and after-school programs, bullying, and student safety. Draw in some collaborators from a local college or university to help.

TIP:

Help from a facilitator

If you want to try an action research project, consider finding an outside facilitator. The facilitator can be a university professor, graduate student, or a staff member from a community organization. Ask the facilitator to be responsible for coordinating and facilitating meetings, following up with staff, offering technical advice about research design and data analysis, and making contact with outside resources.

Creating teams to take action

Action teams (which can go by different names) are a participatory, moderate-cost way to approach school planning and improvement. They can also address problems or concerns in the school or community. If they are aimed at a specific problem or issue, they can be short-term, but they can also take on a long-term responsibility, such as promoting family involvement. This is the mechanism we recommended at the end of Chapter 3 to take on the job of moving a school toward full-fledged partnership.

Every school in the National Network of Partnership Schools (NNPS), developed by Joyce Epstein and her colleagues at Johns Hopkins University, forms an Action Team for Partnerships that develops a comprehensive program of partnership. The program includes activities for the six major types of involvement in Epstein's framework—parenting, communicating, volunteering, learning at home, decision making, and collaborating with community.[5]

The Action Team for Partnerships consists of at least six people—teachers, parents, administrators, counselors, students in the upper grades, and others. The team assesses current practices of partnership, creates a three-year outline, and writes a detailed one-year plan to strengthen partnerships with families.

To organize the work, each Action Team member chairs or co-chairs a subcommittee for each type of involvement. With help from others in the school community, the Action Team puts in place new or improved practices of partnership that meet the schools' needs, interests, and goals. Action Teams are encouraged to evaluate the progress of their programs annually and to improve outreach to all families around activities that are linked to the goals for supporting student success in school.

Empowering Teachers and Parents to Do Action Research

Some action teams gather data about school and community issues, such as traffic safety, low attendance, or problems with communications. The Parent-Teacher Action Research process, developed by the Institute for Responsive Education, includes these steps:

1. Form a team and agree to collaborate.
2. Choose or approve an outside facilitator. (See tip on previous page for more detail.)
3. Agree on goals and more specific objectives.
4. Determine the interests, concerns, and priorities of parents, families, and community members. This can be done through surveys, interviews, home visits, focus groups, or other methods planned and carried out by team members.
5. Design and implement a plan for action or for further study.

6. Compile results, reflect on what has been learned, and design a plan for future action based in what has been learned.[6]

This approach builds positive working relationships between school staff and parents. Families and teachers learn to work together to solve problems that are meaningful to the children and families in that school. They also learn to communicate with and trust each other.

Action research can start with community organizations. In Tucson, Arizona, the Educational and Community Change Project brings organizers, families, and educators together to work on community issues. At Ochoa Elementary, parents and students complained about trash-filled vacant lots in the neighborhood. With help from the Change Project, parents started a campaign to clean up the lots and research city regulations about vacant property. Children petitioned the city council successfully to have the lot turned over to the school. Students, teachers, and parents worked together to design a small urban park and wildlife habitat, with native plants.

EXAMPLE:

Focus on school safety

In Jackson, Mississippi, the local chapter of Parents for Public Schools (PPS) took on a safety campaign triggered by concerns about weapons in schools. PPS collaborated with civic groups, from the Junior League to the Urban League, to organize a public conversation with city officials. PPS brought in experts from the National School Safety Center as a resource. Next, the PPS leaders pulled together a coalition of organizations to sponsor a public meeting to seek solutions. Nearly five hundred people attended. Many of their recommendations became public school policy, such as police-trained school safety officers for each school and training for school staff in crisis management, mediation, and racial sensitivity. (For more information about PPS, see Chapter 10.)

Creating Partnerships Through School-Family Compacts or Agreements

Successful partnerships are based on give-and-take. School, family, and community all share responsibility for children's learning and development. A school-family compact is an opportunity to develop clear, written agreement between parents and teachers about how they should work together. (For advice on linking a compact to improving student learning, see Chapter 5.)

Compacts are required for Title I schools under No Child Left Behind and are a good idea for any school. The compact should describe:

- How the school will "provide high-quality curriculum and instruction in a supportive and effective learning environment"
- How the school and families will build a partnership to help children learn
- How the school and families will communicate regularly with each other
- The responsibilities and rights of families, teachers, and students

Developing a compact requires a few key steps. We recommend involving all families in the school, not just families of Title I students.

1. Ask parents, students, and school staff what they want the compact to cover. Each group should list what it wants the *others* to do, and then list what should be expected of *themselves*.
2. By all means, avoid compacts that apply only to parents and students. Teachers are a key part of the learning triangle, and the rules should apply to them, too.
3. Focus the compact on common concerns (e.g., homework, communication, rules of behavior) and link them to learning. For each topic, list what each partner can do. For example, consider a homework compact:

    Students: I will write down assignments, do my homework every day, and turn it in when it's due.

Parents: I will look over the assignments, talk to my child about them, and make sure he/she does the work and hands it in.

Teachers: I will assign homework that is relevant and interesting, make sure students understand the assignment and what they'll learn from doing it, and grade it promptly.

Make sure the compact is signed by all three parties. A student-led family conference is an opportunity to present, personalize, and sign the compact.

COMPACT DOS AND DON'TS

Do	Don't
• Keep the pledges about equal—no more than ten items for each group.	• List fifteen obligations for parents and only five for teachers.
• Be specific: "I will read to my child twenty minutes a day."	• Be vague: "I will read to my child regularly."
• Be respectful: "I will talk with my child about the need to get at least nine hours of sleep every night."	• Patronize parents: "I will make sure my child is clean and rested." (Parents say: "Why do they think I don't do that?")
• Follow up with tip sheets, such as hints for checking homework, negotiating TV time, and fun math activities.	• Complain that parents aren't doing their job.
• Send home interactive learning kits and reading materials.	• Wonder why parents don't get books from the public library.
• Ask "Are we sticking to our pledges?" at conferences and meetings.	• Hand out the compact at the start of the year and never mention it again.
• Revisit the compact every year.	• Use the same compact year after year.
• Ask families, students, and staff what would make it better. Update it using the current student achievement data.	• Forget to ask whether families and staff actually use the compact.

Build a Broad Base of Involvement by Increasing Families' Connections to Others in the Community

Personal relationships, trust of others, and networks of contacts with people in organizations, government, work, and places of worship make up what researchers call *social capital*. In times of need or transition, social capital is a critical resource. For example, if we lose our job, our network of contacts can help us find a new one.

According to Robert Putnam, author of *Bowling Alone*, social capital is increased by taking part in parent groups at school and in community groups such as local music ensembles, community gardens, churches, sports clubs, and neighborhood councils. This kind of social interaction is the heart of healthy community life.[7]

Just as with financial capital, social capital is not fairly distributed in our society. People with more education usually have more resources—such as social networks, knowledge about how the system works, and confidence in dealing with government agencies, including schools. School leaders and parent organizations in schools can help families develop their social capital, including their knowledge about how to have an impact on the system.

Social capital does not always confer political influence. Parents also need to build what researcher Kavitha Mediratta calls *political capital*. This is the power a community can wield to influence public decisions, in order to obtain resources, services, and opportunities. Using political capital can require setting an agenda and taking group action, such as attending school board meetings, picketing, or holding demonstrations. If residents feel a strong sense of community, they are more likely to risk engaging in collective political action.[8]

Hearing from the Community: Surveys, Focus Groups, Study Circles, and Organizing Campaigns

Parents, teachers, students, and other partners must have opportunities to express their opinions, preferences, ideas, and concerns—to someone who is listening. There are many relatively easy ways for school leaders to find out what people think—and for families and community members to let school leaders know what's on their minds.

- ✦ Place suggestion boxes in the school and in community sites.
- ✦ Set up interactive online chat groups and blogs to allow continuing exchange of ideas on school matters.
- ✦ Request time on community-access cable TV stations, which are obligated to provide public affairs programming and can offer forums on school issues.
- ✦ Hold informal "rap sessions" at sites in the community as a less formal way to connect to the community.
- ✦ Collaborate with an organizing group to elicit the ideas and concerns of families and community members in a listening campaign or neighborhood walk.

Your action team can conduct surveys by phone, mail, online, or door to door. Chapter 11 contains several examples of surveys, and more are available online. (See Chapter 10 for information about survey sources.) Focus groups are a more personal way to bring people together to discuss issues or topics that are important to them. Many say that focus groups are

Even Unpopular Points of View Deserve a Hearing

Being consistent about the values of democracy requires that we recognize the right of parents to advocate for their own interests and preferences, even if their views are unpopular. Opposition to teaching evolution, support for an Afrocentric curriculum, being for (or against) gay and lesbian student organizations, or promoting the distribution of condoms are current controversies. By discussing these issues openly at community forums, study circles, school council meetings, and other public sessions, educators will sharpen their understanding of educational issues and become more effective leaders. Invite local experts to share their views, and ask neutral community organizations to moderate the sessions.

more informative than surveys because they reveal what people are really thinking.

A focus group process involves these steps:

+ In small, two-hour meetings of ten to twenty people, parents meet with parents, teachers with teachers, and so on.
+ The meetings are conducted by neutral facilitators and participants respond to a few, carefully selected questions.
+ The main themes discussed under each question are recorded on chart paper.

After the different groups have met, the participants convene to examine the results from all the discussions and explore options for action.

Study circles provide space for public dialogue about community change. The process begins with community organizing, which is followed by facilitated, small-group dialogue that leads to a range of outcomes. Study circles don't advocate a particular solution. Instead, they invite many points of view around a shared concern. A study circle program is organized by a diverse group of community members and includes a large number of people from all walks of life. Trained facilitators use even-handed discussion materials and group process methods to trigger conversation.

A study circle is a small, diverse group of eight to twelve people that meets for several two-hour sessions. Many such groups can be meeting at the same time on similar or related issues. Using general guidelines, the group sets its own ground rules. Each group is led by an impartial facilitator who manages the discussion. After starting with personal stories, the group examines a problem or issue from many points of view and explores possible solutions. Finally, they make plans for action and change. (For more information about study circles, see Chapter 10.)

Community organizing groups can work with the school action team, or on their own, to draw out family and community members' concerns and ideas for improving schools. Through house meetings, neighborhood walks, and door-to-door listening campaigns, organizers are finding that low-income families and young people of color have a clear, specific agenda. It is often a different agenda from that of professional educators' groups, and is often more directly related to the interests of children.

Reform agenda of low-income families	Reform agenda of professional groups
• More funding for education and better facilities in poor neighborhoods	• Professional collaboration and learning communities
• Smaller class size and smaller high schools so that children get more personal attention	• Authentic assessment of student work
	• Support for new teachers
• Clear pathways to college that are open to all students (i.e., eliminate tracking)	• Site-based management
	• Implementation of high standards
• Quality instruction, better teachers, and more challenging programs	• Greater role for district in school reform
• Translation services and bilingual education	• Academic support programs and interventions
• Equitable and consistent discipline, "decriminalizing" young people of color	• Literacy development
	• Block scheduling and other strategies for creating smaller learning communities
• Extra support so students can catch up if they're behind	
• Youth empowerment	• Instructional strategies for English-learners
• Safety[9]	

Both sides share the same concerns, but their language and approaches differ. Although both agendas are important, parents will need a broad base of community support and power before theirs will be given equal weight. How to work productively with community organizing initiatives is covered later in this chapter.

Parent Leadership Training Programs

Through her observations of how families interact with teachers, sociologist Annette Lareau has found that families are at a disadvantage if

Seven Ways to Build Families' Social Networks and Political Skills

1. Give families information about how the education system and local government work. Take families on field trips to district offices and school board meetings.

2. Keep voter registration forms and information about local government agencies in the school office or family center. For a middle or high school, develop a student-run voter registration drive.

3. During campaign season, invite candidates running for school board and other local offices to speak to families at the school. Work with families to develop an agenda for the meeting so that their concerns will be addressed.

4. Encourage families to lobby local officials about needed funding for community facilities, after-school programs, or better law enforcement.

5. Invite local banks and businesses to talk with families about their services, loan programs, and employment opportunities.

6. Involve families in action research. Ask them to develop and conduct surveys of other families and investigate problems in the community.

7. Make it easy for parents to meet and discuss concerns with the principal, talk to teachers and guidance counselors, and examine their children's school records.

they are not familiar with the language, authority structure, and curriculum of the school. If schools were to promote family-school relationships that emphasize all families' strengths and assets, middle-class culture might not provide such an advantage. Again, knowledge is power.[10]

Many parent leadership programs develop families' social and cultural skills and build a broad base of active parents and community members. These include the Commonwealth Institute for Parent Leadership in Kentucky, the Parent School Partnership Program sponsored by the Mexican American Legal Defense and Educational Fund (MALDEF), and the Parent Leadership Exchange in New England. (The previous chapter, on advocacy, describes several of these programs in some detail. For additional information, see Chapter 10.)

The Tellin' Stories Project of Teaching for Change in Washington, D.C., works in culturally diverse, low-income schools to build strong parent organizations. The program starts by bringing people together to share their stories and come to know each other as fellow parents and community members. During parent meetings that follow, parents gain the knowledge and skills to analyze the school climate, the facilities, and the quality of teaching and learning at their school.[11]

Tellin' Stories Project assumptions about parent involvement	Traditional assumptions about parent involvement
Families and school staff together decide meaningful ways for parents to be involved: as teachers, supporters, advocates, decision makers, ambassadors, and monitors.	Schools determine how parents should be involved. Parents' roles are limited to fund-raising, chaperoning, and attending PTA meetings.
All parents can be resources for their children's schools. Schools must recognize and cultivate the knowledge and strength of each family.	Parents need to have specific skills to be involved. Many lack the capacity or willingness to be involved.
Starting point: Build trust through sharing our stories.	*Starting point:* Hold a PTA meeting and ask parents to sign up for committees.

Tellin' Stories Project assumptions about parent involvement	Traditional assumptions about parent involvement
Diversity is a strength. School culture must reflect the diversity of the school community.	Diversity is a challenge. School culture needs to be imposed on the school community.
Decisions are made collaboratively. Everyone has knowledge and has children's best interests at heart.	Decisions are handed down. School knows best and passes knowledge on to families.
Families, schools, and communities hold each other accountable.	Accountability is determined by a system-chosen standardized test.
Involved parents include those who help their children at home to be ready for school each day.	If parents are not visible at the school, they are not involved.
Clear vision: Parent involvement/family-school collaboration is required for school change.	*Underlying message:* Parent involvement is not important for school success.

© *Tellin' Stories Project of Teaching for Change*

Strengthen Families' Links with Community Organizations and Resources

Think of partnerships as a real exchange between school, families, and the community. Community partners can include businesses, labor unions, hospitals, public housing projects, and social service agencies. Colleges and universities, churches and other faith-based organizations, museums, youth organizations, and service clubs are other good prospects. In addition, consider activist groups and advocacy organizations such as tenant groups and legal service organizations. The federal 21st Century

Community Learning Centers program is an important source of funding for coordinating a program. (See Chapter 10 for more information about resources.)

To ensure that there is a good fit both ways, your action team or school council will have to set priorities and hold serious discussions with potential partners. Parents and students should be involved in these decisions about community connections.

Make your school a community center

The Ford School in Lynn, Massachusetts, serves almost nine hundred children in pre-kindergarten through eighth grade. About 40 percent of its families are recent immigrants from at least twenty countries. It is in the poorest area of a small city that faces many problems.

Under the leadership of Claire Crane, a principal with a background in social work, the school has become a community center for children's learning, adult education, family and social services, recreation, and community development. Features of the school include:

- A year-round program of community education, including morning parent support groups and evening classes for all ages in English as a Second Language, GED, citizenship, and computer training

- An all-day kindergarten, as well as after-school and summer programs that stress both enrichment and academics

- A school chorus and intramural and interschool basketball for grades four to six

- Collaborations with Salem State College to offer educational, social, and health programs for children and families, and with Lynn's public community college to offer pre-college prep and college courses at the school

For more information, see *Becoming a Community School*, a step-by-step guide written by the principal and teachers at the Ford School.[12]

Opening the School to Serve the Community

Schools are an important resource in any neighborhood. Schools can support local merchants and employ neighborhood residents. Community members can benefit from using school facilities such as the school library, gym, meeting rooms, kitchen, cafeteria, and computer lab. Students in vocational programs can set up small businesses, such as catering, a gift shop, carpentry, and home repair, to fill gaps in local enterprise. Well-planned community service programs for students are another low-cost way to strengthen connections between the school and the community.

Drawing Community Resources into the School

An increasing number of schools are collaborating with social service and health agencies to provide needed services to their students and families. In urban areas, scores of "full-service schools," such as those sponsored by the Children's Aid Society and the Beacon Schools program in New York City, are open six days a week, from before school hours until the evening. They offer a safe, secure environment and adult supervision for children.

A few states are funding family resource centers in schools. In Kentucky, these centers offer information and services at the school site. In schools with family resource centers, teachers say there is improved student performance in schoolwork, homework, and peer relationships. Parents report greater satisfaction and involvement with the schools.[13]

Many social service agencies are looking for connections to local communities and places to offer services. If space is available, services can be co-located in the school, nearer to people who need them. Here are some examples of services that community agencies are providing in schools:

✦ Health care, dental treatment, weight management, and family planning
✦ AA/Al-Anon and other programs to treat and combat substance abuse
✦ Individual counseling, mental health services, and crisis intervention

- ESL and other programs to teach English
- Adult education, GED classes, and computer training
- Job training and referrals
- Housing assistance, food banks, and clothing exchanges
- Recreation, sports, and cultural activities
- Mentoring and tutoring
- Child care

If school leaders are aware of what's going on in the community, school resources can be applied to problems that matter. If safety is an issue, a school-community committee can work with local police to build safe areas around the school and post crossing guards at dangerous intersections. Marvelyn Maldonaro, a principal in San Jose, California, says, "A good administrator will know their community. I walk my neighborhood every Sunday—looking for where's the trash, what's happening. I take a different route each time and I take photos. It keeps me centered."

Your action team or council can consider activities like these:

1. Encourage community agencies or institutions such as libraries, housing projects, and religious groups to set up out-of-school programs, and homework and tutoring centers for children and teens.
2. Work with a senior citizens' organization to set up a program to tutor and/or mentor students.
3. Promote more access to community resources for parents and students. Ask museums and cultural agencies to reduce fees for students and families. Ask local colleges to lower tuition for courses and make university facilities available to students and their families.
4. Sponsor family reading programs in public libraries.
5. Ask local corporations and businesses to help. They can offer technical services and equipment, contribute to special projects, provide speakers for classes and special events, and create internship and job opportunities for students.

Tip from a Principal:
Make time to talk with community organizers

"Any good administrator makes time for an organizer to come in. These are your allies—with them you can build a strong support group. If you have that support group as an administrator, you can get a lot of things done," says Marvelyn Maldonaro, a principal in San Jose, California. "I always keep in mind, what is the self-interest of my parents? What are the things that *they* value—their family, education of their children, and safety. We work on those things."

Welcoming Community Organizing for School Reform and Community Development

In the past few years, there has been a revival of civic activism in urban areas and the rural South. New organizing groups with an interest in education are emerging, and older groups that have organized for affordable housing or better jobs are now taking on education issues. In addition, national organizing networks such as ACORN, PICO, and the Industrial Areas Foundation are moving into new sites. (For more information on community organizing, see Chapter 10.)

Unlike many community groups and service organizations, these new groups develop a broad membership base of parents, families, and community residents, explicitly to build their political power. These organizations can become a positive force for school reform. They also can be powerful allies for gaining increased political and financial support for the public schools.

An example of how a community organizing group can be a powerful ally is the Logan Square Neighborhood Association (LSNA) in Chicago. After the Chicago school reform was passed in 1988, LSNA helped parents run for school council posts. The parents then used their positions to lobby the district for new school construction in the heavily overcrowded area. Throughout that campaign, LSNA brought together parents, teachers, and principals to develop a community-centered vision for the new schools.

LSNA has built a broad base of parent involvement throughout the neighborhood in ways that benefit schools and strengthen the community. In 1995, responding to parents' interest in more access to schools, LSNA organizers created the Parent Mentor Program. Parents worked two hours a day in classrooms to support teachers and were paid $1,200 a year. Each Friday, they attended workshops about being school *and* community leaders. The classes covered topics such as nutrition, strategies for teaching reading, housing issues, and group dynamics. This was the first step into the public sphere for many Latino mothers. Over one thousand parents have participated.

As they developed their skills and confidence, parents decided that schools needed to serve community needs. LSNA worked with parents to develop community learning centers in schools. Now at seven schools, learning centers offer evening classes ranging from ESL, citizenship, and

GED preparation to cultural skills such as dancing, quilting, and cooking. Some parent mentors have become teachers in the centers, and one directs a center.

Through the mentor program and learning centers, parents became interested in becoming teachers. In 2000, LSNA collaborated with Chicago State University (CSU) to develop a college-level program to train residents to become bilingual teachers. Federal funds cover the costs, and CSU faculty teach the classes through the learning centers. This program has greatly increased the supply of qualified bilingual teachers.[15]

As the process has continued, new programs are growing. So that teachers could afford housing in the area, LSNA convinced local banks to offer lower-cost loans and other incentives. To promote literacy, volunteers trained by LSNA work with teachers to hold Family Reading Nights, set up bilingual lending libraries for parents, and produce plays about local issues. A health outreach team connects families to affordable health services and state insurance.

LSNA organizer Joanna Brown compares Logan Square schools with the fortresses that many used to be: "Now the schools are full of parents, and many parents are taking leadership roles, organizing cultural events, speaking at teacher staff meetings about the literacy ambassador programs they design and run, and running for local school councils. It changes the way parents think of school. They feel ownership of the schools as they take charge and organize events at the schools."[16]

Mark Warren, a Harvard professor who has studied LSNA, concludes that "experts and educators acting within the four walls of the school cannot solve the problems of urban schools and inner-city communities, because these problems are the result of fundamentally unequal power relationships in our society. We need an active and engaged citizenry to build the kinds of relations and the type of power necessary both to transform education school by school and to address the broader structures of racism and poverty that trap our youth."[17]

A Final Bit of Advice

No one has ever said that democracy is efficient. Winston Churchill once called it the worst form of government in the world—except for all the others. Differences of opinion and potential conflict are a natural part of school life. People have strong views on matters that affect their children. In most disputes, there are several possible points of agreement and compromise.

When a problem arises, openness about the matter from the start is usually the best approach. Attempts to cover up usually backfire. Don't be reluctant to bring in an outside person to help resolve confusion or disagreement about a school issue or policy.

It takes time to hear from all concerned and arrive at a consensus or a solution, but we argue, and experience shows, that the time taken is worth it. People who are involved in making decisions tend to support those decisions. Their buy-in will sustain the work, and that saves a lot of effort in the long run.

In the next chapter, we will discuss how school districts can promote democracy in all schools in the system.

Checklist

How Well Is Your School Sharing Power and Practicing Democracy?

CONSULTING FAMILIES ABOUT DECISIONS

1. The school has a governance council that has a voice in all major decisions and that includes parent representatives elected by a broad base of parents.

    ☐ *Already doing this*   ☐ *Could do this easily*   ☐ *This will take time*   ☐ *This will be hard*

2. Parents and community members sit on the principal selection committee.

    ☐ *Already doing this*   ☐ *Could do this easily*   ☐ *This will take time*   ☐ *This will be hard*

3. The school does an annual survey of parents to get their ideas about programs and policies. The survey is codesigned and tallied by parents.

    ☐ *Already doing this*   ☐ *Could do this easily*   ☐ *This will take time*   ☐ *This will be hard*

4. The parent group is focused on improving achievement for all students.

☐ *Already doing this*   ☐ *Could do this easily*   ☐ *This will take time*   ☐ *This will be hard*

5. Surveys and focus groups are some of the ways that the parent association reaches out to families, builds its membership, and draws out their ideas and concerns.

☐ *Already doing this*   ☐ *Could do this easily*   ☐ *This will take time*   ☐ *This will be hard*

6. The PTA or parent organization invites the principal to report on student academic performance, review the school's scores on the state test, and describe how the school plans to improve.

☐ *Already doing this*   ☐ *Could do this easily*   ☐ *This will take time*   ☐ *This will be hard*

DEVELOPING SOCIAL AND POLITICAL CONNECTIONS

7. Families can learn how to vote and get a voter registration form in the school office.

☐ *Already doing this*   ☐ *Could do this easily*   ☐ *This will take time*   ☐ *This will be hard*

8. The school or parent group invites candidates for office to speak at the school and actively encourages and prepares parents to bring up their issues and concerns.

☐ *Already doing this*   ☐ *Could do this easily*   ☐ *This will take time*   ☐ *This will be hard*

Sharing

Power

. . .

9. Parent leadership and other training is offered, either by the school or by community groups in collaboration with the school.

☐ *Already doing this* ☐ *Could do this easily* ☐ *This will take time* ☐ *This will be hard*

DRAWING ON COMMUNITY RESOURCES

10. The school works closely with local public libraries and takes families on field trips to get library cards and borrow books and media.

☐ *Already doing this* ☐ *Could do this easily* ☐ *This will take time* ☐ *This will be hard*

11. A family resource center, school social worker, and/or other staff help families make connections to social services such as a food bank, a medical clinic, or housing assistance.

☐ *Already doing this* ☐ *Could do this easily* ☐ *This will take time* ☐ *This will be hard*

12. The school taps local businesses and community institutions for technical services, job opportunities for families and students, reduced fees, tutoring and mentoring, and training.

☐ *Already doing this* ☐ *Could do this easily* ☐ *This will take time* ☐ *This will be hard*

COLLABORATING WITH COMMUNITY ORGANIZERS

13. Teachers and parents work with community organizers to research solutions to problems that families and students face, such as bullying, traffic hazards, and gang activity.

☐ *Already doing this* ☐ *Could do this easily* ☐ *This will take time* ☐ *This will be hard*

14. The school hosts "accountability sessions" with local elected officials, so that families can raise their concerns about public services, such as street lights, community policing, drug trafficking, or poor trash collection.

☐ *Already doing this*   ☐ *Could do this easily*   ☐ *This will take time*   ☐ *This will be hard*

15. If community organizers raise issues like class size, teacher qualifications, achievement gaps, and crumbling facilities, the school is willing to work with them to make improvements. If community organizers have not approached the school, the school reaches out to them.

☐ *Already doing this*   ☐ *Could do this easily*   ☐ *This will take time*   ☐ *This will be hard*

In which areas are you doing well? Which ones will need more work?

_____

_____

_____

In what ways does your school share power with parents and build their social and political connections?

_____

_____

What are your concerns?

_____

_____

_____

Reflection: What steps could you take to make your school a laboratory of democracy?

Right away:

_____

_____

Over the long term:

_____

_____

Chapter 9

Scaling Up

Why Can't All Schools in a District Create Strong Partnerships with Families?

So far, this book has been all about what schools can do to welcome families, bridge differences, and promote fair and open ways for working together to improve student achievement. This is what we mean by strong partnerships.

Now it's time to step back and look at the context in which schools operate. All schools are part of a larger school district. What happens—or doesn't happen—at schools depends a great deal on how much the district explicitly expects and supports family and community involvement.

For a district to be serious about closing the achievement gap, it will also have to be serious about closing the gap between Fortress Schools and Partnership Schools.

This chapter explores what a district can do to develop system-wide policies and practices that support families to enhance their children's experience in school. Our leading examples are Boston and New York City. As you will see, both districts took action in three key areas:

1. Creating a culture of partnership throughout the district by setting consistently high standards for family-friendly schools—and expecting district and school staff to meet those standards
2. Connecting family-school partnerships directly to the district's school improvement initiative and to meeting performance goals for students
3. Organizing district resources to create a structure of support so that all schools can and will establish and sustain strong partnerships

The Boston Story

In 2000, superintendent Tom Payzant appointed a Family and Community Task Force and charged it to recommend ways that the Boston Public Schools (BPS) should "more fully include, engage and support families as school partners." The Task Force, a diverse group of parents, members of grassroots community groups, and BPS school committee members, came back with a hard-hitting report that called on the Boston Public Schools to:

1. Expand the definition of parent involvement
2. Make family engagement a BPS priority for which staff will be held accountable
3. Require principals and teachers to develop a family engagement plan against which they will be evaluated
4. Identify a person at each school who is responsible for engaging families
5. Focus family engagement programs on student learning
6. Offer principals and teachers training on how to engage families
7. Make parent support structures more effective, and offer facilitators to help schools[1]

Payzant appointed a working group to get the ball rolling. The working group realized that the job of creating and coordinating a systematic pro-

gram of family and community engagement required senior-level leadership.
In addition to setting priorities for the
Task Force recommendations, the group
insisted that the district appoint a deputy superintendent to oversee the initiative. This deputy was to report directly to
the superintendent and work as an equal
with the deputies in charge of instruction
and supervision of the schools. Such an
appointment, stated the working group,
would establish beyond a doubt that BPS
was fully committed to family and community engagement.

> ## Mission Statement, Office of Family and Community Engagement, Boston Public Schools
>
> To create a *culture of partnership* in the district among schools, families and community members that supports high standards and quality educational outcomes for all students.

The superintendent and school com-
mittee agreed. In 2002, Payzant appointed the first deputy superintendent
for family and community engagement. (Karen Mapp, an author of this
book, served as the second deputy, from 2003 to 2005.)

In the winter of 2003, the Office of Family and Community Engagement
(OFCE), using the recommendations from the Task Force, published a
three-year strategic plan. The plan outlined the OFCE mission statement,
goals, and objectives for its work.

Here is a sample of objectives and initiatives that OFCE created to
improve partnerships between BPS schools and families:

Improved information-sharing. OFCE staff attend community
events during the school year and the summer to provide information to
parents. The first-ever *Guide to the Boston Public Schools for Families and
Students* is available in seven languages.[2]

**Technology-driven and convenient student registration
process.** Preregistration for schools is now available online. The in-
person process is streamlined and improved at the three existing Family
Resource Centers, which serve the three zones of the district.

**Partnership initiatives at each school, with technical assis-
tance to do the job well.** All schools are required to create action
teams to coordinate programs to engage families and community mem-

bers. To support the schools, OFCE created the position of ambassador. Each ambassador is assigned five to eight schools and provides technical assistance and trainings for school staff, as well as practical materials such as sample letters and survey forms. OFCE provides partnership seed grants of $3,000 to schools via an RFP process.

Deeper community partnerships to support children's learning. Face to Face, a BPS collaboration with more than twenty organizations, provides resources to help children succeed in school. These organizations offer kindergarten readiness services; courses in math, computer literacy, and English; training and support groups for parents; and workshops on the BPS special education program for children with disabilities.[3]

Introducing the Boston Public Schools

This clearly written, tabloid-size guide carries this information for each BPS school:

- The address, with the principal's name and phone number

- Special features, such as all-day kindergarten, honors and advanced placement programs, computer resources, and curriculum specialist areas

- MCAS test scores in language arts and math, and whether the school has made adequate yearly progress (AYP) in reading and math

The guide also covers other important information for parents:

- How to register for school, how students are assigned, and how the transportation system works

- Tips for choosing the right school

- BPS programs for students, from kindergarten through high school

- The high school graduation policy

- A directory of BPS and community resources for families, including phone numbers[4]

The New York Story

In October 2002, city schools chancellor Joel Klein and Mayor Michael Bloomberg announced the launch of Children First: A New Agenda for Public Education in New York City. Children First stresses:

+ Improving classroom learning through directing more resources away from administrative bureaucracy and into school instruction
+ Improving principal leadership, empowerment, and accountability
+ Ending social promotion, but with supports to help children succeed
+ Creating new, small schools
+ Making schools safer
+ Partnering with parents by placing a parent coordinator in every school

Boston organized its family engagement efforts from top to bottom. In contrast, New York placed Parent Coordinators (PCs) in schools and built a structure to hire, train, and support them. At community forums held in 2002–3, the fifty thousand parents who attended made it clear that the New York City schools were *not* open and friendly. Bloomberg and Klein saw this as a mandate to make schools welcoming places for families.

Under the reform plan, the city's thirty-two community school districts still remain but are consolidated into ten regions. At the citywide level, an executive director of the Office of Parent Engagement reports directly to the deputy chancellor for teaching and learning. Each region has a Learning Support Center, with satellite offices in the three largest regions. Each center has a Parent Support Office offering technical assistance, training, and support to the PCs and parent volunteers. Parent Coordinators are responsible to:

+ Make schools more welcoming
+ Serve as a main point of contact for parents at the school, help answer their questions and concerns, and resolve issues at the school level

- ✦ Encourage and promote active parent involvement in children's education
- ✦ Hold workshops and activities for families and staff
- ✦ Assist the parent association and parents on the school leadership team

Reporting directly to principals, Parent Coordinators and their support structure are part of the DOE's larger teaching and learning organization. This helps to ensure that PC activities and parent involvement initiatives are closely linked to efforts to improve student achievement.

RESEARCH BRIEF:
District leadership for school, family, and community partnerships

Mavis Sanders, a researcher with the National Network of Partnership Schools (NNPS), is studying districts that are trying "to extend family-school partnerships from the few to the many." Pointing out that going system-wide means going broader and deeper at the same time, Sanders uses a framework developed by Cynthia Coburn to look at "scaling up" from four angles:

1. *Depth:* changing beliefs and practices
2. *Sustainability:* maintaining changes over time
3. *Spread:* increasing the number of participating schools
4. *Ownership:* vesting authority at three levels—district, schools, and teachers

How well districts can extend partnerships, Sanders found, depends on:

- A high priority on family and community involvement
- Adequate funding for school support and facilitation of school teams
- Participation in technical assistance from NNPS and other sources
- Leaders' job titles and responsibilities
- Leaders' passion and commitment[5]

> "The superintendent must demonstrate a commitment to effective family involvement by setting the same high standards and expectations for BPS staff in the area of family engagement as in other areas. Acceptance of poor performance, poor management skills, poor customer service, and lack of professional qualifications sends the message that the BPS does not value and respect parents as important partners in their children's education. This applies to school-based and central office employees."
>
> *(Boston Task Force report, Recommendation 2a)*

These examples illustrate how a district can build a structure to support partnership with families across the system. Both New York and Boston created a culture of partnership, linked parent involvement to school improvement initiatives, and supported all schools so they could become open and welcoming to families.

Creating a Culture of Partnership

Create a culture of partnership throughout the district by setting high standards for family-friendly schools—and by expecting all district and school staff to meet those standards.

Engage Community Members in Setting the Goals for Family and Community Engagement

The first action the Boston Task Force took was to listen to parents and community members. The panel asked three key questions:

1. What services should parents expect from BPS?
2. What is working well now in the schools and in the community to help children succeed in school?
3. What services should BPS add, change, or eliminate to improve parent involvement and communication between home and school?

Instead of holding large public meetings at which only a few could speak, the Task Force reached a variety of audiences through focus groups, surveys, community forums, and a direct mail campaign. The Task Force also asked parents for comments through e-mail and telephone, and interviewed BPS staff, parents, and community leaders.

What did parents say? Although parents praised many BPS practices and programs, they were quite clear about what they did *not* like:

+ Schools with little commitment to involving parents
+ School staff who did not welcome, respect, or listen to them
+ Limited communication in their native language
+ Ineffective parent groups
+ Lack of information about how to help their children
+ Feeling less than equal on School Site Councils

Tip from a Principal:
What should a district do to make it easier for schools to engage families as partners?

Steve Constantino, former principal of Stonewall Jackson High School in Manassas, Virginia, and author of *Engaging All Families*, suggests:

- Develop a statement to answer this question: "What do we believe and value about parent engagement?"
- Take the statement seriously; don't just give it lip service. Offer meaningful professional development in customer service, then make good service a system-wide policy. Do not tolerate Fortress Schools.
- Assess and reward a family engagement mentality. Evaluate employees on this and reward them when they do it well.
- Write achievable goals. Think about what goes into writing a clear, precise reading goal. Put that same level of effort into writing a parent involvement goal.
- For the school board: Understand the impact of a policy. Ask the superintendent to demonstrate how a policy is actually in effect, not just on the books.

Parents were critical of the district, too. Service at the existing Parent Information Centers was inconsistent, they said. They knew nothing about the so-called Parents Support Services Team. They did not believe that parent engagement was a priority for the superintendent. The Task Force report responded to all these concerns.

Analyze School Satisfaction Surveys

Many districts conduct surveys of some sort, but how do they use these data? Just knowing that 60 percent of your families are "very satisfied" doesn't tell you much. Who is satisfied and who isn't? What qualities in a school lead to higher satisfaction? Analyzing which school and district practices are associated with high satisfaction and loyalty can give you a roadmap to improvement.

The Alexandria, Virginia, public schools asked family and faculty their views in four major areas:

✦ Fostering the teacher-parent relationship to support children's progress
✦ The school environment and level of care for children
✦ Parent involvement in learning and decision making
✦ Two-way communication and problem solving

While over half of families said they were "very satisfied" with their schools, and 60 percent would keep their child in the same school, ratings dropped sharply among middle and high school families and varied among ethnic groups. On the whole, the Alexandria families reported that three conditions were highly important to their satisfaction and loyalty:

1. **Being treated fairly and with respect.** Very satisfied families tended to answer "always" to these statements:

   • "My child's school is willing to work with me as a partner."
   • "Students at my child's school are treated fairly no matter what their race or background."
   • "I'm treated with respect at my child's school."

2. Being pleased with the quality of their children's school.
Families who would "definitely" keep their child in the same school were "very satisfied" with:

- A caring and nurturing environment for learning
- The quality of communication
- Their own child's learning and progress

3. Feeling that the district responds well to their problems and concerns.
If families were satisfied with how their concern was handled, they were more than twice as likely to recommend the Alexandria public schools, compared to families who were not satisfied. The complete results of the survey were published in a report, *Listening to Families and Faculty*.[6]

The Alexandria schools are using these findings to develop a problem-solving process. This process includes an advocacy handbook, workshops to help parents use the information, and professional development to assist school staff in working with families to resolve problems. (The School Climate Survey in Chapter 11 is based on the Alexandria survey.)

Set a Clear Standard for What's Expected at Schools and Offer Help to Meet the Standard

In Boston, the Office of Family and Community Engagement Office (OFCE) developed a series of school-family-community partnership initiatives that spanned the district. The initiatives focused on two key goals:

1. Creating family-friendly schools
2. Making sure that students reach proficiency in literacy and math

Schools developed initiatives to align with their annual school improvement plans, with direction and support from the OFCE staff. In August 2004, just before the start of school, all principals attended a three-day institute that included substantive training on how to cultivate partnerships that support children's learning and development. This training also provided what principals called "the stuff"—materials such as sample letters, school climate survey forms, and examples of specific activities for parents and other adult learners.

Every BPS school formed an action team to design its initiative. OFCE planning forms were available on an internal Web site, and school staff were encouraged to file their proposed plans online.

A Walk-Through Process

Fairfax County, Virginia, a large and diverse district in the suburbs of Washington, D.C., has set a standard for parent and family involvement and put it into practice. The Family Services and Involvement Section (FSIS) has developed a voluntary "Welcoming Atmosphere Walk-Through." As Karen Willoughby, the FSIS director, says, "This process allows school staff to look at their school as parents and visitors may see it."

The purpose of the two-hour process is to:

✦ Examine how inviting the school appears to its diverse community
✦ Consider strategies that will make the school more inviting
✦ Increase parent involvement

The walk-through team consists of sixteen people. Twelve are selected by the school: four school staff members and eight parents and community representatives. The other four are facilitators from FSIS. Schools are expected to select team members who represent the diversity of the school's parents, staff, programs, and community. A typical team might include an administrator, teacher, custodian, secretary, bus driver, cafeteria worker, neighbor, community leader, special education parent, PTA board member, ESL parent, general education parent, and business leader.

During the walk-through, the team breaks into four groups. Each group examines an aspect of the school that signals to parents and community members that they are welcomed as partners:

1. **Physical environment**—parking areas, entrance, offices, lobby, hallways, and classrooms

2. **School-wide practices and policies**—for example, tours

for new families, regular family activities, communications, translation services, and community use of the school building

3. **Friendly school staff**—interactions observed in the main office, hallways, and places open to the public

4. **Written materials**—newsletters, handouts, parent handbook, and flyers, as well as Web sites and telephone message lines

During the walk-through, the team uses checklists, interview questions, and comment sheets as they fan out through the building. Based on their observations, the team completes a form that commends the school for its welcoming aspects and offers suggestions for review and consideration. Follow-up assistance from FSIS is available on request.[7]

A Principal's Experience with the Welcoming Walk-Through

Tom Bentson, principal at Olde Creek Elementary School in Fairfax, Virginia, tells this story: "This walk-through process works well in schools in which some level of trust exists between the staff and the community. The walk should be voluntary. School staff have to be ready to hear the recommendations. If more than half the comments will be critical, it may may create bad feeling.

"I spent two years in my community building trust before bringing in district staff to help with the walk-through. I held coffees in different people's houses—mornings, evenings, and weekends—until families felt they knew who I was. After that, we had a strong working relationship with the parent group and a volunteer program that was bringing in all kinds of families. We had a sense of shared purpose.

"One thing I learned from the walk-through was that no one was reading the long newsletter I was sweating bullets over every month! They told me, 'Keep it short, send bulletins out on an as-needed basis, and stick to the point.' It was a good lesson in customer relations."

Staff the Effort with a High-Level Position and Commit Real Resources to It

Appoint someone at the senior leadership level to oversee the district's family and community engagement initiatives. Support the initiatives with hard money from the general operating budget. In many districts, people who work with families are part time and paid only a stipend or minimum wage.

In New York City, a structure to support parent involvement exists from the ground up. At least seven Parent Support Officers (PSOs) staff each region's Parent Support Office. Each PSO works directly with a network of schools and is the go-to person for their Parent Coordinators, principals, and Parent Associations on parent involvement and support matters. The PSOs offer technical assistance, professional development, and "on-site support." This means spending time in schools and getting a sense of what needs to happen to involve and support parents. PSOs also make sure each school has a Parent Association or PTA.

Connecting Family-School Partnerships Directly to the District's School Improvement Initiative and Performance Goals for Students

According to the Boston Task Force Report, "Schools should not confuse good attendance at a spaghetti dinner with family involvement that improves student achievement. Spaghetti dinners and other social and community-building activities are good ways to get families in the building and make them feel welcome, comfortable, and connected. But what happens before, during, and after the activity to call attention to student achievement is the key."

In Boston, the Office of Family and Community Engagement had three goals, all focused on student learning:

1. Cultivate and sustain partnerships to improve student learning among BPS staff, families, and community members.

Put the responsibility for parent involvement at the top

"Don't make parent involvement part of the public relations or communications office, and don't bury it in the bureaucracy (like the federal programs office). Put it
close to the superintendent, and on the instructional side of the organization," suggests Jeana Preston, former director of the Parent Involvement Department in the
San Diego city schools.

"One-way information flow is *not* parent involvement. There is a lot more to it
than persuading parents to support district initiatives. Use parent involvement as a
strategy for improving achievement and closing the achievement gap. Then you can
build parent and community support for your district's reform efforts to improve
achievement."

2. Support families and community members' efforts to be engaged
    in children's learning.
3. Support BPS staff to create strong and effective school, family,
    and community partnerships that support student learning.

The BPS reform initiative is called Focus on Children. To be leaders
in improving schools, parents need information and training about the
reform. BPS provides schools with jargon-free materials to help parents
understand how the system works and what to expect in a high-quality
school. These materials are tied to Focus on Children and the six essential
elements around which it is organized.

The Six Essentials: What to Look For

BPS has adopted an ambitious plan to improve instruction in every classroom, so that all students can meet high standards. To explain the plan, BPS has published *The Six Essentials,* a brochure that anyone from a parent to a researcher can use.[8]

One of the six essentials is "partnering with families and community to support student learning." The *Six Essentials* brochure lists expectations for schools and for central administrators, with a checklist of evidence—what parents and community members should see and hear. This brochure gives parents a tool to understand what's happening in classrooms and around the school.

Expectations for schools and families	Expectations for central administrators
• School staff reach out to show they value all children and welcome families and community members as their partners. • Each school develops a plan to engage families in their children's school life. The plan is shared with families and community members and is posted in the school. • Teachers communicate regularly with families (in English and the home language) about their child's progress and ways families can support students. • Families show interest in their children's schoolwork and learning, monitor their attendance, attend parent conferences, and participate in parent councils if they can.	• The superintendent and deputies hold principals accountable for strong and measurable outreach to families and community members. • The deputy superintendent for family and community engagement shares examples of schools and practices that work effectively with families and community members. • The high school renewal office highlights schools that are effectively soliciting students' concerns and acting in partnership with them on the solutions. • Family resource centers provide technical assistance to schools to develop and implement their family engagement plans.

"Moving" districts know what they're doing

In high-achieving districts, school board members and administrators are familiar with district improvement goals and know how these goals are being carried out in the schools. A study by the Iowa Association of School Boards compared survey data from three high-achieving ("moving") and three low-achieving ("stuck") school districts. The chart below displays some differences in the responses of school board members and superintendents.[9]

"Moving" districts	"Stuck" districts
Understand what leads to productive change. The school board and superintendent can list improvement goals and describe how they are being carried out by administrators and teachers.	*Focus on managing the environment rather than improving it.* The school board and superintendent can name goals sometimes, but seldom can describe actions taken to improve learning.
Link goals to action in buildings and classrooms. They can describe how staff development supports goals and how data are used to monitor student progress.	*Do not focus on school renewal.* They can name very few connections across the system to link the district's goals with practice.
Hold an "elevating" view of students. They say the job of the school is to reach each student's potential: "This is a place for all kids to excel. No one feels left out."	*Hold a "limited" view of students and parents.* They say students' backgrounds limit them: "You can lead a horse to water but you can't make it drink."
Express pride in their community. They can name specific ways the district involves parents and community, and want more involvement.	*Express frustration with low parent involvement.* They tend to blame families for low student achievement and can identify few actions taken to improve involvement.

In New York City, the district links innovations in instruction to tools for parents. For example, let's look at "interim assessments." These are twenty-item assessments given up to three times a year to measure students' progress in meeting state standards. They're not tests and don't count toward a student's grade. Instead, they help teachers and parents gauge whether students are learning new concepts and skills.

Results are available in a week, so teachers can target lessons to meet their students' individual needs. Once a student weakness is identified, teachers can access a special Web site that offers lessons to address it. Parents can also use that same Web site as a tool to help their children. By clicking on a link on the New York City schools' Web site and using their password, parents can see their child's results. Explanations are provided for each question and answer. Parents can even make up their own practice tests, choosing from a list of specific skills. Students complete the assessments online and get results immediately, along with suggestions for further learning.

Advice from a Principal:
"If I were king of the district . . ."

These suggestions are from Thomas Bentsen, a principal in Fairfax, Virginia.

1. Make clear that there is a relationship between having a critical mass of involved parents and improving student achievement.
2. Hire principals with parent and community involvement skills and work with them to develop those skills.
3. Set up discussion and research groups within the district to promote parent involvement.
4. Offer professional development in many settings, including sessions at principals' meetings, leadership academies, and cluster meetings.
5. Feature principals who are successful at this. If the superintendent talks about this, it will get done. If principals talk about this at their schools, it will get done there, too.

Examples from San Diego

When Anthony Alvarado was the district's top academic officer, he put a twist on filling the job of parent coordinator. "Let's not have para-professionals," he said. "Let's hire teachers to do the job instead. They're really qualified to talk with parents about what the district wants kids to be learning." Now, all the lowest-performing schools in the district have a Parent Academic Liaison, or a PAL. PALs are certified teachers pulled out of the classroom to coordinate parent involvement programs. (For more on PALs, see Chapter 5, "Linking to Learning.")

San Diego also offers a Parent University for all parents with children in Title I schools. (Title I is a federal program that provides resources to schools with high numbers of low-income children.) Classes are offered at the district's Parent Center, which offers meeting space and resources to families, advisory groups, and parent support groups. Bus transportation is offered from local schools.

The purpose of Parent University is:
1. To help parents become involved as academic coaches of their children
2. To strengthen parenting skills
3. To improve parent-child relationships

Classes are held in six sessions on weekday mornings. Academic classes support homework, reading, writing, study skills, and math. In parenting skills classes, parents learn to support their children's social, emotional, and physical development. Topics include setting up a learning environment, organizing for homework, and helping children manage their time. Classroom teachers who are retired or on family leave teach the classes.

"We used to have the largest parent conference in the country," notes Bea Fernandez, who directs the Parent University. "Now we have gone to a new model, which has moved away from once-a-year large events to a series of smaller classes. We want to change the way parents interact with their kids, and this is much more effective." (The San Diego School District is an award-winning member of the National Network of Partnership Schools.)

Organizing District Resources So All Schools Can Establish and Sustain Strong Partnerships

In New York City, the structure of support starts with the Parent Coordinators (PCs). The PCs build positive working relationships with members of the school community and create a welcoming school environment for all parents. They assist parents with concerns about their child's education or needs at school, and offer workshops and other information about supporting students' learning at home.[10]

In Region 1, for example, the Parent Support Office deploys seven Parent Support Officers (PSOs) to work with clusters of schools. The PSOs are accountable for making sure that the PCs do their job and that the structure of parent involvement in the district is functioning. In addition to spending time in schools, PSOs:

> "There must be someone at the top of the district in charge of this endeavor to engage families, and someone at the school level who can organize people to get the job done."
>
> *(Yvonne Torres, associate superintendent for District 9, New York City)*

◆ Work with the President's Council, composed of Parent Association (PA) presidents, which meets monthly

◆ Send out flyers about meetings

◆ Support the district education council, which advises the district superintendent (the city's thirty-two school districts still have their own superintendents, but community school boards were replaced with district councils)

◆ Observe PA elections (because the PA president sits on the school leadership team, he or she must be elected in a fair and open process)

◆ Offer professional development for the PCs

Because the PCs and their support officers are part of the teaching and learning structure, they're linked to other staff who are working to improve student achievement. Each region employs Local Instructional Supervisors (LISs) to monitor the quality of instruction at schools. Because they are part of the accountability process, the LISs also monitor what's going on for parents in the schools.

Parent Coordinators on the Move

The Citywide Best Practice Fair in July 2005, sponsored by Washington Mutual Bank, brought together the city's Parent Coordinators to share their projects and ideas with each other. Here is a sampling:

+ *Prepare for standardized tests.* Curriculum-related workshops help parents and children get ready for the tests and understand what the tests cover.

+ *Discovering New York.* A series of workshops identifies family activities that parents can do with their children (over two hundred parents signed up).

+ *Community awareness fair.* High school parents and students learn about a variety of local community organizations, organized by ten high school PCs.

+ *Learn Spanish.* Spanish classes, requested by English-speaking parents, break the language barrier and forge relationships between parents of different cultures.

+ *Get dads involved.* A core group of men who were specially recruited attend meetings, serve on the PA executive board, and become Learning Leaders.

+ *Create a safe haven for parents.* Parents of special needs children formed a support group to share challenges in confidence and learn where to get help and information.

+ *Borough parties for high school parents.* Instead of asking parents to turn out at a central location, meetings come to parents hosted by parent volunteers at their homes.

+ *Baby-and-me play group.* These groups introduce families to each other and draw them into the school's pre-kindergarten program, reducing tension in an ethnically diverse neighborhood.

Across New York City, there has been a flowering of activities and programs for parents and families. Parent Coordinators have organized book clubs and workshops to give parents information about what their children are learning in class. PCs in neighboring schools are teaming up to offer advice to teachers about engaging parents from different cultures. Parents are learning how to recruit other parents, especially those who are bilingual.

Boston is also experimenting with a parent coordinator program. In May 2005, the Boston Public Schools launched a Family and Community Coordinator (FCOC) Initiative, which placed full-time, school-based positions dedicated to family and community engagement at thirteen Boston public schools for the start of the 2005–6 school year. Two more FCOCs split their full-time positions between two schools each, for a total of fifteen full-time FCOC positions. Seven elementary schools, three middle schools, one K–8 school, and five high schools were selected to participate in this pilot program. 2005–6 was a pilot year for the FCOC program.

The external evaluation preliminary report indicated that the FCOC program is succeeding. Not only was the program re-funded for the 2006–7 school year, but the Boston Public Schools increased the number of full-time positions to seventeen.

Offer Technical Assistance, Funding, and Other Supports

Why is there so much variation in parent involvement from one school to the next? Even in the same neighborhood, one school can be a Fortress while another is an Open-Door school. If the district doesn't make clear what's expected, the extent to which schools collaborate with families is left up to the school. Without professional development on creating partnerships, and commendation of principals' efforts to engage families, the disparities will persist.

The Los Angeles school district has a partner in Families in Schools (FIS), a Parent Information Resource Center funded by the U.S. Education Department. FIS works with the city's regional districts to create activities and programs for families, such as the Parents as Learning Partners program (PLP). PLP aims to support parents to create and contribute to the school community; to train teachers to work with parents as partners at home and at school; and to persuade administrators to use staff and budget resources for meaningful parent involvement.[11] (FIS is another award-winning member of the National Network of Partnership Schools.)

Other programs sponsored by FIS and adopted in local districts include:

- **Read with Me/Lea Conmigo,** an early childhood program, encourages a culture of reading in the home. A typical middle-class child enters first grade with over a thousand hours of one-to-one picture book reading, while a low-income child averages only twenty-five hours. This program is aimed at eliminating that gap.

- **Blueprints for Living** offers workshops covering universal values—such as responsibility, respect, caring, trust, honesty, and courage—in which parents learn how to encourage these qualities in their children.

- **Going On to College** encourages students to set career goals that include going to college. It also offers parent workshops on how to ensure that their children take courses that will put them on the pathway to college.

- **Transitions to Middle School and High School** work-shops help parents understand what to expect at the next level. Parents learn how to get answers to key questions, such as the meaning of standardized test scores and report card grades, types of classes needed for higher education, and supplemental services.

In their local districts, parents attend classes on how to use computers, English as a Second Language, and Latino leadership. Workshops on immigration status give parents information about work permits and residency requirements. A mother-daughter college prep program begins in middle school and recruits girls from families in which no one has yet attended college.[12] (For more information about the mother-daughter program, see Chapter 10.)

When Richard Alonzo, former superintendent of a regional district in Los Angeles, interviewed aspiring principals, he always asked what they have done to improve relations with parents. "Holding open houses was not an adequate answer," he said. To back up the principals, Alonzo appointed a full-time coordinator for family-school partnerships, Linda Ariyasu. A former elementary school principal, Ariyasu recruited, trained, and supported school-community liaisons in every school. (See Chapter 11 for the Family Involvement Coordinator Sample Job Description.)

In Ariyasu's tool box was a list of the knowledge and skills expected of school-community liaisons, and a four-part performance scoring guide. The highest performance level in the guide lists these competencies:

✦ **Attitude.** Always maintains positive, professional attitude. Demonstrates a strong belief in the importance of parents as partners.

✦ **Parent Center.** Focuses on support for what's being taught in class. Experts in the school facilitate workshops that are well attended, and outreach has led to increased parent engagement. The Parent Center is viewed as the "heart of the school."

✦ **School information.** Knows all staff, programs, and resources available, and is able to refer parents to the right people and services.

> "Whether you're a preschool or a high school parent, everyone wants his or her child to have the option to go to college. I've learned that their children's class schedules, and whether they are taking the courses they'll need to prepare for college, rank as parents' biggest concerns."
>
> *(Linda Ariyasu, former coordinator of family-school partnerships, District F, Los Angeles Unified School District)*

✦ **Leadership.** Excels in communicating and collaborating and is seen as an effective leader by the whole school community. Takes part in all school activities.

Support Parent Decision-Making Structures at Schools

To show Boston's commitment to sharing power with parents, twenty-two FCE staff acted as "BPS ambassadors" to parents and school staff.

They visited schools to collect and share information with parents and principals about opportunities for parents to get involved in councils. Information about school councils is included in the parent manual and was a key component of the three-day training that principals in Boston attended in August 2004.

New York City has several structures to support parent involvement in decision making:

Parent Associations. Every school must have a Parent Association/ Parent Teacher Association (PA/PTA), which is expected to:

+ Give parents the latest information about the school
+ Share ideas about what's going on and what can be improved
+ Work with the principal, PC, and other staff to create a welcoming environment for all families
+ Bring parents' needs to the attention of the principal and PC.

Presidents' Council. The council brings together all the PA/PTA presidents in a region or district, giving them a chance to exchange ideas and concerns. The council meets with the district and regional superintendents on a regular basis.

School Leadership Teams. Each school's team must be composed of parents, the principal, the PA/PTA president or co-president, and the teachers' union chapter leader. The team sets the school's educational goals and draws up a comprehensive plan that aligns school budget and priorities.

Community Education Councils. Every community school district (there are thirty-two) has a council of nine elected parents, a student, and two community members appointed by the borough president. Elections are held every two years. The councils advise the superintendent and give feedback to the chancellor, meet with the district's PAs/PTAs, connect with School Leadership Teams, and evaluate the district superintendent and instructional supervisors in the district.

Three Ways Districts Can Help Struggling Schools

Christine Lamb, a principal who turned around the lowest-achieving school in her district in Groveton, Virginia, says that districts can do three things to help a struggling school:

1. Provide funding for school-family liaisons and train them at the district level so principals don't have to do that, then have staff who can step in if the principal is having a problem with the liaison.

2. Offer high-quality professional development for teachers, and deliver it when they need it.

3. Make it easy to develop relationships with district offices, so schools can get services for families as needed, such as an early literacy class.

Citywide Councils on Special Education and on High Schools. These councils include parents of special education and high school students, students, and community members. The councils hold regular public meetings, make recommendations for improvement, and publish annual reports.

Sustain Teacher Action Research

Action research allows teachers to look at their own practice, reconsider their teaching methods, or solve a problem. A team of educators studies a problem or issue and tests out ways to approach it. Fairfax County, Virginia, has committed serious resources to encourage such teacher research. (For more about action research, see Chapter 8, "Sharing Power.")

When teachers at Annandale High School embarked on an action research project to learn more about immigrant students and their families, they applied for help from the Fairfax County school district. Support they received from the Office of Staff Development and Planning included:

✦ An experienced researcher to work with their group to develop research questions and methods
✦ Substitute time to conduct and write up their studies
✦ Workshops on topics such as grant writing to support further research, and tips for publishing projects
✦ Online support and a newsletter linking their research to work of colleagues in other schools
✦ Professional development credits and recertification points
✦ An end-of-the year conference at which teachers presented displays about their research to their colleagues, students, families, and other members of the community

Bill Brock, a tenth grade English teacher, used student journals to obtain more insight into the family background of his students: "Student journals provided me with a broader picture of life inside the immigrant parent household. There is a great deal more than meets the eye. . . . Family priorities usually take center stage. . . . Reading journal entries provided me with greater understanding of both student and parent outside the classroom."[13]

Develop Written District Policies

In 1988, San Diego adopted a written parent involvement policy that applied to all schools in the district, not just Title I schools.[14] It was one of the first big-city school districts to do this. The policy is supported by central office staff and local funding. The San Diego policy affirms the school board's commitment to:

✦ Involve parents as partners in school governance, including shared decision making
✦ Establish effective two-way communication between home and school

+ Develop structures and strategies in each school to empower parents to participate actively in their children's education
+ Provide K-12 district coordination and support
+ Use schools to connect students and families to community resources

Other activities to support family involvement include San Diego Parent University, a district-level Title I Parent Center, Parent Academic Liaisons at the lowest-performing schools (see Chapter 5), and a district-level Parent Congress. In addition, the San Diego district has provided grants on a competitive basis to schools to develop new parent and community outreach strategies.[15] (See Chapter 11 for the District Policy on Family-School Partnerships tool.)

Leadership is key. When a superintendent demonstrates a serious, consistent commitment to parent and community engagement, everyone in the district gets the message. Jorge Izquierdo is the former superintendent of District 6 in New York City, where a majority of families come from the Dominican Republic, most students speak limited English, and many schools are low-performing. He believed that a large number of parents were disenchanted with the schools.

What did he do about it? Izquierdo decided to commit himself "to find ways to bring families back and show them there is hope." First, he invited parents to come into the schools with him. To make them more comfortable, he conducted weekly "walk-throughs" with about fifteen parents to tour a school building and learn about how teachers teach. "We had rich conversations about how schools might be different from those they attended," he comments. "What people also realized after the visit is that we did a good job with limited resources."

Izquierdo also involved parents in school restructuring. A big challenge that faced the district was what he called "student flight"—because the schools had a poor reputation, higher-income parents enrolled their children elsewhere. Parts of the district were attracting upper-income families, however, and his goal was "to bring them in and have them stay." To do this, the district converted two middle schools into smaller academies. Parents have been part of this planning process. "Parents must be interested, because if they're not, the children won't succeed," he insists.

"My goal was to educate parents so they understood good instruction and could support our schools and our children," says Izquierdo. "We had to focus our sights on instruction and we needed the entire community involved in doing it. The parents were key." Izquierdo is currently the local instructional superintendent in Region 9, one of ten in New York City.

To make sure that every one of our children meets high standards of achievement, all of us—teachers, parents, administrators, office holders, community members, students, family members, and local organizations—must work together to make it happen. This requires strong leadership, constant and open communication, and a passion for partnership.

Checklist

How Well Does Your District Support Family and Community Engagement?

FAMILY ENGAGEMENT POLICY

1. The district has a strong policy that sets standards for what partnerships in schools should include and lays out a process for making sure that schools meet the standards.

☐ *Already doing this*   ☐ *Could do this easily*   ☐ *This will take time*   ☐ *This will be hard*

2. Parent involvement is clearly defined and means more than parents' being their children's "first teachers."

☐ *Already doing this*   ☐ *Could do this easily*   ☐ *This will take time*   ☐ *This will be hard*

3. The policy commits the district to offer certain programs and opportunities for families, staff, and community members.

☐ *Already doing this*   ☐ *Could do this easily*   ☐ *This will take time*   ☐ *This will be hard*

4. Parents have the right to observe in classrooms, attend faculty meetings, and take part in professional development.

☐ *Already doing this*   ☐ *Could do this easily*   ☐ *This will take time*   ☐ *This will be hard*

Scaling

Up

· · ·

5. The director of family and community engagement is an assistant or deputy superintendent and reports directly to the superintendent.

    ☐ *Already doing this*   ☐ *Could do this easily*   ☐ *This will take time*   ☐ *This will be hard*

6. The director's staff are full-time and can cover all schools in the district. They have the skills to offer professional development to schools on engaging families effectively.

    ☐ *Already doing this*   ☐ *Could do this easily*   ☐ *This will take time*   ☐ *This will be hard*

7. Principals are required to have credentials and experience in engaging diverse families.

    ☐ *Already doing this*   ☐ *Could do this easily*   ☐ *This will take time*   ☐ *This will be hard*

8. Schools with high levels of parent, family, and community involvement are recognized and rewarded.

    ☐ *Already doing this*   ☐ *Could do this easily*   ☐ *This will take time*   ☐ *This will be hard*

ACCOUNTABILITY

9. All schools are required to appoint an action team of staff and parents who represent the school's diversity to build and sustain parent involvement.

    ☐ *Already doing this*   ☐ *Could do this easily*   ☐ *This will take time*   ☐ *This will be hard*

10. Principals are evaluated, in part, on how well the school engages families and community members and organizations.

    ☐ *Already doing this*   ☐ *Could do this easily*   ☐ *This will take time*   ☐ *This will be hard*

11. An annual survey assesses families' opinions about the school and what supports they need to become more involved.

    ☐ *Already doing this*   ☐ *Could do this easily*   ☐ *This will take time*   ☐ *This will be hard*

12. The annual survey data are correlated with student outcome data (including test scores) to develop programs for families that are linked to student learning.

☐ *Already doing this*   ☐ *Could do this easily*   ☐ *This will take time*   ☐ *This will be hard*

13. The district uses a walk-through process to help schools assess how family-friendly they are.

☐ *Already doing this*   ☐ *Could do this easily*   ☐ *This will take time*   ☐ *This will be hard*

SUPPORT AND RESOURCES

14. Professional development and technical assistance on all aspects of family and community engagement are available for administrators, teachers, and parents.

☐ *Already doing this*   ☐ *Could do this easily*   ☐ *This will take time*   ☐ *This will be hard*

15. Funding to plan and carry out family involvement activities is built into the district budget. Family involvement is not dependent on discretionary grants or other "soft money."

☐ *Already doing this*   ☐ *Could do this easily*   ☐ *This will take time*   ☐ *This will be hard*

16. The district has a well-developed and easy-to-use Web site so that schools and families can contact staff, obtain important information, and download useful materials.

☐ *Already doing this*   ☐ *Could do this easily*   ☐ *This will take time*   ☐ *This will be hard*

17. The district offers incentives, such as small action grants, to develop new programs and activities.

☐ *Already doing this*   ☐ *Could do this easily*   ☐ *This will take time*   ☐ *This will be hard*

18. The district showcases best practice, such as at conferences where schools exhibit their programs and describe the results, and in publications and on the Web site. There are awards for schools and staff that have made the most progress.

☐ *Already doing this*   ☐ *Could do this easily*   ☐ *This will take time*   ☐ *This will be hard*

Which areas are you doing well in? Which ones will need more work?

_____

_____

_____

How are parents and community members involved at the district level to promote effective family and community engagement?

_____

_____

_____

What are your concerns?

_____

_____

Reflection: What steps could you take to develop a district-wide initiative?

Right away:

_____

_____

Over the long term:

_____

_____

Chapter 10

Help! Where Can You Find Useful Resources to Build Your Partnership?

This chapter is a list of annotated resources. Because of the huge abundance of material on this topic, a great deal of which is available on the Internet, we have been highly selective in the interest of space. The selected bibliography at the end of this book also lists useful resources.

This chapter is organized into three sections:

I.   **Chapter Topics**

    1.   Developing Relationships
    2.   Linking to Learning
    3.   Addressing Differences
    4.   Supporting Advocacy
    5.   Sharing Power
    6.   Scaling Up

I. Chapter Topics

1. Developing Relationships

Guides and Publications

Collaborative for Academic, Social and Emotional Learning (CASEL) at the University of Illinois in Chicago has resources for developing relationships, including the *SEL Parent Packet: Ideas and Tools for Working with Parents and Families.* This packet contains research, examples of practice, parent handouts, tips, books, interviews, and resources. For the packet in English: www.casel.org/downloads/parentpacketLSS.pdf and Spanish: www.casel.org/downloads/parentresourcespanish.pdf
   Web site: www.casel.org

Northwest Regional Educational Laboratory (NRWEL) has published a guidebook, *Building Relationships for Student Success: School-Family-Community Partnerships and Student Achievement in the Northwest,* by Diane Dorfman and Amy Fisher (2002). The booklet includes a review of the literature, practical suggestions, and examples of practices to enlist families in their children's successful learning.
   Web site: www.nwrel.org/partnerships/cloak/booklet2.pdf

Sacramento Area Congregations Together (ACT) is a community organizing group affiliated with the PICO network. *Connecting Families and Schools: Sacramento ACT* tells the story of the ACT home visiting program to train teachers and help schools reach out to families. This case study is available from the Center for Community Change. (For more on PICO, see Section II, Topic 5: "Community Organizing.") Go to www.community change.org/issues/education/publications/downloads/actionguide_08.pdf.

Web-Based Resources

National Fatherhood Initiative offers programs, workshops, publications, and materials to encourage men to be involved, responsible, and committed fathers.

Web site: www.fatherhood.org

Programs

Parents and Teachers Talking Together (PT3) is a discussion process developed by the Prichard Committee for Academic Excellence. It includes a series of questions that participants discuss in small groups, then as one large group. The conversation begins when parents and teachers answer two questions: "What do we want for our students?" and "What do we need to do to get what we want?" These local conversations help parents and teachers work together to improve education. Results include increased focus on school initiatives, deeper involvement, ideas for projects in individual schools, and increased understanding and appreciation of each group's perspective.

Web site: www.prichardcommittee.org/pt3.html or call 1-800-928-2111.

Security Dads is a program that gives fathers and other men a positive role to play in school as role models and peacekeepers. For more information, contact Anthony Wallace, 11041 Turfgrass Way, Indianapolis, IN 46236, phone 317-371-4094, e-mail alaw54@ameritech.net.

Web site: www.securitydads.com

Tellin' Stories Project, of Teaching for Change in Washington, D.C., involves families as purposeful partners in the education process. Tellin' Stories workshops use the power of story to connect people from diverse backgrounds, to pass on valuable information and experiences, and to organize collective action. The project has published a reader-friendly guidebook, *Between Families and Schools: Creating Meaningful Relationships*, written by D.C. parents and teachers. It includes tips, stories, and checklists based on an action research project.

Web site: www.teachingforchange.org/DC_Projects/Telling_Stories

2. Linking to Learning

Guides and Publications

Focus on Families! How to Build and Support Family-Centered Practices in After School, published by the Harvard Family Research Project, provides a research base for why family engagement matters. It includes concrete program strategies for engaging families, case studies of promising family engagement efforts, and an evaluation tool for improving family engagement practices. Read the guide online or print it as a PDF at: www.gse.harvard.edu/hfrp/projects/afterschool/resources/families.

PASS Project Parent Kits, developed by SAY San Diego, are videotape and print materials in English and Spanish. They include "Developing Better Homework Habits," "Preparing for College," and "Understanding Academic Standards." For ordering information, contact Ellen Yaffa, e-mail ellen@saysandiego.org.

Student-Led Conferences is a handbook on planning and implementing student-led conferences, developed by parents and teachers at Conway Middle School. It is available from the Prichard Committee for Academic Excellence in Kentucky.

Web site: www.prichardcommittee.org/pubs/cat/student-led_confer ences.pdf

Useful Web sites

American Federation of Teachers (AFT) provides information on topics that parents frequently ask about and ideas about how families can help their children be successful in school—from improving homework time to selecting rigorous courses. The magazine *The American Teacher*

includes articles on parent-relevant topics, such as "Does K-5 Homework Mean Higher Test Scores?" A recent AFT publication is *What Parents Can Do at Home to Help Their Children Meet High Standards*.

Web site: www.aft.org

Education Trust works for high academic achievement of all students, pre-K through college, and for closing achievement gaps that separate low-income students and students of color from other youth. This national organization has several resources that link parent involvement to student learning.

Web site: www2.edtrust.org. Click on the Parent and Community tab for more information about these resources.

Florida Partnership for Family Involvement in Education at the University of South Florida offers a wealth of family-friendly tip sheets and handouts on engaging families in improving achievement on its Web site. The site also has ideas for workshops and other professional development on engaging families.

Web site: www.floridapartnership.usf.edu/resources.html

National Network of Partnership Schools at Johns Hopkins University offers an online collection of Promising Partnership Practices, which document family and community partnerships that support children's learning from preschool through high school.

Web site: www.csos.jhu.edu/p2000/PPP/2005/index.htm

National PTA and its state affiliates have many resources for schools and parents. National PTA has produced a set of standards for family-community-school partnership, which schools and parent groups can use to assess their own efforts. The PTA Web site has materials for parents on how to help their children learn.

Web site: www.pta.org. Click on the Parent Resources tab.

Programs

TIPS, Teachers Involving Parents in Schoolwork, is a program developed by Joyce Epstein, teachers, and colleagues at the National Network of Partnership Schools (NNPS) at Johns Hopkins University. TIPS features homework assignments that require students to talk to someone at home about something interesting that they are learning in class. TIPS homework creates a three-way partnership among students, families, and teachers. The Web site lists several resources for TIPS, including training tools and a CD with hundreds of ideas for interactive homework assignments at the elementary, middle, or high school levels.

Web site: www.csos.jhu.edu/P2000/tips/tipsresources.htm

Title I, No Child Left Behind. For a complete review of the parent involvement requirements in Title I of the NCLB law, see *No Child Left Behind: What's in It for Parents* (Lexington, KY: Prichard Committee, 2003) by Anne Henderson. It is available from the Center for Parent Leadership in Kentucky.

Web site: www.centerforparentleadership.org/publications.html

Understanding All Kinds of Minds fosters an alliance between parents (and other caregivers), educators, and children to support a child's success in school and at home. Online support about learning issues is offered to the public through a parent tool kit located on the Web site. The tool kit provides a better understanding of learning processes, interactive insights into difficulties, video clips, and strategies to foster success in developing proficiency in math, reading, and writing.

Web site: www.allkindsofminds.org. Click on the Parents tab.

3. Addressing Differences

Guides and Publications

Culturally Responsive Parent Involvement: Concrete Understandings and Basic Strategies, by Sabrina Hope King and A. Lin Goodwin, is available from the American Association of Colleges of Teacher Education. This fifteen-page booklet offers basic operating assumptions and a set of concrete strategies for educators. Go to www.aacte.org/Publications/kinggoodwin.pdf.

Diversity: School, Family, and Community Connections is a review of sixty-four research studies that covers three aspects of diversity: race or ethnicity, culture (including language), and socioeconomic status. The report explores barriers to involvement for minority and low-income families, strategies that have been used to address those barriers, and recommendations for local education leaders to address specific needs. Go to www.sedl.org/connections/research-syntheses.html.

Family Involvement Network of Educators (FINE) carries back issues of its electronic newsletters, many of which address issues of diversity. For example, go to www.gse.harvard.edu/hfrp/projects/fine/announcements/04jun.html.

MiddleWeb offers a transcript of an in-depth online discussion among educators about class and cultural differences held in 2003. Go to www.middleweb.com/MWLISTCONT/MSLparentsAH.html.

Reaching out to Diverse Populations, by Chris Ferguson, is a strategy brief from the Southwest Educational Development Laboratory. The brief recommends that schools adopt plans for parent involvement that build on cultural values, stress personal contact, foster communication, and include accommodations such as child care, translation, and transportation. Go to www.sedl.org/connections/resources/rb/rb5-diverse.pdf.

Web-Based Resources

Teaching for Change offers an online and print catalog of multicultural teaching resources and its own and other publications. Two of its own titles are *Putting the Movement Back into Civil Rights Teaching* and *Beyond Heroes and Holidays*. The Web site also offers timely resources on current issues such as immigration.
Web site: www.teachingforchange.org/

Teaching Tolerance, a project of the Southern Poverty Law Center, is a Web site devoted to combating bigotry and creating communities that value diversity. The site offers downloadable public service announcements, daily news coverage about groups and individuals working for tolerance, guidebooks for adult and youth activists, resources for parents and teachers, and educational games for young children.
Web site: www.tolerance.org

Hispanic Mother-Daughter Program supports Hispanic girls to help them succeed in college. It is sponsored by the Junior League and the School of Social Work at the University of Texas in Austin. Girls are recruited through teachers and counselors at middle and high schools. About 75 percent have gone on to college. The program helps students and parents understand that a college degree is attainable and learn steps to achieve that goal. In addition to counseling, mentoring, and tutoring, program activities include college field trips for students and parents, and mother-daughter conferences on issues such as peer pressure, self-esteem, and goal setting.

Web site: www.jlaustin.org/?nd-mom_kid

Pacific Educational Group, directed by Glen Singleton, offers programs, workshops, and institutes to address racism and racial issues. Beyond Diversity, for example, is a two-day workshop to help teachers, parents, and administrators consider the impact of racism, exclusion, and prejudice on student learning. Participants explore racism and how it manifests in our culture and in schools, becoming aware of how racism and other diversity issues are part of educational failure. Participants learn to identify and address policies and practices that hinder students' ability to meet rigorous academic standards.

Web site: www.pacificeducationalgroup.com/who_glenn.html

4. Supporting Advocacy

Guides and Publications

The Advisory Guide: Designing and Implementing Effective Advisory Programs in Secondary Schools helps secondary educators design and implement a student advisory program tailored to their school. Design chapters describe advisory models and help planning teams think through major issues. Implementation chapters offer facilitation tips and suggestions for using different formats. Over 130 sample activities are organized around ten advisory themes, including student orientation, community building, goal setting and assessment, and career exploration.

The guide is by Rachel A. Poliner and Carol Miller Lieber and was published in 2004 by Educators for Social Responsibility in New York.

Web site: www.esrnational.org

Creating Partnerships, Bridging Worlds: Family and Community Engagement (2004), by the Center for Collaborative Education, offers research-based tools and strategies for helping schools, teachers, families, and communities partner to deepen student learning and engagement. The guide is part of the Turning Points program for middle school reform, developed by the Carnegie Corporation.

Web site: www.turningpoints.org

Intercultural Development Research Association (IDRA), based in Austin, Texas, conducts research, development, and training activities. IDRA offers professional development and training for educators and parents and provides technical assistance in schools and communities. In addition to publications and other material on intercultural topics, IDRA has a package of bilingual materials to help Latino families plan for college. These publications are available in English and Spanish at www.idra.org.

- *Hacia Adelante—Pathways to College—A Guide for Latino Families*, by Rosana Rodriguez and others, informs parents and students on how to plan together for college. This guide includes steps for choosing high school courses, selecting a college or university, financial planning, and an action calendar.
- *I'm Going to College—Fun Activities and Pictures to Color for Children in Elementary Grades* (2002). This activity book is designed to foster interest in going to college. The activities for children (ages four to ten) and parents include puzzles, word games, connect-the-dots, mazes, word scrambles, and coloring pages.

Making the Most of Middle School: A Field Guide for Parents, by Anthony Jackson, Gayle Andrews, Holly Holland, and Priscilla Pardini (New York: Teachers College Press, 2004). This useful guide gives parents practical advice about young adolescents and the world of the middle school. The book is available at the National Middle School Association online store. Go to http://store.nmsa.org/index .asp?PageAction=VIEWPROD&ProdID=237.

Speaking Up! A Parent Guide to Advocating for Students in Public Schools, published by the British Columbia Confederation of Parent Advisory Councils in Vancouver, offers practical, reader-friendly advice about how to resolve problems. Go to www.bccpac.bc.ca/advocacy/parents_speak.htm.

Working Together: A Guide to Positive Problem-Solving for Schools, Families and Communities, published by the Manitoba Department of Education, is available online as a fifty-six-page guide, a two-page brochure, and a ten-page pamphlet. The guide is designed to help parents, educators, and community members take part in the cooperative problem-solving process of informal dispute resolution. Go to www.edu.gov.mb.ca/ks4/specedu/documents.html.

Web-Based Resources

Individual Graduation Plan, a resource from the Kentucky Department of Education, is a plan of study that emphasizes academic and career development for middle and high school students. This tool helps students set learning goals based on academic and career interests. The KDE Web site offers folders that can be downloaded for students to use in academic and career planning.

Web site: www.education.ky.gov/KDE/Instructional+Resources/Career+and+Technical+Education/Individual+Graduation+Plan/default.htm

Schools to Watch, a Web site from the National Forum to Accelerate Middle Grades Reform and the Education Development Center, shows how award-winning schools have incorporated three important criteria for excellent middle schools: academic excellence, developmental responsiveness, and social equity.

To be selected as a School to Watch, a school must develop alliances with families to enhance and support the well-being of their children, involve families as partners in their children's education, keep families informed and involved in their children's learning, and ensure family participation in decision making.

Web site: www.schoolstowatch.org/what.htm

Programs

Advancement Via Individual Determination (AVID) is an in-school academic support program for grades five through twelve that prepares students to be eligible for college. The goal is to level the playing field for students without a college-going tradition in their families. AVID identifies students with academic potential and gives them a class on study skills and support to achieve in advanced classes. Parents of AVID students agree to support AVID academic requirements and to attend AVID parent meetings. Some AVID programs organize tours of college campuses for students' families.

Web site: www.avidonline.org

First Things First, a reform framework, was developed by the Institute for Research and Reform in Education (IRRE) in Rochester, New York. IRRE offers research and technical assistance to support First Things First. Schools adopting the program keep students with the same teachers for two or more years in high school. Large high schools break into smaller "learning communities" of no more than 325 students and twelve to fifteen teachers. Each community has a learning theme. Each student is assigned a teacher advocate to meet with weekly. The advocates also meet with the students' parents at least twice a year.

Web site: www.irre.org

Parents and Counselors Together (PACT) is a program of the National Association for College Admissions Counseling. The program strongly encourages middle and high school staff to help parents and students be aware of middle school courses needed to pursue challenging studies in high school and to provide information about high school courses required for admission to college and other postsecondary programs. Other recommendations for school staff include discussing with parents and students topics such as college admission requirements (good grades, advanced classes, and extracurricular activities), how to prepare for college admissions tests (ACT or SAT), and how to get financial aid for higher education.

Web site: www.act.org/research/policy/pdf/involve_parents.pdf

5. Sharing Power

Guides and Publications

Community Engagement Review and Planning Guide—Field Test Version (2002), developed by the Intercultural Development and Research Association (IDRA), is available in English and Spanish. This guide is designed to help schools and universities plan and strengthen community engagement. It includes a school-community engagement model covering eight categories, as well as analysis and planning worksheets for monitoring progress.
Web site: www.idra.org/resource

Pathways to Parent Leadership/Senderos a un liderazgo de padres (2002), by Action Alliance for Children, describes nine parent leadership programs, including Parent School Partnerships (PSP), Parent Institute for Quality Education (PIQE), and the Right Question Project (RQP). (See also the resources on Parent Leadership Training and Community Organizing in Section II of this chapter.)
Web site: www.4children.org/parents.htm#path

School Family and Community Partnerships: Your Handbook for Action (Second Edition), by Joyce L. Epstein et al. (Thousand Oaks, CA: Corwin Press, 2002), provides detailed information for schools already involved in the national partnership program and those who would like to join.

Web-Based Resources

National Issues Forum helps to sponsor public forums on community issues and offers workshops and a starter kit on how to organize a forum.
Web site: www.nifi.org

Council for Public Deliberation, at Ohio State University, offers resources and information about holding public forums.
Web site: www.cpdohio.org

Kettering Foundation conducts research on what it takes to make democracy work and is a strong advocate for public discussion of common problems. Its Web site contains reports, protocols, and other resources for public deliberation.

Web site: www.kettering.org

Programs and Organizations

Study Circles Resource Center in Pomfret, Connecticut, offers assistance with facilitating study circles. Study circles are a process for public dialogue and community change that begins with community outreach, which is followed by facilitated small-group conversations. The Web site offers examples of the study circle process in communities across the country.

Web site: www.studycircles.org

Parents United for Responsible Education (PURE), a nonprofit advocacy group in Chicago, informs parents about educational issues, brings the views of parents into the decision-making process through testimony and press conferences, and acts as an advocate for parents with the school administration. Each year, PURE provides direct assistance or referrals to hundreds of parents and local school council (LSC) members calling its hotline for help and information. Other services offered by PURE include workshops on topics suggested by parents and newsletters about developments in Chicago public schools.

Web site: www.pureparents.org/about.php

6. Scaling Up

Web-Based Resources

Center for Public Education examines models for, and school district experiences with, a range of community engagement activities, including focus groups, advisory boards, and community education programs.

Web site: www.centerforpubliceducation.org

Programs

College Partnership Program is a collaboration among the Fairfax County, Virginia, public schools, colleges and universities, local businesses, and parents to increase the number of minority students who enroll and succeed in college. Nearly 98 percent of graduating seniors in the program enroll in college. Participating colleges and universities sponsor activities to increase students' and parents' understanding of higher education programs and college life. The school district's Education Foundation links local business employees with students to provide work experiences and mentors.

Web site: www.fcps.k12.va.us/DSSSE/StudentServices/CollegePartnership/colpart2.htm

Math and Science Equity Program, a collaboration among parents, educators, researchers, and community activists in the Charlotte-Mecklenburg, North Carolina, school district, is aimed at reducing academic disparities between African American and white students. Home meetings with families enhance parent involvement by (1) expanding parents' knowledge about their rights, (2) encouraging networking among parents within schools and communities, and (3) stressing the importance of higher-level math and science courses.

Web site: www.msep.unce.edu

Parents for Public Schools (PPS), a national organization with local district chapters, supports school improvement efforts and parent involvement. PPS is committed to sustaining productive family involvement and advocating community-wide support of public education. The PPS Web site has information on starting an organization and getting involved, as well as links to many other sites.

Web site: www.parents4publicschools.com

Survey Resources

Comer School Development Program (SDP) offers surveys for sale. SDP will tally and analyze them for a fee. Go to http://info.med.yale.edu/comer/research_evaluation/schoolclimatesurvey.html.

Dade County Public Schools in Florida includes the questions and results from its parent surveys on its Web site. Select any school to see the results. Go to http://drs.dadeschools.net/ClimateSurvey/2002-03/Schools_0203.htm.

Intercultural Development and Research Association (IDRA) has developed the *Family and Community Engagement Survey—Field Test Version* (2002). The survey can be used by teachers, administrators, and parents to assess a school's effectiveness in partnering with families and communities. It is a useful tool for planning strategies in student achievement, access and equity, organizational support, and quality of interaction. It is available in English and Spanish. Go to www.idra.org/resource.

North Central Regional Educational Laboratory (NCREL) includes surveys for elementary and high school students. Go to http://goal.ncrel.org/winss/scs/sample.htm. How to participate in a survey project: http://goal.ncrel.org/winss/scs.

Zoomerang offers an online survey service, with options to use its templates or to create your own surveys. Go to http://info.zoomerang.com/quicktour/createsurvey.htm.

II. Selected Resources

1. Academic Standards

Academic Development Institute houses the federally funded Parent Information Resource Center (PIRC) for Illinois. ADI works with families, schools, and communities so that children become self-directed learners, avid readers, and responsible citizens. ADI promotes the school as a community, in which students, parents, teachers, and staff share common values and assume responsibility for one another. Parents are not external agents but full partners in the education of their children and of each other's children. ADI offers professional development and materials and publishes *The School Community Journal*.

Web site: www.adi.org

The Education Trust, a national organization supporting high academic standards, has a Web site that contains valuable reports on student achievement and a link in the section on data tools to an interactive database (Education Watch Online) on achievement gaps and national achievement trends. Education Trust publications include:

- **"Improving Your Child's Education: A Guide for Latino Parents"** offers a number of suggestions for how Latino parents can get involved and be a better advocate for the education of Latino children. It is available in English or Spanish.
- **"Improving Your Children's Education: A Guide for African American Parents"** gives African American parents the tools needed to advocate for and improve their child's education.
- **"Making Data Work: A Parent and Community Guide"** gives parents and the public easy-to-use tools to collect and analyze school data to improve student achievement.

Web site: www.edtrust.org

The Efficacy Institute, Inc., is a nonprofit training and consulting organization that works with schools, businesses, and community organizations. The institute provides training, tools, and other services that committed adults can use to accelerate academic achievement and character development of all students.

Web site: www.efficacy.org

KSA Plus Communications in Arlington, Virginia, a public relations firm that specializes in education, has developed reader-friendly school report cards, guides on academic standards, and other publications about educational issues. Its Parent Leadership Group offers products and services to strengthen parent-school partnership, including workshops, consulting services, and materials.

Web site: www.ksaplus.com

National Urban League has developed *Putting Standards into Action: A Guidebook for Parent Educators and Workshop Facilitators* (2001), which includes a videotape and four modules.

Web site: www.nul.org/

Prichard Committee for Academic Excellence offers resources for community leaders, educators, parents, and community activists, including numerous reports, studies, guidebooks, and newsletters. The Prichard Committee sponsors the Commonwealth Institute for Parent Leadership and the Center for Parent Leadership.

Web site: www.prichardcommittee.org

2. Community-Focused Organizations

Coalition for Community Schools is an alliance of education, youth development, human services, community development, and local government organizations that are involved in the development of community schools. The Coalition advocates for community schools as the most effective vehicle for strengthening schools, families, and communities so that together they can improve student learning.

Web site: www.communityschools.org

Communities in Schools, Inc. (CIS) is a network of local and state programs that establish the community school model to connect schools and their communities to students and families. Schools partner with community service agencies to provide a variety of health, social, and family services, as well as programs to engage parents, volunteers, mentors, and tutors.

Web site: www.cisnet.org

Charles Stewart Mott Foundation began its focus on community education in Flint, Michigan, by sponsoring the after-hours use of school facilities for learning and recreation programs for youth and adults. The foundation supports the 21st Century Community Learning Centers program, a federal initiative to expand before- and after-school programs for children. The foundation offers a listserv (Mott After School) and links for individuals interested in the Community Learning Centers program. The foundation also supports community organizing.

Web site: www.mott.org

National Community Education Association (NCEA) promotes all aspects of community education, including parent involvement through its many affiliated state organizations. NCEA holds a national conference and publishes a quarterly journal, which often deals with issues related to school-family-community partnership. The organization's Web site has links to many other organizations and their publications.

Web site: www.ncea.com

National Center for Community Education (NCCE) in Flint, Michigan, offers workshops at their center and online, including reports and publications, lists of books and videos, and links to other community education resources. NCCE also provides training and assistance for the after-school program efforts of the federal 21st Century Community Learning Centers program.

Web site: www.nccenet.org

Search Institute in Minneapolis provides leadership, knowledge, and resources to promote healthy children, youth, and communities. Search Institute has created a framework of forty Developmental Assets, which are positive experiences and personal qualities that young people need to grow up healthy, caring, and responsible.

Web site: www.search-institute.org

Youth Development Institute (YDI) of the Fund for the City of New York collaborated with the New York City Department of Youth and Community Development to create the Beacon Schools Initiative in 1991. Beacon Schools are active community centers for use after school, on weekends, and during the summer, in which community agencies provide services such as education, language classes, job training, counseling, and cultural and recreational activities for youth and families. YDI consults nationally with cities, communities, and community organizations to develop programs based on the Beacon Centers.

Web site: www.fcny.org

3. *Community Organizing*

ACORN, the Association of Community Organizations for Reform Now, is a national network that supports local community organizing efforts. ACORN provides support and training to local affiliates campaigning for the improvement of public services, including education, in low- and moderate-income neighborhoods.

Web site: www.acorn.org

Boston Parent Organizing Network (BPON) connects more than thirty grassroots organizations in Boston to build their effectiveness as advocates for improvement in the Boston Public Schools. BPON represents an effort to engage and empower parents and other community members for school reform. The Network has attracted the interest of civic leaders and major area foundations, which have provided start-up funding. It has a collaborative relationship with the Institute for Responsive Education.

Web site: www.bpon.org

Center for Community Change helps to establish and develop community organizations across the country, focusing on issues related to poverty and ensuring that government programs respond to community needs. The Center supports community organizing in low-income and immigrant communities. In addition to technical assistance and training, the Center offers reports, news updates, and publications. *Action Guide for Education Organizing* (2004) is a Web-based tool for organizers just starting to work on education reform issues.

Web site: www.communitychange.org/issues/education/publications

Community Involvement Program, Annenberg Institute for School Reform (formerly affiliated with the Institute for Education and Social Policy at New York University) conducts studies and publishes materials about community organizing as a form of democratic participation that holds local school officials accountable for results. CIP also provides technical assistance, data analysis, and other support to community and youth organizing groups in New York and other cities to promote school reform.

Web site: www.educationorganizing.org

Cross City Campaign for Urban School Reform (CCCUSR) is a national network of school reformers, parents, community members, teachers, and principals working to improve urban public schools. CCCUSR conducts studies and publishes reports, and offers training and technical assistance.

Web site: www.crosscityorg

The Interaction Institute for Social Change, with offices in

Cambridge, San Francisco, and Ireland, has developed *Community Building Curriculum: Skills for Emerging Grassroots Leaders*. The curriculum is delivered in three workshops and focuses on building networks of leaders in low-income communities. The workshops, available in Spanish and English, are based on principles of community building.

Web site: www.interactioninstitute.org/services/training.php

Pacific Institute for Community Organization (PICO) is a national network of faith-based community organizations working to solve problems facing local communities. PICO chapters work to expand access to health care, improve public schools, make neighborhoods safer, build affordable housing, and redevelop communities.

Web site: www.piconetwork.org

Southern Echo is a leadership education, training, and development organization based in Jackson, Mississippi. Echo training builds the working tools of community organizing, including political skills, organizational development, and policy formation at the local level. Echo staff work with and support African American and working-class community leadership and organizations in rural Mississippi and eleven other Southern states.

Web site: www.southernecho.org

4. Current Developments and News

Gadfly is a free e-mail newsletter about education sponsored by the Thomas B. Fordham Foundation. It reflects a generally conservative perspective on issues yet offers a variety of points of view. *Gadfly* occasionally has reports and comments relevant to school-family-community relationships.

Web site: www.edexcellence.net/gadfly

George Lucas Educational Foundation includes in its Web site a section for parents, with articles, research summaries, video clips, and resources. The Web site also contains interviews with school professionals about how to build partnerships with families. Although the foundation emphasizes technology-related topics, it also covers other areas. *Edutopia*, a free magazine published by the Lucas Foundation, covers exemplary programs and practices that use multimedia. For articles and information about the involvement of parents, families, and communities, go to www.edutopia.org/getstarted/parents.php.

Web site: www.glef.org

MiddleWeb carries information, news updates, links to other sites, and a listserv feature, all about middle grades reform, including material on parent-community involvement. In addition to the collection of reform-oriented materials, MiddleWeb includes hundreds of articles and links about curriculum, teaching strategies, professional development, parent involvement, and classroom assessment.

Web site: www.middleweb.com

The Kappan, Phi Delta Kappa's monthly magazine, often includes articles on partnership topics as well as notes on current news and developments.

Web site: www.pdkintl.org

Public Agenda offers regular e-mail reports about domestic and world news, with attention to educational issues. Its Web site carries reports on its focus groups and surveys on educational topics.

Web site: www.publicagenda.org

Rethinking Schools, a monthly newsletter available in print and online, focuses on topical issues of education reform, the realities of the classroom, and the importance of teaching for social justice.

Web site: www.rethinkingschools.org

5. Government Sources

Web sites

U.S. Department of Education (USDE) and state education agencies carry information about laws, regulations, available funding, and other assistance, as well as links to other sites. The USDE site has special sections for parents and students. The Web site of the Council of Chief State School Officers carries links to every state education agency. Nearly all these sites have material on NCLB, partnerships, and school reform.

Web sites: www.ed.gov and www.ccsso.org

Local school and school district Web sites contain basic information such as school and bus schedules, as well as examples of innovative practices. Many district sites publish information about test score performance and school climate survey results for each school. Checking sites of nearby districts can reveal how they provide information and help to parents and community residents.

Parent Information and Resource Centers (PIRCs), funded by the U.S. Department of Education, provide parents, schools, and local organizations with training, information, and technical assistance. Operating in all states, PIRCs work with parents, educators, and community organizations to strengthen partnerships so that children can reach high academic standards. RMC Research Corporation provides a complete list and links to every PIRC.

Web site: www.pirc-info.net

Regional Educational Laboratories

North Central Regional Educational Laboratory (NCREL) has conducted projects and issued publications over the years on topics related to this book. Their Web site has a section on parent and community involvement topics and resources.

Web site: www.ncrel.org/8drs/areas/pa0cont.htm

Northwest Regional Educational Laboratory (NWREL) provides information about publications and projects, including material about full-service schools and other aspects of school-community partnerships. Publications of interest include *Building Relationships for Student Success: School-Family-Community Partnerships and Student Achievement in the Northwest* and *Partnerships by Design: Cultivating Effective and Meaningful School-Family-Community Partnerships*.

Web site: www.nwrel.org

Southwest Educational Development Laboratory (SEDL) offers a Web site with information and descriptions of their publications and projects. The site also has interactive features, including online courses to facilitate family and community connections with schools. Two courses are "What do we mean by family and community connections with schools?" and "What structures can help schools create effective family and community involvement that supports learning outside of school?" *Beyond the Building: A Facilitation Guide for School, Family and Community Connections* (2006) is a multimedia tool kit composed of four interactive modules. SEDL offers training for facilitators to use the tool kit to build partnerships in local sites. SEDL has published research syntheses on school, family, and community connections, including *A New Wave of Evidence*.

Web site: www.sedl.org

6. Key National Networks

National Center for Family Literacy (NCFL) offers professional development for practitioners who work in children's education, adult education, English as a Second Language, and related literacy fields. Other services include model program development, policy analysis, advocacy to expand family literacy practices through the Family Literacy Alliance, and a membership program.

Web site: www.familylit.org

National Coalition for Parent Involvement in Education (NCPIE), a national coalition of more than seventy-five organizations, offers a Web site that is a good starting place to search for information. The database of organizations and resources links to the Web sites of most member groups: organizations, government agencies, higher education and research organizations, consultants, and federally funded parent information centers. NCPIE serves as a clearinghouse for resources created by its partners and maintains an archive of reports. NCPIE also produces its own materials, such as bulletins on the various components of NCLB.

Web site: www.ncpie.org

National Network of Partnership Schools (NNPS) at the Center on School, Family, and Community Partnerships at Johns Hopkins University has conducted scores of studies and projects. Directed by Joyce Epstein, NNPS includes more than a thousand schools, districts, state and other educational agencies, and university partners. The NNPS Web site describes membership requirements.

Member schools commit to developing a comprehensive program of partnership using Epstein's framework of six types of involvement: parenting, communicating, volunteering, learning at home, decision making, and collaborating with community. Services that members receive include training workshops, handbooks, newsletters, a national conference, research reports and abstracts, notices about funding opportunities, and telephone assistance. The NNPS Web site is a rich and accessible resource for research reports, publications, information, and services.

Center Web site: www.partnershipschools.org

NNPS Web site: www.csos.jhu.edu/P2000

Family Involvement Network of Educators (FINE), sponsored by the Harvard Family Research Project (HFRP), offers a Web site and a free monthly newsletter via e-mail that includes current reports and articles. Many items can be downloaded without cost. Some FINE/HFRP publications include:

- *Taking a Closer Look: A Guide to Online Resources on Family Involvement* (2005) is a practical, well-annotated catalog of organizations and Web sites. (We drew on the guide for this chapter, but its listings are far more extensive.)
- *Preparing Educators to Involve Families: From Theory to Practice,* by H. B. Weiss, H. Kreider, M. E. Lopez, and C. M. Chatman (2005), prepares educators to partner effectively with elementary school families. The book uses teaching cases that reflect critical dilemmas in family-school-community relations, especially among families for whom poverty and cultural differences are daily realities.
- *Concepts and Models of Family Involvement,* available on the Web site, identifies four approaches to family involvement—parenting practices, school-family partnerships, democratic participation, and school choice—and illustrates them in case studies.

Web site: www.finenetwork.org and e-mail: hfrp@gse.harvard.edu

Public Education Network (PEN) is a national association of local education funds working to improve public school quality. The weekly *PEN NewsBlast,* a free e-mail newsletter, features discussion on a variety of topics, including partnerships, civic engagement, and accountability, plus coverage of news media reports about innovative programs. PEN also produces publications and special reports, many of which can be downloaded without charge from their Web site or purchased in hard copy. The PEN Web site includes links to other organizations' Web sites.

Web site: www.publiceducation.org
E-mail: pen@publiceducation.org

7. No Child Left Behind (NCLB), Title I

An Action Guide for Community and Parent Leaders: Using NCLB to Improve Student Achievement is published by the Public Education Network. The guide gives specific advice and action steps for both parent and community activists.

Web site: www.PublicEducation.org

"Title I as a Tool for Parent Involvement," an article by the Center for Law and Education, offers a summary of the law and its parent involvement requirements. Go to www.cleweb.org/issues/title/tool.htm.

Improving Your Schools: A Parent and Community Guide to No Child Left Behind, published by the Education Trust, provides user-friendly information on NCLB that parents and communities can understand and use, and highlights key aspects of the law that can help parents and communities use NCLB for advocacy.

Web site: www.edtrust.org

No Child Left Behind: What's in It for Parents, a guide to the parent involvement requirements in the federal law, is available from the Prichard Committee's Center for Parent Leadership. It includes six key leverage points for parents, as well as advice from the research on designing Title I parent involvement programs. A Spanish version is also available.

Web site: www.centerforparentleadership.org/publications.html

NCLB Action Briefs, a project of Public Education Network (PEN) and the National Coalition for Parent Involvement in Education (NCPIE), are designed to keep community and parent leaders up to date on various provisions of NCLB. The briefs are written in reader-friendly language focused on specific sections of the law, such as compacts, teacher quality, standards and assessment, and public school choice. Each one includes pertinent regulations, a glossary of terms, action steps, and additional resources.

Web site: www.ncpie.org/Resources/nclbactionbriefs.html

A Practical Guide to Talking with Your Community About No Child Left Behind and Schools in Need of Improvement is published by the Learning First Alliance, a coalition of a dozen leading national education organizations. The guide gives tips about communicating with parents and the public about the law and its effects.

Web site: www.learningfirst.org/publications/nclb

8. *Parent, Teacher, and Administrator Associations*

American Federation of Teachers (AFT) has brochures and publications about school-parent partnership and a Web site with a special section for parents. The Web site stresses AFT's belief that strong family-school partnerships are essential to students' academic well-being. The parent section provides information on topics that parents frequently ask about, as well as ideas for families to help their children in school. The magazine *The American Teacher* also includes articles on parent-relevant topics, such as "Does K-5 Homework Mean Higher Test Scores?" A recent AFT publication is *What Parents Can Do at Home to Help Their Children Meet High Standards*.

Web site: www.aft.org

National Association of Elementary School Principals (NAESP) publishes articles about parents and the community in *Principal* magazine and its newsletters. NAESP has an online National Principal's Resource Center with a section on family involvement and offers a book, *Strengthening the Connection Between School and Home*.

Web site: www.naesp.org (click on "Resources")

National Association of Secondary School Principals (NASSP) devotes time at its conferences to relevant topics and offers mini-grants to principals to strengthen ties between schools and communities. The *NASSP Bulletin*, a scholarly publication, occasionally includes articles on school-family partnership.

Web site: www.nassp.org

National Education Association (NEA) offers publications and reports on many subjects such as testing, reading, and supplementary services in NCLB. NEA has developed a series of parent guides jointly with the National PTA. These are available in both English and Spanish. Some examples:

- *Helping Your Student Get the Most Out of Homework*
- *A Parent's Guide to Helping Your Child with Today's Math*
- *A Parent's Guide to Raising Scientifically Literate Children*
- *A Parent's Guide to Improving School Achievement*

The NEA Web site has a section about and for parents and community that gives the NEA point of view about the importance of parent involvement and describes available resources.

Web site: www.nea.org

National PTA has produced a set of standards for family-community-school partnership, which schools and parent groups can use to assess their own efforts. The standards encourage two-way school-home communication, parenting skills, participation in decision making, and school-community collaboration. National PTA offers a program, "Building Successful Partnerships," to train local, state, and national leaders to conduct workshops about parent involvement and the PTA standards. Some state PTAs also have resources to offer online or by phone. The National PTA Web site includes access to resources, including tips for schools and parents on topics such as student achievement, school safety, and media and technology. An example is *10 Ways for Parents to Help Teachers*.

Web site: www.pta.org

9. Parent Training and Professional Development

This is a small sample of the hundreds of organizations and agencies that provide training for school staff and parents about school-family-community partnerships. When searching beyond our list, bear in mind that some sources are commercial; others are nonprofit. The costs, quality, and content vary widely. We urge consumer caution in selecting a program.

Parent Training

The California PARENT Center, located at San Diego State University, is a state-level parent training resource. The Center also offers professional development for teachers and administrators. Their publications, curricula, and approaches, including a free e-newsletter, apply to schools and parents in other states as well.

Web site: http://parent.sdsu.edu

Campaign for African American Achievement and other programs such as Achievement Matters, Opportunity Works, and College Access are available via the National Urban League and its local affiliates. *Read and Rise*, a resource guide that offers research-based information and practical tips to help parents engage their children in reading and literacy-building activities, is available to download in PDF.

Web site: www.nul.org

Families and Schools Together (FAST), developed by the Wisconsin Center for Education Research, helps parents to establish their own support system. FAST builds social capital and supports children's learning by creating relationships among parents and between parents and teachers.

Web site: www.wcer.wisc.edu/fast

The Home and School Institute, founded by Dorothy Rich, offers the MegaSkills program, which provides fee-based training and handbooks for school personnel and parents. Emphasis is on helping parents to support their children's learning at home.

Web site: www.megaskills.org

National Council of La Raza sponsors Parents as Partners, a nine-week parent education program modeled on PIQE (see below).

Web site: www.nclr.org

Parent Expectations Support Achievement (PESA), developed by the Los Angeles County Office of Education, is a twelve-week parent education program based on the belief that parents' expectations predict children's achievement, relationships, and ultimate success. PESA is modeled after the Teacher Expectations and Student Achievement (TESA) program, which trains teachers to have high expectations for all students. The program uses a trainer-of-trainers approach.

Web site: www.lacoe.edu/pesa

Parent Institute for Quality Education (PIQE) provides a nine-week parent education program. Over three hundred thousand parents have graduated from PIQE in California alone, and research shows that parents use the information to their children's benefit. The initial planning session asks parents what they would like to include in the course. Curriculum topics include school-home collaboration; the home, motivation, and self-esteem; communication and discipline; drugs, gangs, school, and community; how the school system functions; and college and career selection.

Web site: www.piqe.org

Professional Development

Family Friendly Schools, founded by Steve Constantino, works with schools and districts to increase student achievement by developing networks of relationships between leadership, staff, and families to create a culture of high performance. Constantino has written *Engaging All Families: Creating a Positive School Culture by Putting Research into Practice* (Lanham, MD: Scarecrow Press, 2003).

Web site: www.familyfriendlyschools.com

Institute for Responsive Education (IRE), now at Cambridge College in Cambridge, Massachusetts, conducts studies and sponsors projects on school, family, and community partnerships, including participatory action research. Following is a sample of IRE training programs:

- Achievement Through Partnership (ATP) includes a three-day interactive institute. School teams (principal, teachers, parents, community members, and students) develop a long-term plan that involves all stakeholders and is connected to improved student learning.
- Principal Partnership Institute (PPI) helps principals explore core beliefs about partnership, work with community partners and family-school coordinators, and evaluate the success of their work.

- Partnering for Student Success (PSS) offers training for school teams about school-based family centers, a school-wide welcoming atmosphere, home visiting programs, parent-teacher conferences focused on student learning, and after-school links to learning.
- Parent Leadership Program (PLP) offers workshops for emerging parent leaders who work on family involvement initiatives with the schools.

Web site: www.responsiveeducation.org

National Center for Conflict Resolution Education promotes the development of conflict resolution education programs in schools by offering professional development programs, materials, and workshops. The Web site offers links to related organizations.

Web site: www.nccre.org

National Professional Organizations

American Federation of Teachers (AFT) offers *School-Home Connection: Partnerships Supporting Student Learning,* a sixty-hour course to help school staff understand how they can assist parents to support their children's learning. Topics include using effective communication strategies, designing more productive homework assignments to involve families, explaining classroom work and grading systems, and developing school-wide parent involvement plans. Go to www.aft.org/topics/teacher-quality/downloads/schoolhome.pdf.

Association for Supervision and Curriculum Development (ASCD) offers professional development videos and audiotapes on working with families. Two online training courses also cover family involvement, and one part of a guide for instructional leaders offers strategies for communicating about instruction to parents and the community. ASCD's annual conference offers sessions on collaborations and partnerships.

Web site: www.ascd.org

National Education Association (NEA) offers the Family-School-Community Partnerships initiative to train educators to improve student learning by involving parents, families, and communities. This two-and-a-half-day program presents current research, theory, and practice to build local partnerships. Go to www.nea.org/priorityschools/famschoolpartner ships.html.

National Association for the Education of Young Children (NAEYC) offers *Supporting Teachers, Strengthening Families*, a leadership program for early childhood professionals, to prevent child abuse and neglect, promote children's social and emotional development, and support families. Go to www.naeyc.org/ece/supporting.asp.

National Staff Development Council (NSDC) has set standards for high-quality professional development and offers publications and an annual conference. The Web site carries a section about parent and community engagement. Go to www.nsdc.org/library/parentspartners/ parents.cfm.

Parent Leadership Training Programs

ASPIRA Parents for Educational Excellence Initiative (APEX) trains parents to become informed advocates for education in their communities. APEX is a series of ten workshops in Spanish and English that cover why education is important, the home connection, school structure, what parent involvement means, communication, organizing parent networks, and group dynamics. A training manual for the APEX workshop series also is available.

Web site: www.aspira.org

Commonwealth Institute for Parent Leadership (CIPL) is sponsored by the Prichard Committee for Academic Excellence, a statewide education advocacy organization in Kentucky. CIPL has trained over thirteen hundred parents to understand the state's standards-based education system and what it requires of schools, students, and teachers. Participants gain information and skills to expand their role in their children's education and the larger community. All CIPL fellows are expected to design and carry out projects to improve student learning. Many have gone on to assume leadership roles and run for local office.

Web site: www.cipl.org

Center for Parent Leadership was formed by the Prichard Committee to respond to requests for technical assistance on designing parent leadership training programs. The Center offers consulting to states, community groups, schools, and school districts as well as workshops, seminars, and publications.

Web site: www.centerforparentleadership.org

Parent Leadership Program (PLP), sponsored by the Institute for Responsive Education, offers workshops for emerging parent leaders who work on family involvement initiatives with the schools.

Web site: www.responsiveeducation.org

Parent Leadership Training Institute (PLTI) is a twenty-week institute that reaches a diverse audience of adults raising children. It is sponsored by the Connecticut Commission on Children, an arm of the state legislature. The curriculum is focused on citizenship skills that can be used to improve education and other services for families. Graduates have gone on to take better jobs, enroll in higher education, run for public office, testify before the state legislature, and train teachers, parents, and administrators to become partners in school reform.

Web site: www.cga.ct.gov/coc/plti.htm

Parent School Partnership Program (PSP), developed by the Mexican American Legal Defense and Education Fund (MALDEF), trains parents, school staff, and community organizations to promote the educational attainment of children. The training manual and curriculum provide trainers with sixteen weekly sessions, procedures, and best practices to conduct a parent leadership program. The curriculum covers parent rights and responsibilities, structure and function of schools, the parent-teacher partnership, understanding group process, principles of leadership, and the road to the university.

Web site: www.maldef.org/education/partnership.htm

Right Question Project (RQP) emphasizes participants' working together to name the information that they want and need, formulate questions, reflect on the knowledge that they gain, and develop plans for advocacy and accountability. The trainers use simulations, role playing, and discussion. RQP emphasizes three roles that parents can play: support their children's education, monitor their educational progress, and advocate for meeting their needs when necessary.

Web site: www.rqp.org

10. Special Needs Information

Educating Our Children Together: A Sourcebook for Effective Family-School-Community Partnership is published by the National Center on Dispute Resolution in Special Education. Available online and in CD format, this guide offers tips and principles about family-school-community involvement in K-12 schools and includes a self-assessment tool to determine current practices.

Web site: www.directionservice.org/cadre

Center for Law and Education carries an online catalog of school improvement resources, including material on parent involvement. The Web site also is a source of information for advocates on special education, Title I, and other educational policies.

Web site: www.cleweb.org

National Dissemination Center for Children with Disabilities is a federally funded clearinghouse that provides information to assist families, educators, caregivers, advocates, and others to help students with disabilities participate as fully as possible at home, in school, and in the community.

Web site: www.nichcy.org

The Pacer Center provides information, support, and advocacy for families of special needs children.

Web site: www.pacer.org

11. System-wide Reform

The Annenberg Institute for School Reform works in collaboration with education reform organizations, school districts, school improvement networks, and education funds to develop the capacity of urban communities to build and sustain programs and policies that improve teaching and learning. Public engagement in school reform is an important part of its work. *Public Engagement Watch* is a monthly online digest that includes publications, a featured tool, and funding alerts.

Web site: www.annenberginstitute.org

ATLAS Communities is a comprehensive school reform design that incorporates five elements: teaching and learning, assessment, professional development, management and decision making, and family and community. The ATLAS Web site and available resources provide information on how the program involves families and communities in improving student achievement.

Web site: www.atlascommunities.org

Center for Comprehensive School Reform and Improvement occasionally offers articles in its newsletter to help schools and districts foster successful parent involvement.

Web site: www.centerforcsri.org

Coalition of Essential Schools aims to create and sustain equitable, intellectually vibrant, personalized schools, and to make such schools the norm of American public education. CES maintains a family collaboration section of its Web site with books and articles on parent-teacher communication and family collaboration. Go to its site map and click on "Family collaboration."

Web site: www.essentialschools.org

The Comer School Development Program (SDP) at Yale University, developed by James Comer, is based on principles of healthy child development, which are seen as essential for academic achievement and life success. The SDP gives parents a major role in planning and management for school reform. SDP offers parent and staff surveys for sale, and will tally them for a fee.

Web site: www.comerprocess.org

12. Tool Kits and Guidebooks

The How-to Guide for School-Business Partnerships, published by the Council for Corporate and School Partnerships, is designed for school officials and business leaders who are interested in engaging in school-business partnerships. Partnership programs can involve staff and curriculum development, guidance, mentoring, tutoring, incentives, and awards, or they may provide material and financial resources. The guide provides tips, guidelines, and worksheets to develop effective programs.

Web site: www.corpschoolpartners.org

The Knowledge Loom: School, Family and Community Partnership is offered by the Education Alliance at Brown University. This Web resource, developed with RMC Research Corporation, focuses on involving parents and communities in the learning process. It includes bibliographies, posters, and resource links as well as case studies.

Web site: www.knowledgeloom.org

Met Life Tri-Connecting Action Kit is a tool kit focused on school-family-student-community communication offered by the Families and Work Institute.

Web site: www.familiesandwork.org

The Parent Institute, founded by a former school administrator, offers informational materials, on a fee basis, for parents and educators in both English and Spanish. These include newsletters and over two hundred parent guides, booklets, brochures, and videos on parent involvement. They are written in practical, down-to-earth language and cover topics such as children's school success, responsibility, homework skills, self-esteem, study skills, test skills, attention span, self-discipline, ability to handle peer pressure, and bullies.

Web site: www.parent-institute.com

Strengthening Families, Strengthening Schools, an online tool kit, provides information and resources to help schools work in partnership with families and communities. The tool kit is offered by the Annie E. Casey Foundation.

Web site: www.aecf.org/initiatives/mc/sf

Taking a Closer Look: A Guide to Online Resources on Family Involvement, produced by the Harvard Family Research Project, is an online guide with Web links to research, information, programs, and tools about parenting practices to support children's learning and development. The guide covers home-school relationships, parent leadership development, and collective engagement for school improvement and reform.

Web site: www.gse.harvard.edu/hfrp/projects/fine/resources/guide/guide.html

III. Recommended Reading from the San Diego PALs

Book clubs and reading groups are an increasingly popular way to explore important topics with colleagues. The Parent Academic Liaison (PAL) program in San Diego has an active book club. Melissa Whipple, the program director, says, "As a group of twenty-five professionals working in this area on a daily basis, we do not want to become complacent and start to think we already know it all when it comes to effective family engagement."

The PALs select books of interest and discuss them in various ways. Topics explored include parent involvement, positive school culture, effective leadership, asset development, and linking with community. To this group, the book club is a part of their regular professional development.

At monthly PAL meetings, Whipple sets aside time for book groups to meet and discuss the readings. Sometimes they read research summaries and other related articles and break into mixed groups to share and discuss them. Every so often, Whipple sets a date when reading groups list the big ideas they've learned and report to the rest of the group.

Here are their recommendations for other book clubs. Some of these titles are cited in the endnotes of this book. All except the first are available from online bookstores such as Amazon and Barnes and Noble.

1. *Including Every Parent: A Step-by Step Guide to Engage and Empower Parents at Your School* by Parents and Teachers at the O'Hearn School in Boston and the Project for School Innovation (available from www.psinnovation.org)

2. *The Parent Project: A Workshop Approach to Parent Involvement* by James Vopat

3. *Teachers and Parents Together* by Maureen Botrie and Pat Wenger

4. *A Path to Follow: Learning to Listen to Parents* by Patricia Edwards

5. *Parent to Parent: Our Children, Their Literacy* by Gerald R. Oglan and Averil Elcombe

6. *Creating a Positive School Culture: How Principals and Teachers Can Solve Problems Together* by Marie Nathalie Beaudoin and Maureen Taylor

7. *Involving Latino Families in Schools: Raising Student Achievement Through Home-School Partnerships* by Concha Delgado Gaitan

8. *Parents Are Lifesavers: A Handbook for Parent Involvement in Schools* by Carol S. Batey

9. *Building Trust for Better Schools: Research Based Practices* by Julie Reed Kochanek

10. *Parents and Teachers Working Together* by Carol Davis and Alice Yang

11. *The Essential Conversation: What Parents and Teachers Can Learn from Each Other* by Sara Lawrence-Lightfoot

12. *Dealing with Difficult Parents and with Parents in Difficult Situations* by Todd Whitaker and Douglas J. Fiore

Chapter 11

Tools to Support Your Work

Where Do We Start?

Throughout this book, we have attempted to share what we have learned from our own experience and from practitioners—people like you—who are working to strengthen partnerships among school staff, families, and community members. Before we send you off armed with all the information and tools from this text, we thought it important to discuss one final topic: how will you keep track of your work and evaluate your progress?

Many of the tools in this chapter and the checklists throughout the book will help you collect data on your programs and assess how well they're working. With the increasing emphasis on accountability, you'll want to measure the effectiveness of your interventions and report on your successes and challenges using concrete data.

We know that many of you struggle to make the case that parent and community initiatives are important. The following information offers some guidance on tracking your program outcomes in ways that are easy to do and make sense.

Creating a Logic Model

Setting up procedures to evaluate your work may sound daunting, but it can be fun and exciting to record your progress. A good place to start is the creation of a *logic model*. A logic model gives you a picture of how your program works and what you are trying to accomplish. Developing a logic model, whether your program is large or small, helps to plan better programs and design smart and effective ways to keep track of your accomplishments and challenges. Logic models create a visual representation of your program and help you document both the process and products of your program. In other words, you will be asking yourself: "What did we do? How well did we do it?" and "What difference have we made?"

Our friends at the Harvard Family Research Project have developed several helpful tools to assist you in creating logic models and tracking the progress of your programs. The first tool, "Learning from Logic Models: An Example of a Family/School Partnership Program," offers tips on how to construct your own logic model using an example from a family-school partnership. This tool is available at www.gse.harvard.edu/hfrp/pubs/onlinepubs/rrb/learning.html.

The second tool will help you learn how to create and use indicators to measure the progress and outcomes of your work. "Indicators: Definition and Use in a Results-Based Accountability System" provides an overview of different types of indicators, criteria for selecting them, and links to additional resources for child and family indicators. It is available at www.gse.harvard.edu/hfrp/pubs/onlinepubs/rrb/indicators.html.

The third tool will help you identify family involvement measures that you can adopt. The Harvard Family Research Project staff have assembled a catalog of measures that you can use to evaluate changes in family processes, such as shifts in parent-child relationships, parenting practices, and parent involvement in children's learning in the home and at school. A "Catalog of Family Process Measures" is available at www.gse.harvard.edu/hfrp/eval/issue28/pp5.html.

This chapter contains tools for engaging families mentioned throughout this book. They are listed in alphabetical order. With each tool is a brief note suggesting how it might be used. We invite you to modify the tools to suit your own setting and purposes, and to think of new and interesting ways to use them.

1. Attitude Check
2. Conference Checklist
3. Developing a Code of Conduct
4. District Policy on Family-School Partnership
5. Family Involvement Coordinator—Sample Job Description
6. Family Welcome Questionnaire
7. Homework Survey
8. Needs Assessment Survey
9. Parent Review
10. Parent Volunteer Survey
11. School Climate Survey
12. Tips for Developing a School Family Involvement Policy

1. Attitude Check

This one-hour exercise is designed to explore and discuss staff and parent attitudes about working together and sharing responsibility. It's intended to spark discussion, not to force final decisions. Pick a neutral facilitator to lead the exercise.

Post four large pieces of paper around the room. Number them from 1 to 4.

+ On #1 write: "Parents can do this on their own."
+ On #2 write: "Parents can do this with active assistance from school staff."
+ On #3 write: "Parents should do this with advice from school staff."
+ On #4 write: "School staff should do this alone."

Ground Rules

1. Read aloud one of the statements in the list below. You can use three or four of the statements or make up your own. Ask par-

ticipants to stand under the paper that expresses their view on that statement.

2. Ask participants to explain why they're standing where they are. They may try to win people over to their part of the room. Remind people that they can move to another part of the room if they change their mind.

3. Use a ball as a "floating microphone"—only the person holding the ball can speak. After some debate, proceed to another statement.

4. The facilitator should hold his or her comments until the end to encourage participant discussion. Participants should be encouraged to interpret the statements themselves and questions should be given a minimal response.

Statements

+ Developing activities for classes
+ Representing the school at meetings, conferences, and other events
+ Setting the rules and regulations for the school
+ Developing the budget for various activities
+ Deciding on disciplinary action for staff and students
+ Conducting staff training
+ Planning trips
+ Hiring staff
+ Fund-raising (such as bake sales or candy sales)

Wrap-up

Mention key things that people said. Point out that there is no right or wrong answer. Explain that by stressing different words (such as *active assistance* versus *input*), you can see the different ways that schools can encourage or hinder parent involvement. Point out that the comments made, such as "It depends on the existing level of parent involvement in the school" or "What matters is the expertise the parents come in with," are exactly what people should think about when promoting engagement in schools. Also, highlight issues around training needed for different types of parent involvement or other suggestions that may have come up during this discussion.

—Adapted from *Advancing Youth Development Curriculum,*
Youth Development Institute/Fund for the City of New York

2. Conference Checklist

This checklist was developed by Melissa Whipple, the coordinator of the Parent Academic Liaison (PAL) program in San Diego, as a tool to help teachers prepare for conferences with families.

Before the conference

__ 1. **Notify parents and students about:**
   - Purpose
   - Place, time, length of time
   - Child care arrangements
   - Parent planning sheet (questions to ask)

__ 2. **Prepare:**
   - Review student's folder
   - Gather samples of work
   - Gather input from students
   - Prepare materials
   - Think about what to say; avoid "educationese"

__ 3. **Plan agenda:**
   - Draw up a plan for the conference
   - Emphasize cooperation—what can both sides do?

__ 4. **Arrange environment:**
   - Place seating away from the desk
   - Make sure there will be privacy
   - See that things look welcoming and comfortable

During the conference

1. **Welcome.** Establish rapport.
2. **Set terms.** State the purpose, mention any time limits, encourage note taking, and mention options for follow-up.

3. **Lead with the positive.** Share what you see as the child's major strengths and unique qualities.

4. **Encourage.** Share information ("What do you think your child does well?") and invite comments and questions ("Do you have any questions for me?").

5. **Show.** Point out areas where there has been academic and social growth.

6. **Listen.** Pause and restate parents' words; look for verbal and nonverbal clues; invite questions.

7. **Develop an action plan.** Choose one or two areas on which to focus.

8. **Summarize.** Review the conversation and plan follow-up to check progress on the action plan.

9. **End on a positive note.** Express confidence in the child's ability to be a successful learner.

After the conference

___ 1. **Review** the conference with the child.
___ 2. **Share information** with other school staff, if needed.
___ 3. **Put it in writing**—send a follow-up note or letter.
___ 4. **Mark calendar** for planned follow-up.

3. Developing a Code of Conduct

This interactive process can ease tension and build broad agreement about student, staff, and parent conduct in and around the school.

Pick a safe place and a neutral facilitator to develop rules that will be accepted by the school community. Invite school staff, family members, student representatives, and community members to take part. Expect controversy.

Set ground rules to create a climate of respectful dialogue. Some suggestions:

+ Everyone should be encouraged to speak and be heard.
+ Listen when another person is talking—avoid side conversations.

+ If you disagree with what someone is saying, express your point of view politely when it's your turn to speak.
+ No one may insult another person.

Post these rules and ask for other ideas. When everyone agrees on the rules, start the process.

1. **Ask families, students, and staff what's important to them.** What rules would they like to set? The rules can cover a dress code, punctuality, music (what, when, and where it's appropriate to play), body art, makeup, and other aspects of style. Be prepared for rules about how teachers and staff should dress and be punctual and prepared. The rules should apply to everyone. Participants can discuss their ideas in small groups.
2. **Brainstorm proposed rules.** Write down each idea. After all the ideas are given, consolidate the duplicates.
3. **Set priorities.** Give everyone three to five colored dots to place on the proposed rules. They may put one dot on each rule they support, or put all their dots on one. Choose the rules that receive the most votes.
4. **Decide how to let people know about the rules and dress code, how they should be enforced, and what the penalties should be.** This can be done by committee or by another process similar to the one for setting the rules. Some schools will draft rules and circulate them for comment, then revise after the community has had its say. We think it's better to involve both parents and students at the start. The school council or other governance group should approve the final rules.
5. **Publish the rules, in print and on the school Web site.** Many schools publish the rules in a Code of Conduct handbook, which all teachers, families, and students receive at the beginning of the year.
6. **Determine a process for reviewing and modifying the Code of Conduct,** with participation from staff, students, families, and community members.

4. District Policy on Family-School Partnership

A district policy should be a statement of the district's commitment to the partnership concept. The policy also should be specific about how the district will support partnership, including providing on-site support and help from central office. These suggestion are modeled on the family involvement policy in San Diego public schools.

A strong policy should cover:

1. **Personnel policies that support partnership.** Cover how families may take part in staff selection, evaluation, promotion, and development. Specify expectations for the preparation of new teachers to work with families, contract time available for meeting with families, and rewards and incentives for partnership activities. We recommend that the policy support family liaison positions at each school (or at least each Title I school). Tool 5 is a job description for a family involvement coordinator.

2. **A partnership plan.** Require that every school appoint an action team and develop a plan for family-school partnership. Specify some mechanisms that schools should consider: family/parent centers, home visiting, action research teams, and mentoring programs.

3. **School-home communication.** Encourage varied approaches, such as class meetings, home visits, portfolio exhibitions, interactive newsletters, cell phones for teachers, e-mail and Web sites, automated telephone systems, use of community media and facilities, and messages in families' home languages.

4. **Ground rules for agreements with health and social service providers.** Encourage school-linked service programs, and relationships with community agencies and institutions to offer community learning opportunities for children and families, including community service by students.

5. **District- and school-level decision making.** Set requirements and guidelines for planning, decision making, and school governance entities, including parent associations and school site councils.

6. **Learning materials for families.** Authorization and encouragement for teachers to provide guidance and learning materials to aid families in supporting the learning of their own children at home and the community.

7. **Business partnerships.** Suggest guidelines for developing and implementing partnerships with local business and industry.

8. **Adult and community education.** Set guidelines that regulate and encourage the use of school facilities for out-of-school-time programs.

9. **Parent choice.** Encourage parent choice for programs within schools, between schools, between districts, and with charter or alternative schools. Provide family/consumer information services.

To add items that will satisfy the requirements for a Title I district parent involvement policy under No Child Left Behind, go to www.ed.gov/programs/titleiparta/parentinvguid.doc to see the Education Department's nonregulatory guidelines.

About the Process

San Diego's policy was developed by a task force of parent leaders, community representatives, and district staff. Meetings attracted wide interest in the community, with as many as twenty to thirty people attending. The process took a few months to develop, and the draft was then widely circulated to parent groups, community organizations, outside experts, and the teachers' union for comment.

The task force then prepared a final version for the superintendent to present for board approval, which included a request to establish and staff a parent involvement department. Jeana Preston, who facilitated the process, became the first director for parent and community involvement in the district after the policy was approved.

About the process, Preston comments, "As I recall, just about every word was discussed and negotiated, because when you want a clear, brief document without miles of explanation, individual words become powerful expressions of intent." (To see the entire policy, go to www.sandi.net/parents/parent_facts.pdf.)

Tools to Support
Your Work

· · ·

5. Family Involvement Coordinator Sample Job Description

This description lists seven major tasks that family involvement coordinators are expected to accomplish, along with some ideas for activities and programs to carry them out. The coordinator will need to enlist volunteers—it will take more than one person to do all these tasks well.

1. **Help the school to develop a family-friendly school climate. This should be done in cooperation with the principal, teachers, parent organization, and other staff. For example:**

- Conduct an annual "Welcoming School Walk-Through" with parents and teachers to make sure the school welcomes families and treats them with respect. (For more information about the walk-through, see Chapter 10.)
- Work with school staff to use the walk-through results to make improvements (e.g., signs, directions, greeting at front office, displays of student work, regular visiting hours).
- Create a comfortable family resource room where families can meet, get to know each other, and discuss their interests and concerns. Stock the family room with books, games, and learning materials that families can borrow.
- Develop a school family involvement policy with input and approval from parents and teachers. (To satisfy the requirements for a school parent involvement policy under Title I of No Child Left Behind, go to www.ed.gov/programs/titleiparta/parent invguid.doc. For ideas on developing a policy, see tool 12.)

2. **Develop programs and activities designed to engage families in improving student achievement. Plan these in collaboration with an action team of families, teachers, parent organizations, business-community partners, and the principal. For example:**

- Design two family involvement programs/activities each quarter to help families participate more effectively in improving their children's learning. For example, family reading activities, math and science trainings, and career and college planning events. Use student achievement data to target skills that need to be strengthened.

- Help families understand standards and assessments, students test scores, rubrics, and the school report card.
- Facilitate and organize other parent meetings and workshops, as parents request.
- Collaborate with school staff, community members, partners and families to develop programs and activities geared to reach families who are underrepresented because of social, economic, racial, and/or language barriers.

3. **Help teachers/staff and families develop strong partnerships and enhance communication between parents/families and school staff. For example:**

- Encourage and support school staff to reach out to families. Create ways for families and teachers to meet face-to-face and to know each other, such as class meetings, breakfasts with the principal, and getting-to-know-you activities at PTA meetings.
- Develop monthly family contact logs for teachers with families' telephone numbers, so that teachers can be in touch with families at least once a month.
- Work with teachers and other staff to develop learning kits that families can take home to use with their children.
- Provide administrators, teachers, and support staff with research articles and handouts for parents. Staff can develop their own resource kits and notebooks with this material.
- Be a liaison between families and teachers when problems arise, more information needs to be shared, or cultural differences are a barrier.
- Develop a "room parent" or "department parent" (in middle and high schools) system to help teachers communicate important information and deadlines to parents.
- Arrange for translation and interpretation services for meetings, parent-teacher conferences, telephone calls, and notes home.
- Organize tours of the community for school staff to get know

families and neighborhoods better and to identify families' concerns and ideas for improvement. (You might partner with parents and community organizations to help organize this event.)

• Communicate regularly with principal about parents' and families' ideas and concerns.

4. **Develop and implement effective family involvement strategies and activities to empower students and their families. For example:**

✦ Invite parents to participate in school committees and in the school's parent organization. Work with those groups to help them be welcoming and supportive of new members.

✦ Recruit parents to be a part of school/district decision-making committees and meetings. Be sure they have information and background materials to be informed members.

✦ Document parent/community activities through visual portfolios that include sign-in sheets, flyers, and pictures.

✦ Invite families to participate in professional development training along with staff.

✦ Ask parents to evaluate parent meetings and parent/family workshops.

✦ Survey families/school community and school personnel to assess the effectiveness of your school's partnership program.

5. **Take part in opportunities for professional development. For example:**

✦ Attend all meetings and training activities for family involvement coordinators and share ideas and experiences.

✦ Keep school staff updated about family involvement activities in your school. For example, create a bulletin board about the activities, with pictures.

✦ Maintain a portfolio of all major activities, with sign-in sheets and photographs.

✦ Take advantage of professional development to learn new knowledge and skills.

✦ Identify and take part in learning opportunities, such as conferences and meetings.

6. **Participate in and support district activities and programs for families. For example:**

✦ Work closely with district family involvement and community resources coordinator.
✦ Help organize and recruit for district events and activities.
✦ Publicize and promote district programs for families, such as advocacy workshops and literacy activities (as it applies to your school).
✦ File quarterly reports on the family involvement activities at your school.

7. **Help to recruit partners to become part of the district's family involvement program. For example:**

✦ Reach out to local community groups and businesses to find out how they would like promote family involvement in your school.
✦ Work with community partners and families to identify resources for families in the community. Make sure that teachers and counselors have up-to-date referral information on community services to give families.
✦ Attend community meetings that will help you connect to community resources for families in your school.

Qualifications and skills:

✦ Understands class and cultural backgrounds of families and how to interpret culture of school to them
✦ Thinks and acts in ways that respect ethnic, cultural and language diversity
✦ Communicates successfully with teachers, families, administrators, and students (including being bilingual, if needed)
✦ Is computer-literate
✦ Has experience in collaborative leadership
✦ Displays interpersonal skills

- ✦ Advocates for children and parents
- ✦ Shows organizational skills
- ✦ Writes and speaks clearly and well

This job description was developed by Anne Henderson and Karen Parker Thompson, coordinator of family involvement and community resources for the Alexandria City Public Schools in Virginia, with advice from Jeana Preston of the Parent Center in San Diego.

6. Family Welcome Questionnaire

This questionnaire is designed to help school staff learn more about their students' families. We recommend that the questions below be asked face-to-face, rather than in a written survey. This can be done in several steps and places, such as when students enroll in the school, at the school open house, at parent-teacher conferences, and at parent activities. The family-school coordinator or parent liaison can do this, and community groups can help. **(It is important to emphasize that this information will be kept strictly confidential.)**

Dear Families:

Our school wants to know more about its families and their rich and interesting cultural heritage. With this information, the Family and Community Involvement Action Team can plan better programs to build on our students' home cultures. We also want to learn more about how families would like to help.

First, tell us about your cultural background:

- • What languages are spoken in your home?
- • In what country (or state) were you born?
- • Tell us about your family's beliefs about the importance of education.
- • What does your family do to help your children learn?
- • What are your family's traditions? What activities do you do as a family? How do you celebrate birthdays and other important family events?

- Who is in your extended family (grandparents, aunts and uncles, cousins, close friends)?

Second, tell us how you would like to be involved at home and at school, and what would help you be more involved.

- What are some ways you would like to be involved?
- What could the school do to help you be more involved?
- What are your working hours?
- When are the most convenient times for activities and meetings at school?
- What are your transportation needs?
- What are your hobbies, skills, talents, and interests?

Finally, tell us about your concerns, perspectives, and ideas:

- What would you like us to know about your child? What are his/her interests?
- What is working well for your child at school? What isn't?
- What are some ways you would like to school to recognize and teach about your child's culture?
- Are there any ways that you feel your culture could be better respected at the school?
- Do you have some things that reflect your culture and background that you could share with us (for example, pictures, weavings, carvings, stories, musical instruments, songs, traditions, naming ceremonies)?
- How could you help the school reach out to other families in your community?

Many questions suggested here appear in Sabrina Hope King and A. Lin Goodwin, *Culturally Responsive Parent Involvement* (Washington, D.C.: American Association of Colleges of Teacher Education, 2003). For a free copy, go to www.aacte.org/Publications/kinggoodwin.pdf.

7. Homework Survey

This survey was developed by staff at Wyman Elementary School in St. Louis, Missouri, in collaboration with students and faculty in the Education School at St. Louis University. A committee of teachers, the parent coordinator, and administrators used the results to plan activities for families and design learning materials that families can use at home. The following questions were designed to find out several things about what families do at home to support and encourage children's learning:

1. When parents are available to help with homework
2. What children do after school
3. What control and structure parents exercise over homework
4. How aware of homework parents are on a daily basis
5. Parents' experience of and attitudes toward homework
6. Supports parents would like in order to help their children with homework

Survey Questions:

1. Is a parent home after school? ☐ Yes   ☐ No

2. Do parent(s) work outside the home? ☐ Yes   ☐ No

3. What time do parents get home after work?   ☐ 1–3:30 P.M.
   ☐ 4–6 P.M.   ☐ 6:15–7:30 P.M.   ☐ 7:45 P.M.–8 A.M.

4. What do children do after school? (Circle all that apply)
   Study   Practice music   Watch TV   Play
   Do chores (list) _____
   (*Tip: use pictures to show choices*)

5. Do you have a set time for homework?
   ☐ Yes   ☐ Sometimes   ☐ No

6. Do your children do their homework together?
   ☐ Yes   ☐ Sometimes   ☐ No

7. Is homework done in the same place every day?
    ☐ Yes   ☐ Sometimes   ☐ No

8. How many times do you have to tell your children to do their homework?
    ☐ 3+   ☐ 2   ☐ 1   ☐ none

9. How do you know when your children have homework?
    ☐ I ask   ☐ They tell me   ☐ Teacher sends home a schedule

10. Does your child have time at school to do homework?
    ☐ Yes   ☐ Sometimes   ☐ No

11. Where are you when homework is being done?
    ☐ Close by   ☐ In house   ☐ At work
    ☐ Other _____

12. What are you (or other adult) doing while child is doing homework?
    ☐ Helping child   ☐ Preparing food
    ☐ Cleaning house   ☐ Watching TV
    ☐ Other _____

13. Do you think your kids are just like you were about homework?
    ☐ No
    ☐ Yes, I usually enjoyed my homework
    ☐ Yes, I usually hated doing homework

14. When I was in school, I had someone to help me with homework.
    ☐ Yes   ☐ Sometimes   ☐ No

15. Who helped you?
    ☐ Parent   ☐ Other relative   ☐ Older child
    ☐ Someone else _____

16. Do you have a high school diploma or a GED?
    ☐ Yes   ☐ No

17. If no, would you like to obtain a GED?   ☐ Yes   ☐ No

18. What do you need to help your children with their homework?

19. Which types of homework do you like to help with? (Circle all that apply.)

    History   Math   Reading   English   Science   Art   Building things

20. Which ones do you *not* like to help with? (Circle all that apply.)

    History   Math   Reading   English   Science   Art   Building things

21. In which subjects would you like to improve your skills? (Circle all that apply.)

    History   Math   Reading   English   Science   Art   Building things

8. Needs Assessment Survey

This survey is based on one used in the Boston Public Schools to find out from parents what help they would like to support their children's learning.

Dear Parents and Families:

We'd like to hear from you about how we can help you support your child's learning. Please use this checklist to tell us where you could use extra information, advice, and guidance from our school staff. Check as many boxes below as you wish.

For all grades:

Academics:
○ Helping my child with reading
○ Helping my child with writing
○ Helping my child with math
○ Helping my child with other subjects _____

Homework and out-of-school time:
- ○ Helping my child to complete homework
- ○ Helping my child with how to manage time
- ○ Helping my child perform well on the [name of state test]

Motivation and behavior:
- ○ Helping my child with his/her attitude about school
- ○ Helping my child improve behavior at school and at home
- ○ Helping my child with social relationships and peer pressure

Other Supports:

_____

_____

Add for middle and high school students:

Planning for the future:
- ○ Helping my child with college and career planning
- ○ Helping my child choose courses and programs

9. Parent Review

This review consists of questions to ask parents about their children's interests and talents, strengths and fears. It also asks parents to provide a personal message about their child, if they wish to. This can be done as an interview, which we recommend, or a survey form. An interview builds the personal relationship and will yield more information. For parents with limited English or formal education, an interview in their home language is a must.

Tell us about your child

Who is your child's best friend?

What does your child like about school?

What are your child's successes in school? What are your child's challenges in school?

Does your child feel liked and accepted at school? If not, why not?

What are some of your child's interests and hobbies?

What does your child feel is his/her greatest talent or skill? Do you agree?

Does your child enjoy reading and being read to?

Does your child enjoy doing math?

What challenges does your child have in math/in reading?

Is there anything you want me to know about your child?

What does your child want to do and be when he/she grows up?

What are some of your child's favorite activities?

What chores does your child like to do?

Follow-up

How should we stay in touch about how your child is doing?

Please let me know how to contact you:

Here is my contact information:

Final Question

Please tell me about your hopes and dreams for your child this year. (Please write it here, or contact me.)

(Note to teacher: When you ask this final question, be quiet and really listen. Then paraphrase what the parent has said, to make sure you understand each other. Some of the other questions could be used during any silences. The point is to provide parents ways of offering information that would be of help to the teacher, as well to create a positive way to focus on the child.)

This review was developed with advice from Melissa Whipple, the director of the Parent Academic Liaison program in San Diego.

10. Parent Volunteer Survey

This survey was designed by East Boston High School to find out how parents would like to contribute to the high school and to learn about what would encourage them to come to the school.

Dear Families:

[Name of school] and its Family Center are conducting this survey to better serve parents, with the ultimate goal of improving your student's and family's education.

Parent's Name _____ Student's Name _____

Address _____

Phone # _____ E-mail address _____

Work phone, cell phone, beeper, etc. _____

What are the best times for you to come to the school?
☐ Mornings ☐ Afternoons ☐ Evenings ☐ Weekends

[Name of school] encourages parent involvement. Would you like to be involved with the school? ☐ Yes ☐ No
If yes, check what you would feel comfortable doing:
☐ Make phone calls to other parents ☐ Classroom speaker/assistant
☐ Help out in the offices or library
☐ Work on important school topics ☐ Attend field trips
☐ Help plan events ☐ Join school site council
☐ Other _____

Is there anything that prevents you from becoming involved that we could help you with?
☐ Getting excused from work, work hours ☐ Child care
☐ Transportation issues ☐ Interpretation needed
☐ Other _____

Do you know how much time high school students should spend on homework each day?
   What do you think is the correct answer?*
   ☐ 1 hour ☐ 1 $\frac{1}{2}$ hours ☐ 2 $\frac{1}{2}$ hours

Are you worried about your son or daughter passing the state test?
☐ Yes ☐ No

What do you need to know about the state test? _____

_____

Students and families have many talents. What can you share with
[name of school]?

☐ Cooking ☐ Languages spoken ☐ Art ☐ Computer skills
☐ Sewing ☐ Trade skills (such as carpentry) ☐ Music
☐ Other _____

What is your opinion of [name of school]? _____

_____

Would you like to be notified of various meetings and events?

☐ Yes ☐ No

What is the best way to notify you? ☐ Call on phone
☐ Mail a letter home ☐ Put notices in the newspaper

Do you mind if you are called at work for these notices?

☐ Yes, call me ☐ No, not at work
Work telephone number _____
Best time to reach you at home _____

If the school offered classes, what would you be interested in?

☐ Computers ☐ General education
☐ English as a Second Language ☐ College/advanced level courses
☐ Job skills (interviewing, resume writing)
☐ How to help my student succeed at school
☐ Parent training (such as Leadership Academy, Title I workshops,
  other workshops)
☐ Other _____

Thank you for taking the time to complete this survey. Please return
to the homeroom teacher or mail/fax to: [Family Center Coordinator's
name, address of school, telephone number, fax number]

* The correct time is ___ hours. (East Boston High recommends 2 ½
hours.) If you do not see your student spending time on homework, ask

both the student and teacher why. The school administration needs to know if there is a problem with students not doing homework or teachers not giving it/correcting it.

11. School Climate Survey

This tool can be used to develop an action plan, to plan activities for staff and families, and to set priorities for the school improvement team, school council, or other committees.

Dear Families:

We want our school to be the best it can be. Please fill out this survey and tell us what you think are the school's strong points and what you think could be better. Your comments and ideas will be very welcome. If you would like to help tally and analyze the results, please let us know.

—The Family and Community Involvement Action Team
[list names and contact information]

Caring Environment

1. When I walk into this school, I feel welcome.
   - ◯ Always   ◯ Almost always   ◯ Sometimes
   - ◯ Rarely   ◯ Never

2. I am treated with respect at this school.
   - ◯ Always   ◯ Almost always   ◯ Sometimes
   - ◯ Rarely   ◯ Never

3. This school respects my cultural heritage.
   - ◯ Always   ◯ Almost always   ◯ Sometimes
   - ◯ Rarely   ◯ Never

4. Students at my child's school are treated fairly no matter what their race or cultural background.
   - ◯ Always   ◯ Almost always   ◯ Sometimes
   - ◯ Rarely   ◯ Never

5. I feel welcome at PTA/parent group meetings.
   ○ Always   ○ Almost always   ○ Sometimes
   ○ Rarely   ○ Never

Problem Solving

6. I have a good working relationship with my child's teacher.
   ○ Always   ○ Almost always   ○ Sometimes
   ○ Rarely   ○ Never

7. I can talk to the school principal when I need to.
   ○ Always   ○ Almost always   ○ Sometimes
   ○ Rarely   ○ Never

8. This school has a clear process for addressing my concerns.
   ○ Always   ○ Almost always   ○ Sometimes
   ○ Rarely   ○ Never

9. If the school can't help me, I know they will refer me to someone who can.
   ○ Always   ○ Almost always   ○ Sometimes
   ○ Rarely   ○ Never

Communication

10. My child's teacher lets me know right away if my child is having a problem with (circle all that apply):
    Behavior
    Fitting in with other students
    Homework
    Special projects
    Tests

11. It's easy to get a translator if I need one.
    ○ Always   ○ Almost always   ○ Sometimes
    ○ Rarely   ○ Never

12. Staff at my child's school consult me and other families before making important decisions.
  - ○ Always   ○ Almost always   ○ Sometimes
  - ○ Rarely   ○ Never

13. I understand the rules and requirements about student dress, language, and behavior.
  - ○ Always   ○ Almost always   ○ Sometimes
  - ○ Rarely   ○ Never

Student Progress

14. My child's teacher keeps me well informed about how my child is doing in school.
  - ○ Always   ○ Almost always   ○ Sometimes
  - ○ Rarely   ○ Never

15. I understand the standards my child is supposed to meet.
  - ○ Always   ○ Almost always   ○ Sometimes
  - ○ Rarely   ○ Never

16. My child's teacher and the school give me useful information about how to improve my child's progress.
  - ○ Always   ○ Almost always   ○ Sometimes
  - ○ Rarely   ○ Never

17. At this school, students feel challenged to do their best.
  - ○ Always   ○ Almost always   ○ Sometimes
  - ○ Rarely   ○ Never

Satisfaction

18. I am very satisfied with the quality of this school.
  - ○ Always   ○ Almost always   ○ Sometimes
  - ○ Rarely   ○ Never

19. I would recommend this school to family and friends with children.
  - ○ Always   ○ Almost always   ○ Sometimes
  - ○ Rarely   ○ Never

What grade is your child in? List all if you have more than one child in the school. _____

My child is (check only one box):
- ☐ African American
- ☐ Asian American
- ☐ Caucasian/White
- ☐ Latin American/Hispanic
- ☐ Native American
- ☐ Other (please specify) _____

What is the school doing that is most helpful to you as a parent?

_____

Share one thing that you wish the school would do to improve the learning experience for you and your child. _____

_____

Thank you for your participation.

Please return this survey to:

This survey is adapted from one used in Alexandria, Virginia, public schools in 2003. It was developed by Karen Parker Thompson, coordinator of family involvement and community resources for the Alexandria City Public Schools, Anne T. Henderson, and Scott Broetzmann of Customer Care Management and Consulting.

12. Tips for Developing a School Family Involvement Policy

A policy commits a school to certain goals and actions. A family involvement policy describes effective partnership between the school and its families, and lays out how and when that will happen and who will do what.

What Questions Should Your Policy Answer?

- What is the school's vision of the importance of working closely with families?
- How will the school be family-friendly?
- In what ways will teachers be expected to communicate with families on student progress?
- How will the school build personal relationships with families?
- How will the school honor families' contributions and build on their strengths?
- How will the school work with families to improve student achievement, and what does the school expect families to do?
- How will the school help and support families to do what's expected?

What Should the Policy Include?

1. **A vision statement** that says what the school community believes about the importance of family-school partnership to high student achievement.
2. **Specific steps** that the school and families will take to work as partners to improve achievement, such as a school-family compact, family learning activities, personal learning plans, and student support teams. Include indicators to look for as evidence that the school is really doing this.
3. **Terms of engagement,** such as times for parents to observe in classrooms, availability of interpreters and translation, principal's office hours, opportunities for parent-teacher communication, and so on.
4. **An indication of who will be responsible** for carrying out the policy, including school staff, parents, and community members.
5. **Resources,** such as funding, space, equipment, and staff time and positions.

The policy also needs to spell out how it will be developed, promoted, and assessed:

- How parents, school staff, community members, and students will be involved in developing and approving the policy
- Guidelines for measuring whether the policy is working, such as increased parent involvement in school activities and improved student attendance
- How parents, school staff, and community members will learn about what the policy says

Steps to Develop a Policy

1. Bring together an action team that represents the people who will carry out the policy, including parent leaders who reflect the diverse families in the school.
2. Find out how families and school staff want to work together to improve achievement. What they are interested in doing and learning about? What supports do they need? Focus groups, surveys, and interviews are good ways to do this.
3. Revise the existing policy to respond to current needs and interests. Focus on action—what needs to happen and when.

What Practices Should a Policy Promote?

Above all, the policy must focus on improving student achievement. The research on family involvement and student achievement finds that these practices can improve student learning:

- Being family-friendly—staff are warm, helpful, and welcoming to families of all backgrounds, and form relationships with families through one-to-one and small group contact
- Offering activities and programs for families that are clearly linked to improving achievement
- Providing opportunities for families to volunteer or contribute both at home and at school
- Informing families through workshops and other activities on how to improve their children's learning
- Bridging cultural differences by understanding families' home cultures, identifying their strengths and assets, and making sure all have chances to contribute

- Encouraging families to be effective advocates for their children: help them take more challenging classes and plan for postsecondary education and a career
- Building the capacity of teachers, parents, and other school staff to work together through training and professional development

Sample Sections of an Elementary School Policy

Vision

Parents are their children's first and most important teachers. Research tells us that parent involvement makes a big difference. When schools welcome families, establish personal relationships among families and staff, help parents understand how the system works, and encourage family-staff collaboration to improve student achievement, students do better in school—and the schools get better.

Our school is committed to being family-friendly and to working as partners with our families to help *all* our students learn to high levels. Our school encourages families to be:

- Teachers of their children at home
- Supporters of our school and of public education
- Advocates for their own and other children
- Decision makers in school policy and practice

Expectations

Here is what we expect of the school for it to be fully family-friendly:

1. **A welcoming environment**
- Friendly signs welcome visitors and explain how to get around the building.
- Standards of welcoming behavior apply to *all* staff, including front office staff, bus drivers, security guards, custodians, and cafeteria workers.
- Visitors and callers are greeted politely and right away and can get information easily.

- A comfortable family resource room is maintained as a place for parents to meet, and lends books, games, and educational information for families to use at home.

2. **Programs and activities to engage families in improving student achievement**
- Current student work is displayed throughout the building, so that visitors can understand the purpose of the work and the high standards it is to meet.
- Programs and activities help families understand what their children are learning and promote high standards.
- Workshops, learning kits, and other activities show families how to help their children at home—and respond to what families say they want to know about.
- The school reports to parents about student progress and how teachers, parents, and community members can work together to make improvements.

3. **Strong relationships between teachers and families**
- The school welcomes new families, offers tours, and introduces them to staff and other families. Bilingual speakers are available to help families.
- Teachers and families meet face-to-face and get to know each other through class meetings, breakfasts, home visits, and class observations.
- Teachers or advisors make personal contact with each family at least once a month.
- A family liaison helps teachers connect to families and bridge barriers of language and culture.

4. **Opportunities for families to develop their skills, self-confidence, and contacts**
- Families are involved in planning how they would like to be involved at the school.
- School committees and the PTA/PTO reflect the diversity of the school community and actively recruit and welcome families from all backgrounds.

- The school is open and accessible—it is easy for parents to meet with the principal, talk to teachers and counselors, and bring up issues and concerns.
- Parents develop school improvement projects and do action research—survey other families, observe in classrooms, review materials, and visit other schools and programs.

5. **Professional development for families and staff on how to work together productively**

- Families learn how the school system works and how to be effective advocates for their children.
- Teachers learn about successful approaches to working with families of diverse cultural backgrounds.
- Families and staff can learn together how to collaborate to improve student achievement.
- The school reaches out to identify and draw in local community resources that can assist staff and families.

About Process

This policy was developed by a committee of parents, teachers, support staff, and community members. Here is what they did:

1. They conducted focus groups with families, staff, and community members, and did a school climate survey to find out what was important to them. (See tool 11 for a sample School Climate Survey.)
2. They drafted a policy and distributed it widely for comment.
3. They revised the policy using the comments and had it ratified by the school council, the parent organization, and the faculty.
4. They pledged to revise the policy every two years, using the process described above.

To be sure that your policy will satisfy the requirements for a school parent involvement policy under Title I of No Child Left Behind, go to www.ed.gov/programs/titleiparta/parentinvguid.doc to see the Education Department's nonregulatory guidelines.

Selected Bibliography

Bryk, Anthony S., and Barbara Schneider. *Trust in Schools: A Core Resource for Improvement.* New York: Russell Sage Foundation, 2002.

Chavkin, Nancy, ed. *Families and Schools in a Pluralistic Society.* Albany: State University of New York Press, 1993.

Clark, Reginald. "Ten Hypotheses About What Predicts Student Achievement for African-American Students and All Other Students: What the Research Shows." In Walter Allen et al., eds., *African American Education,* 155–77. Oxford, UK: Elsevier Science, 2002.

Comer, James et al. *Rallying the Whole Village: The Comer Process for Reforming Education.* New York: Teachers College Press, 1996.

Constantino, Steven M. *Engaging All Families: Creating a Positive School Culture by Putting Research into Practice.* Lanham, MD: Scarecrow Press, 2003.

Cortes, E., Jr. "Making the Public the Leaders in Education Reform." *Education Week,* November 22, 1995, 34.

Crane, Claire et al. *Becoming a Community School.* Dorchester, MA: Project for School Innovation, 2004.

Cushman, Kathleen. *Fires in the Bathroom: Advice for Teachers from High School Students.* New York: The New Press, 2003.

Davies, Don. "Family Participation in Decision-Making and Advocacy." In Diana Hiatt-Michael, *Promising Practices in Family Involvement in Schools,* 107–51. Greenwich, CT: Information Age Publishing, 2001.

Decker, Larry, and Virginia Decker. *Home, School, and Community Partnership.* Lanham, MD: Scarecrow Press, 2003.

Delgado Gaitan, Concha. *Involving Latino Families in Schools.* Thousand

Oaks, CA: Corwin Press, 2004.

Delpit, Lisa D. *Other People's Children: Cultural Conflict in the Classroom.* New York: The New Press, 1995.

————."The Silenced Dialog: Power and Pedagogy in Educating Other Peoples' Children." In Lois Weis and Michele Fine, eds., *Beyond Silenced Voices: Class, Race and Gender in the United States.* Albany: State University of New York Press, 1993.

Diamond, John B. et al. "Teachers' Expectations and Sense of Responsibility for Student Learning: The Importance of Race, Class, and Organizational Habitus." *Anthropology and Education Quarterly* 35, no. 1 (2004): 75–98.

Dryfoos, J. G. *Full Service Schools.* San Francisco: Jossey-Bass, 1994.

Ellis, Debbie, and Kendra Hughes. *Partnerships by Design: Cultivating Effective School-Family-Community Partnerships.* Chicago: Northwest Regional Educational Laboratory, 2002.

Epstein, Joyce L. "Effects on Student Achievement of Teachers' Practices of Parental Involvement." *Advances in Reading/Language Research* 10 (1991): 261–76.

————. *School, Family, and Community Partnerships: Preparing Educators and Improving Schools.* Boulder, CO: Westview Press, 2001.

Epstein, Joyce L., Mavis G. Sanders, Beth S. Simon, Karen Clark Salinas, and Natalie R. Jansorn. *School Family and Community Partnerships: Your Handbook for Action,* 2nd ed. Thousand Oaks, CA: Corwin Press, 2002.

Ferguson, C. *Developing a Collaborative Team Approach to Support Family and Community Connections with Schools: What Can School Leaders Do?* Austin, TX: Southwest Educational Development Laboratory, 2005.

Gutman, Leslie M., and Carol Midgely. "The Role of Protective Factors in Supporting the Academic Achievement of Poor African American Students During the Middle School Transition." *Journal of Youth and Adolescence* 29, no. 2 (2000): 223–48.

Henderson, Anne T. *No Child Left Behind: What's in It for Parents.* Lexington, KY: Prichard Committee for Academic Excellence, 2003.

Henderson, Anne T. et al. *The Case for Parent Leadership.* Lexington, KY: Prichard Committee for Academic Excellence, 2004.

Henderson, Anne T., and Karen L. Mapp. *A New Wave of Evidence: The Impact of School, Family and Community Connections on Student Achievement.* Austin, TX: Southwest Educational Development Laboratory, 2002.

Hiatt-Michael, Diana. *Promising Practices for Family Involvement in Schools.* Greenwich, CT: Information Age Publishing, 2001.

Hoover-Dempsey, Kathleen, and Howard Sandler. "Why Do Parents Become Involved in Their Children's Education?" *Review of Educational Research* 67, no. 1 (1997): 3–42.

Institute for Responsive Education. *Supporting Parent Leaders: Stories of Dedication, Determination, and Inspiration.* Boston: Institute for Responsive Education, 2002.

Jackson, Anthony W. et al. *Making the Most of Middle School: A Field Guide for Parents and Others.* New York: Teachers College Press, 2004.

Johnson, Vivian R. "The Family Center: Making Room for Parents." *Principal Magazine,* September 2000, 27–31.

———. "Replicating What Works." In *New Ways of Thinking About Parental Involvement*, 7–8. Baltimore, MD: Center on Families, Communities, Schools and Children's Learning, 1994.

King, Sabrina Hope, and A. Lin Goodwin. *Culturally Responsive Parent Involvement*. Washington, DC: American Association of Colleges of Teacher Education, 2003.

Kretzmann, Jody, and John L. McKnight. *Building Communities from the Inside Out: A Path Toward Finding and Mobilizing a Community's Assets*. Evanston, IL: Institute for Policy Research, Northwestern University, 1993.

Kugler, Eileen G. *Debunking the Middle Class Myth: Why Diverse Schools Are Good for All Kids*. Lanham, MD: Scarecrow Press, Inc., 2002.

Ladson-Billings, Gloria. *The Dreamkeepers: Successful Teachers of African American Children*. San Francisco: Josey-Bass Publishers, 1994.

Lareau, Annette. "Social Class Differences in Family-School Relationships: The Importance of Cultural Capital." *Sociology of Education* 60 (1987): 73–85.

Lareau, Annette, and Erin Horvath. "Moments of Social Inclusion and Exclusion: Race, Class and Cultural Capital in Family-School Relationships." *Sociology of Education* 72, 1 (1999): 37–53.

Lewis, Ann, and Anne T. Henderson. *Urgent Message: Families Crucial to School Reform*. Washington, DC: Center for Law and Education, 1997.

Lightfoot, Sara Lawrence. *The Essential Conversation: What Parents and Teachers Can Learn from Each Other*. New York: Random House, 2003.

Mapp, Karen L. "Having Their Say: Parents Describe Why and How They Are Engaged in Their Children's Education." *School Community Journal* 13, 1 (2003): 35–64.

Mathews, David. *Is There a Public for Public Schools?* Dayton, OH: Kettering Foundation Press, 1996.

Mediratta, Kavitha et al. *Constituents of Change: Community Organizations and Public Education Reform*. New York: Community Involvement Program, Institute for Education and Social Policy, New York University, 2004.

———. *Organizing for School Reform: How Communities Are Finding Their Voices and Reclaiming Their Public Schools*. New York: Institute for Education and Social Policy, New York University, 2002.

Mediratta, Kavitha, and Norm Fruchter. *From Governance to Accountability: Building Relationships that Make Schools Work*. New York: Institute for Education and Social Policy, New York University, 2003.

Moore, Don. *What Makes These Schools Stand Out: Chicago Elementary Schools with a Seven-Year Trend of Improved Reading Achievement*. Chicago: Designs for Change, 1998.

Moulthrop, Daniel, Nínive Clements Calegari, and Dave Eggers. *Teachers Have It Easy: The Big Sacrifices and Small Salaries of America's Teachers*. New York: The New Press, 2005.

National Coalition for Parent Involvement in Education. *Developing Family-School Partnerships: Guidelines for Schools and School Districts*. Washington, DC: National Coalition for Parent Involvement in Education, 2001.

National PTA. *Building Successful Partnerships: A Guide for Developing Parent and Family Involvement Programs*. Bloomington, IN: National Educational Service, 2000.

———. *National Standards for Parent/Community Involvement Programs*. Chicago: National PTA, 1998.

O'Hearn Parents and Teachers. *Including Every Parent*. Dorchester, MA: Project for School Innovation, 2003.

Patrikakou, Evanthia N. et al., eds. *School-Family Partnerships for Children's Success*. New York: Teachers College Press, 2005.

Perry, Theresa, Claude Steele, and Asa G. Hilliard III. *Young, Gifted and Black*. Boston: Beacon Press, 2003.

Polite, Lillian, and Elizabeth Baird Saenger. "A Pernicious Silence: Confronting Race in the Elementary Classroom." *Phi Delta Kappan*, 85, 4 (2003): 274–78.

Putnam, Robert. *Bowling Alone*. New York: Touchstone, 2000.

Rich, Dorothy. *MegaSkills*. Boston: Houghton Mifflin Company, 1992.

Rothstein, Richard. *Class and Schools: Using Social, Economic and Educational Reform to Close the Black-White Achievement Gap*. Washington, DC: Economic Policy Institute, 2004.

Salinas, Karen, and N. Jansorn. *Promising Partnership Practices 2004*. Baltimore: Johns Hopkins University Center on School, Family, and Community Partnerships, 2004.

Scribner, Jay D. et al. "Building Collaborative Relations with Parents." In P. Reyes et al., eds. *Lessons from High-Performing Hispanic Schools*. New York: Teachers College Press, 1999.

Seeley, David S. *Education Through Partnership*. Cambridge, MA: Ballinger, 1981.

Shirley, Dennis. *Community Organizing for Urban School Reform*. Austin: University of Texas Press, 1997.

Swap, Susan M. *Developing Home-School Partnerships: From Concept to Practice*. New York: Teachers College Press, 1993.

Weiss, Heather, Holly Kreider, M. Elena Lopez, and Celina M. Chatman, eds. *Preparing Educators to Involve Families: From Theory to Practice*. Thousand Oaks, CA: Sage Publications, 2005.

Notes

Chapter 1: Introduction

1. Anne T. Henderson and Karen L. Mapp, *A New Wave of Evidence: The Impact of School, Family and Community Connections on Student Achievement* (Austin, TX: Southwest Educational Development Laboratory, 2002), 7. Available at www.sedl.org/connections/research-syntheses.htm.

2. Public Agenda, "A Lot Easier Said than Done: Parents Talk About Raising Children in Today's America," 2002. The article is available in the Research Studies tab at www.public agenda.org.

3. Atelia Melaville, "Learning Together: The Developing Field of School-Community Initiatives," in Larry Decker and Virginia Decker, eds., *Home, School, and Community Partnership* (Lanham, MD: Scarecrow Press, 2003), 12.

4. Randy Capps et al., *The New Demography of America's Schools: Immigration and the No Child Left Behind Act* (Washington, DC: Urban Institute, 2005), 5. For the complete report, go to www.urban.org/UploadedPDF/311230_new_demography.pdf.

5. National Center for Children in Poverty, Columbia University, www.nccp.org/fact.html (accessed May 2, 2006).

6. Gary Orfield, Daniel Losen, Johanna Wald, and Christopher B. Swanson, *Losing Our Future: How Minority Youth Are Being Left Behind by the Graduation Rate Crisis* (Washington, DC: Urban Institute, 2004). For the complete report, go to: www.urban.org/url.cfm?ID=410936.

7. For more information, go to www.nces.gov.

8. Arthur Reynolds and Melissa Clements, "Parental Involvement and Children's School Success," in Evanthia N. Patrikakou et al., eds., *School-Family Partnerships: Promoting the Social, Emotional, and Academic Growth of Children* (New York: Teachers College Press, 2005).

9. H. L. Hodgkinson, *Leaving Too Many Children Behind* (Washington, DC: Institute for Educational Leadership, 2003), 1–2, 4. Available at www.iel.org/pubs/manychildren.pdf.

10. Joyce L. Epstein, "Effects on Student Achievement of Teachers' Practices of Parental Involvement," *Advances in Reading/Language Research* 5 (1991): 261–76.

11. Center for Community Change, "Organized Teachers, Organized Parents," in *Education Organizing* 16 (2004): 9.

12. Anne T. Henderson, *No Child Left Behind: What's in It for Parents* (Lexington, KY: Prichard Committee, 2003), 7–15.

Chapter 2: What Is a Family-School Partnership Supposed to Look Like?

1. Other versions of this four-part framework appear in Anne Henderson, Bonnie Jacob, Adam Kernan-Schloss, and Bev Raimondo, *The Case for Parent Leadership* (Lexington, KY: Prichard Committee for Academic Excellence, 2003), 11–12, and in Center for Law and Education, *Urgent Message for Parents* (Washington, DC: CLE, 1999), 9–10.

Chapter 3: Ready, Set, Go!

1. Sara Lawrence Lightfoot, *The Essential Conversation: What Parents and Teachers Can Learn from Each Other* (New York: Random House, 2003), 109.
2. John Immerwahr, "Great Expectations: How the Public and Parents—White, African-American and Hispanic—View Higher Education" (New York: Public Agenda, May 2000, #4).
3. Luis Moll, C. Amanti, D. Neffi, and N. Gonzalez, "Funds of Knowledge for Teaching: Using a Qualitative Approach to Connect Home and Classrooms," *Theory into Practice* 31, no. 2 (1992): 132–41.
4. Cited in Susan Black, "Respecting Differences: Diverse learners can blossom in culturally responsive classrooms," *American School Board Journal*/ASBJ.com, January 2006. Go to http://asbj.com/2006/01/0106research.html.
5. Kathleen Hoover-Dempsey and Howard Sandler, "Why Do Parents Become Involved in Their Children's Education?" *Review of Educational Research* 67, no. 1 (1997): 3–42.
6. Richard F. Elmore, "The Politics of Education Reform," *Issues in Science and Technology,* fall 1997, 13.
7. Rick Dufour, "Leading Edge: Are You Looking Out the Window or in a Mirror?" *Journal of Staff Development* 25, no. 3 (2004).
8. Joyce L. Epstein, Mavis G. Sanders, Beth S. Simon, Karen Clark Salinas, Natalie Rodriguez Jansorn, and Frances L. Van Voorhis, *School, Family and Community Partnerships: Your Handbook for Action,* 2nd ed. (Thousand Oaks, CA: Corwin Press, 2002), 86–87.

Chapter 4: Developing Relationships

1. Anthony S. Bryk and Barbara Schneider, *Trust in Schools: A Core Resource for Improvement* (New York: Russell Sage Foundation, 2002), 94–97.
2. Ibid., 22–26.
3. Karen L. Mapp, "Having Their Say: Parents Describe Why and How They Are Engaged in Their Children's Education," *School Community Journal* 13, no. 1 (2003): 35–64. For a free copy of this article, contact Lori Thomas at lthomas@adi.org or 217-732-6462, ext. 30.
4. Susan Dauber and Joyce Epstein, "Parents' Attitudes and Practices of Involvement in Innercity Elementary and Middle Schools," in Nancy Chavkin, ed., *Families and Schools in a Pluralistic Society* (Albany: State University of New York Press, 1993), 53–71.
5. Steven M. Constantino, *Engaging All Families: Creating a Positive School Culture by Putting Research into Practice* (Lanham, MD: Scarecrow Press, 2003), 16–17.
6. O'Hearn Parents and Teachers, *Including Every Parent* (Dorchester, MA: Project for School Innovation, 2003), 72. For more information or to order a copy, go to www.psinnovation.org.
7. Bryk and Schneider, *Trust in Schools,* 85.
8. Ibid., 81–86.
9. Vivian R. Johnson, "Family Centers in Schools," in Diana Hiatt-Michael, ed., *Promising*

Practices for Family Involvement in Schools (Greenwich, CT: Information Age Publishing, 2001), 88, 85–106. (Dr. Johnson, an author of this book, is a leading proponent of and researcher on family centers.)

10. Vivian R. Johnson, "The Family Center: Making Room for Parents," *Principal Magazine*, September 2000, 27–31.

Chapter 5: Linking to Learning

1. Anne T. Henderson and Karen L. Mapp, *A New Wave of Evidence: The Impact of School, Family and Community Connections on Student Achievement* (Austin, TX: Southwest Educational Development Laboratory, 2002), 7.

2. San Diego City Schools, "Walton Family Annual Report" (on the PAL program), October 2005.

3. Westat and Policy Studies Associates, *The Longitudinal Evaluation of School Change and Performance in Title I Schools, Volume I: Executive Summary* (Washington, DC: U.S. Department of Education, Office of the Deputy Secretary, Planning and Evaluation Service, 2001). Go to www.ed.gov/offices/OUS/PES/esed/lescp_highlights.html.

4. Henderson and Mapp, *New Wave*, 8.

5. Joyce Epstein, Beth S. Simon, and Karen Clark Salinas, "Involving Parents in Homework in the Middle Grades," *Phi Delta Kappan Research Bulletin* 18 (1997).

6. Frances Van Voorhis, "Interactive Science Homework: An Experiment in Home and School connections," *NASSP Bulletin* 85, no. 627 (2001): 20–32. For more information about TIPS, go to www.csos.jhu.edu/p2000/tips/OVERVIEW.htm.

7. For more information about the parent involvement requirements in Title I of NCLB, see Anne T. Henderson, *No Child Left Behind: What's in It for Parents* (Lexington, KY: Prichard Committee for Academic Excellence, 2003). Available in pdf at http://www.centerfor parentleadership.org/publications.html

Chapter 6: Addressing Differences

1. Jay D. Scribner, Michelle D. Young, and Anna Pedroza, "Building Collaborative Relations with Parents," in P. Reyes, Jay D. Scribner, and A. Paredes-Scribner, eds., *Lessons from High-Performing Hispanic Schools* (New York: Teachers College Press, 1999).

2. K. Salinas and N. Jansorn (eds.), *Promising Partnership Practices 2000* (Baltimore: Johns Hopkins University Center on School, Family, and Community Partnerships, 2000). (Note: Annual collections of *Promising Practices* are available on the Web site of the National Network of Partnership Schools at www.partnershipschools.org in the section "In the Spotlight.")

3. P. Bak-Fun Wong, "Reflections on Diversity" (2001), Family Involvement Network of Educators (FINE) Forum, 2. To see the entire article, go to http://www.gse.harvard.edu/hfrp/ projects/fine/fineforum/forum 2/reflections.html.

4. National Alliance of Black School Educators, *Addressing Over-Representation of African American Students in Special Education* (Arlington, VA: Council of Exceptional Children, 2002), 26–27. For more information, go to www.nabse.org/publications.htm.

5. "Latino Learning Links," National Council of La Raza (May 2004). See related story at http://www.arlington.k12.va.us/SCR/news/9899/022399-kithmath.shtml (accessed May 3, 2006).

6. The concept of cultural broker was developed by Concha Delgado Gaitan. For information and examples, see Concha Delgado Gaitan, *Involving Latino Families: Raising Student Achievement Through Home-School Partnerships* (Thousand Oaks, CA: Corwin Press, 2004).

7. For more information about the Parent Institute for Quality Education, go to www.piqe. org and see the parent training section in Chapter 10.

8. K. Salinas and N. Jansorn, eds., *Promising Partnership Practices 2004* (Baltimore: Johns Hopkins University Center on School, Family, and Community Partnerships, 2004).

9. John B. Diamond, "Diversity and Cultural Setting: Contextual Issues in Student Achievement." This paper was presented at Family, School, and Community Connections Symposium: New Directions for Research, Practice and Evaluation, sponsored by National Center for Family and Community Connections with Schools and the Harvard Family Research Project, Boston, December 2004. Available at www.gse.harvard.edu/hfrp/projects/ fine/resources/conference/con nections.html.

10. Gerardo R. Lopez, "On Whose Terms? Understanding Involvement Through the Eyes of Parents," paper presented at AERA annual meeting, Seattle, 2001.

11. Sherik Hughes, "How Can We Prepare Teachers to Work with Culturally Diverse Students and Their Families?" in FINE Member Insights, 2005. Go to www.gse.harvard.edu/ hfrp/projects/fine/memberinsights.html#diverse.

12. Diamond, "Diversity and Cultural Setting," 2004.

13. K. Salinas and N. Jansorn, eds., *Promising Partnership Practices 2003* (Baltimore: Johns Hopkins University Center on School, Family, and Community Partnerships, 2003).

14. Vivian R. Johnson, "Replicating What Works," in *New Ways of Thinking About Parental Involvement* (Baltimore, MD: Center on Families, Communities, Schools and Children's Learning, 1994), 7–8.

15. Lisa D. Delpit, "The Silenced Dialog: Power and Pedagogy in Educating Other Peoples' Children," in Lois Weis and Michele Fine, eds., *Beyond Silenced Voices: Class, Race and Gender in the United States* (Albany: State University of New York Press, 1993), 125.

16. For more information about Glen Singleton and the Pacific Educational Group, go to www.pacificeducationalgroup.com/who_glenn.html (accessed May 2, 2006).

17. Elizabeth Armstrong, "Meeting on the Same Page," *Christian Science Monitor*, March 18, 2003.

18. Lillian Polite and Elizabeth Baird Saenger, "A Pernicious Silence: Confronting Race in the Elementary Classroom." *Phi Delta Kappan*, 85, no. 4 (2003): 274–78.

19. This example is based on Mark Richardson, "Principal's Special Coffee," in *Attractions*, the newsletter of the Chantilly Pyramid Minority Student Achievement Committee, winter 1999, 5–6.

20. John B. Diamond, Antonia Randolph, and James Spillane, "Teachers' Expectations and Sense of Responsibility for Student Learning: The Importance of Race, Class, and Organizational Habitus," *Anthropology and Education Quarterly* 35, no. 1 (2004): 75–98.

21. Theresa Perry, "Up from the Parched Earth: Toward a Theory of African American Achievement," in Theresa Perry, Claude Steele, and Asa G. Hilliard III, *Young, Gifted and Black* (Boston: Beacon Press, 2003), 11.

22. Reginald Clark, "Ten Hypotheses About What Predicts Student Achievement for African-American Students and All Other Students: What the Research Shows," in Walter Allen et al., eds., *African American Education* (Oxford, UK: Elsevier Science, 2002), 155–77. Another version of this article is available at http://www.ncrel.org/gap/clark/index.html. Also see Reginald Clark, "Homework-focused Parenting Practices That Positively Affect Student Achievement," in Nancy Feyl Chavkin, ed., *Families and Schools in a Pluralistic Society* (Albany: State University of New York Press, 1993), 85–105.

23. Cara Solomon, "Schools Try to Build Bridges to Immigrant, Poor Parents," *Seattle Times*, September 15, 2003.

24. Jody Kretzmann and John L. McKnight, *Building Communities from the Inside Out: A Path Toward Finding and Mobilizing a Community's Assets* (Evanston, IL: Institute for Policy Research, Northwestern University, 1993).

25. Polite and Saenger, "A Pernicious Silence," 276.

26. Annette Lareau and Erin Horvath, "Moments of Social Inclusion and Exclusion: Race, Class and Cultural Capital in Family-School Relationships," *Sociology of Education* 72, no. 1 (1999): 37–53.

27. For a transcript of this online discussion about class and cultural differences held in Summer, 2003 on MiddleWeb, go to www.middleweb.com/MWLISTCONT/MSLparentsAH .html (accessed May 3, 2006).

Chapter 7: Supporting Advocacy

1. Lee Shumow and Richard Lomax, "Parental Efficacy: Predictor of Parenting Behavior and Adolescent Outcomes," paper presented at the annual meeting of the American Educational Research Association, Seattle, 2001.

2. Tatsha Robertson, "Black Parents Tackle a Gap," *Boston Globe*, March 28, 2005, A-1. For more information about the report that led to the initiative described in this story, *All Students Reaching the Top: Strategies for Closing Academic Achievement Gaps (A Report of the National Study Group for the Affirmative Development of Academic Ability)*, go to www.ncrel .org/gap/studies/allstudents.pdf.

3. Kathleen Cushman, *Fires in the Bathroom: Advice for Teachers from High School Students* (New York: The New Press, 2003), 56–57.

4. Kristen Admundson, "Questions and Answers," *Ideas Staff Can Use to Promote Parent Involvement (Elementary Edition)*, Parent Institute, January 2006, 2.

5. Linda Peterson, *Supporting Parents as Leaders: Stories of Dedication, Determination and Inspiration* (Boston: Institute for Responsive Education, 2002). Available at www.responsive education.org/pdf/supporting.pdf.

6. Action Alliance for Children, *Pathways to Parent Leadership, A Bilingual Report* (2002). The report is available on the AAC Web site, www.4children.org. This report describes nine parent leadership programs, including Parent School Partnerships (developed by MALDEF, the Mexican American Legal Defense and Education Fund), Parent Institute for Quality Education (PIQE), and the Right Question Project (RQP).

7. For more information about the Family Advocate System, go to the Kansas City, Kansas, public schools Web site: www.kckps.org/parents/fas.

8. Center for Law and Education, *Urgent Message for Parents* (Washington, DC: CLE, 1999), 13–14. Go to www.cleweb.org.

9. See www.schoolstowatch.org/barrencounty (accessed May 3, 2006).

10. Anne Henderson, Bonnie Jacob, Adam Kernan-Schloss, and Bev Raimondo, *The Case for Parent Leadership* (Lexington, KY: Prichard Committee for Academic Excellence, 2004), www .prichardcommittee.org. Also available from KSA Plus Communications, www.ksaplus.com.

11. Leslie M. Gutman and Carol Midgely, "The Role of Protective Factors in Supporting the Academic Achievement of Poor African American Students During the Middle School Transition," *Journal of Youth and Adolescence* 29, no. 2 (2000): 223–48.

12. George L Wemberly and Richard J. North, "Schools Involving Parents in Early Postsecondary Planning," in *Policy Report, 2004* (Iowa City: American College Testing Corporation, 2004). Go to www.act.org/path/policy/pdf/involve_parents.pdf.

13. "Career Portfolio Night," in K. Salinas and N. Jansorn, eds., *Promising Partnership Practices 2003* (Baltimore: Johns Hopkins University Center on School, Family, and Community Partnerships, 2003).

14. Eileen Gale Kugler and Erin McVadon Albright, "Increasing Diversity in Challenging Classes: A Multicultural High School Expands Opportunities for Its Diverse Student Body," *Educational Leadership* 62, no. 5 (2005): 42–45. Eileen Kugler has written a book based on the experience at Annandale High School, *Debunking the Middle Class Myth: Why Diverse Schools Are Good for All Kids* (Lanham, MD: Scarecrow Press, 2002).

Chapter 8: Sharing Power

1. Anne T. Henderson, *No Child Left Behind: What's in It for Parents* (Lexington, KY: Prichard Committee for Academic Excellence, 2002). For a free copy in PDF, go to www.prichard committee.org. This book was co-published by KSA Plus Communications in Arlington, Virginia. For more information, go to www.ksaplus.org.

2. Don Moore, *What Makes These Schools Stand Out: Chicago Elementary Schools with a Seven-Year Trend of Improved Reading Achievement* (Chicago: Designs for Change, 1998), 1–16. Available online at www.Designsforchange.org/pubs.

3. Anne Henderson, Bonnie Jacob, Adam Kernan-Schloss, and Bev Raimondo, *The Case for Parent Leadership* (Lexington, KY: Prichard Committee for Academic Excellence, 2004), 31–32, www.prichardcommittee.org. Also available from KSA Plus Communications; go to www.ksaplus.com.

4. Parents and teachers at the Patrick O'Hearn Elementary School in Boston, *Including Every Parent* (Dorchester, MA: Project for School Innovation, 2003). For more information, go to www.psinnovation.org.

5. For more information about Action Teams, see J. L. Epstein, M. G. Sanders, B. S. Simon, K. C. Salinas, N. R. Jansorn, and F. L. Van Voorhis, *School, Family, and Community Partnerships: Your Handbook for Action*, 2nd ed. (Thousand Oaks, CA: Corwin Press, 2002). For more information about the National Network of Partnership Schools, go to www.partnership schools.org.

6. Don Davies, "Family Participation in Decision-Making and Advocacy," in Diana Hiatt-Michael, ed., *Promising Practices in Family Involvement in Schools* (Greenwich, CT: Information Age Publishing, 2001), 107–51, 132.

7. Robert Putnam, *Bowling Alone* (New York: Touchstone, 2000).

8. Eric Zachary and shola olatoye, *A Case Study: Community Organizing for School Improvement in the South Bronx* (New York: Community Involvement Program, Institute for Education and Social Policy, New York University, 2001), 5. Available online at www.educationorganiz ing.org. Also see Kavitha Mediratta and Norm Fruchter, *From Governance to Accountability: Building Relationships That Make Schools Work* (New York: Institute for Education and Social Policy, New York University, 2003). Available online at www.educationorganizing.org.

9. Kavitha Mediratta, Norm Fruchter, and Anne C. Lewis, *Organizing for School Reform: How Communities Are Finding Their Voices and Reclaiming Their Public Schools* (New York: Institute for Education and Social Policy, New York University, 2002), 13. Available online at www .educationorganizing.org.

10. Annette Lareau, "Social Class Differences in Family-School Relationships: The Importance of Cultural Capital," *Sociology of Education* 60, no. 2 (1987): 73–85.

11. Shared with permission from the Tellin' Stories Project. For more information about the Tellin' Stories Project in the District of Columbia, go to www.teachingforchange.org.

12. Claire Crane et al., *Becoming a Community School* (Dorchester, MA: Project for School Innovation, 2004). For more information, go to www.psinnovation.org.

13. Joy Dryfoos, *Evaluations of Community Schools: Findings to Date* (Hastings-on-Hudson, NY: Coalition for Community Schools, 2000). For more information, go to www.community schools.org/evaluation/evalprint.html.

14. Mediratta, Fruchter, and Lewis, *Organizing for School Reform*, 27–28. For more information about community organizing research, see Anne T. Henderson and Karen L. Mapp, *A New Wave of Evidence* (Austin, TX: Southwest Educational Development Laboratory, 2002), 53–60.

15. Mark R. Warren, "Communities and Schools: A New View of Urban Education Reform," *Harvard Education Review* 75, no. 2 (2005): 20–23.

16. Ibid., 22.

17. Ibid., 32.

Chapter 9: Scaling Up

1. To see *The Family and Community Engagement Task Force Report to the Boston School Committee* (June 23, 2000), go to www.bostonpublicschools.com/info/task_force.asp (accessed May 5, 2006).

2. To see the *Guide to the Boston Public Schools for Families and Students* (2005–2006), go to http://boston.k12.ma.us/info/Guide.pdf (accessed May 5, 2006).

3. For information about Face to Face, go to www.thehome.org/site/content/FACETOFACE/facetoface_partners.asp (accessed May 6, 2006).

4. To see *Introducing the Boston Public Schools* (2005–2006), go to http://boston.k12.ma.us/schools/assign.asp (accessed May 6, 2006).

5. Mavis Sanders, "Helping Schools Leave No Child Behind: A Case Study in District Leadership for School, Family and Community Partnerships," paper presented at the annual meeting of the American Educational Research Association, Montreal, 2005. See also C. Coburn, "Rethinking Scale: Moving Beyond Numbers to Deep and Lasting Change," *Educational Researcher* 32, no. 6 (2003): 3–12.

6. To see Alexandria City Public Schools, *Listening to Families and Faculty* (December 2004), go to www.acps.k12.va.us/Familyinvolvement/index.php (accessed May 5, 2006).

7. For information about the "Welcoming Atmosphere Walk-Through" process, go to www.fcps.k12.va.us/DIS/OECFS/FLI/welcome.htm (accessed May 5, 2006).

8. To see the *Six Essentials* brochure, go to http://boston.k12.ma.us/teach/offices.pdf. The example listed is on page 1 (accessed May 5, 2006).

9. Ron Rice et al., "The Lighthouse Inquiry: School Board/Superintendent Team Behaviors in School Districts with Extreme Differences in Student Achievement," paper presented at the American Educational Research Association annual meeting, Seattle, 2001. The work was sponsored by the Iowa Association of School Boards.

10. New York City Board of Education, *A Guide for Parents and Families*, 2003–2004; go to www.nycenet.edu/childrenfirst/CFParentGuide.pdf (accessed May 6, 2006).

11. For more information on Families in Schools (FIS), go to www.familiesinschools.org/pirc/index.php (accessed May 6, 2006).

12. Linda Jacobson, "Putting the 'Parent Piece' in Schools," *Education Week* 21, no. 5 (2002): 1, 14.

13. For more information on Fairfax County's Teacher Action Research program, go to www.fcps.edu/DIS/OSDT/StaffDevelopment/trn.htm (accessed May 6, 2006).

14. For more information about San Diego policies affecting parents, go to http://www.sandi.net/indices/parents.htm For a copy of the entire parent involvement policy handbook, go to http://www.sandi.net/parent_facts.pdf (accessed May 6, 2006).

15. For more information on San Diego's Parent University, go to http://prod031.sandi.net/parent/programs/parentuniversity/parent.html. For information about the programs of the California Parent Center, go to http://parent.sdsu.edu (accessed May 5, 2006).

Notes

. . .

Index

academic achievement, 20–21; community involvement and, 3; family involvement and, 2–3, 81–111, 135, 175; preparing parent advocates to focus on, 168–69; resources, 265–67; school district goals, 231–36; teacher support and, 175

Academic Development Institute, 265

Achievement Gap Initiative, Harvard, 158

ACORN, 10, 210, 268

Action Alliance for Children, 162

An Action Guide for Community and Parent Leaders, 275

action research, 196–97, 243–44

Action Team for Partnerships, 196

action teams, 44–46, 188, 195–96

advanced placement (AP) classes, 176, 180; qualifying for, 181

The Advisory Guide, 258

advisory system, 178

advocacy, supporting, 151–85, 152; angry parents, dealing with, 164; benefiting many or all students, 161–65; checklist, 182–86; collaborating with parents, 165–66; community services and, 159; definition of advocate, 153; good advocacy compared to going over the line, 155; helping families understand how to resolve school problems, 155–62, 183; "power parents," 165; "press for success," 154; programs for, 166–72; resources, 258–61; roles of the advocate, 153; school organization and staff, informing parents about, 156–58, 182; school policy for, 166; setting goals for the future, 176–81, 184–85; training for parents, 162–63; training for teachers, 171; transition practices and programs, 173–75, 184; workshops, 170–72. *See also* power, sharing of

African Americans, 164; advocacy by parents, 158; family involvement in children's education, 124–25; racial tensions and bias, addressing, 128–39

Alonzo, Richard, 240–41

Alvarado, Anthony, 236

Amato, Mary Lou, 85, 90, 191–92

American College Testing (ACT) service, 176

American Federation of Teachers (AFT), 254–55, 276, 280

Amundson, Kris, 160

The Annenberg Institute for School Reform, 269, 283–84

Ariyasu, Linda, 241

arts, parent-child involvement in the, 87

Asian-American families, 123–24

ASPIRA Parents for Educational Excellence Initiative (APEX), 281

Association for Supervision and Curriculum Development (ASCD), 280

Index

. . .